Spirituality in Transition

James J. Bacik

Sheed & Ward
Kansas City

For my sister, Patricia Bacik Wallace,

faithful conserver of family traditions,

master teacher and health educator,

spontaneous witness to the graciousness of the Mystery.

Sheed & Ward™ is a service of The National Catholic Reporter Publishing Company.

Library of Congress Cataloguing-in-Publication Data

Bacik, James J., 1936-
    Spirituality in transition / James J. Bacik.
        p.   cm.
    ISBN: 1-55612-857-6   (alk. paper)
    1. Spirituality--Christianity. 2. Christian life. 3. Church and the world.   I. Title.
    BV4501.2.B248 1996
    248--dc20   96-17809
                                                       CIP

Published by: Sheed & Ward
             115 E. Armour Blvd.
             P.O. Box 419492
             Kansas City, MO 64141-6492

To order, call: (800) 333-7373

Contents

Chapter 3
Love of Neighbor: Deepening Personal Relationships

Introduction

We are living through one of the great transition periods in human history. Scientific advances have given us unprecedented control over our own destiny. Genetic engineering holds out the possibility of eliminating certain diseases and improving the human race. Nuclear weapons threaten civilization and the very existence of humanity. The electronic media have radically altered the way people perceive the world and process information. The Internet has transformed the global village into a vast communications network. Given such drastic changes, it is not surprising that many people are experiencing so much discontinuity, disruption and fragmentation in their lives.

Furthermore, tragic events of the 20th century including world wars, assassinations of major leaders and unexpected terrorist attacks have undermined the modern faith in progress and have contributed to a new mood which is more somber, pessimistic and in some cases cynical.

As the Second Vatican Council taught us, Christians have a special responsibility to participate in the process of creating a more humane world. This requires a spirituality which is rooted in tradition and alert to the signs of the times. To manage rapid change we need to tap the power of the Holy Spirit residing at the very center of our being. To deal with the fragmentation so prevalent in contemporary society, we need communities of faith which bring us together and exemplify the ideal of unity in diversity. Believers need a rich interior life nourished by prayer in order to work effectively for peace and justice in a world still plagued by racism and sexism. In a culture threatened by discouragement and cynicism, Christians have the crucial task of proclaiming in word and deed a message of hope. This message is based not on an optimistic assessment of human possibilities, but on the faith conviction that the often hidden God remains with us in the struggle against evil.

This book is part of a widespread effort to develop a viable contemporary spirituality which is faithful to the great Christian tradition and responsive to the changing world. Chapter One offers a broad overview of our current situation and suggests some general directions for spirituality today. The first part of the chapter begins by describing the impact of massive changes on ordinary people in the United States, highlighting the fragmentation and somber mood so prevalent in our culture. It goes on to summarize scholarly opinion on the character of our transitional period, concluding that we are living through a major paradigm shift from the modern world to a postmodern situation which is still fluid and is fundamentally open to spiritual concerns.

The second part of the chapter insists that an authentic postmodern spirituality must maintain family ties with traditional forms of Christian piety and should retrieve valuable insights from the spiritualities which flourished in previous eras. For example, spirituality today will maintain its traditional Christocentric character and will retain the modern emphasis on self-fulfillment, while placing it in a more communal context. But Christians must also respond to the distinctive challenges presented by postmodernity. The chapter discusses these responses in the framework of the threefold love of self, neighbor and God. To cultivate a healthy love of self today we must attend to our longings for the Infinite as well as our concrete socio-economic situation. Love of neighbor demands that we respect the uniqueness of other people and pay special attention to those pushed to the sidelines by the modern world. Finally, a postmodern spirituality invites us to deepen our love of God by praising the inexhaustible

Source of love and by trusting in the hidden One who is revealed more through story and symbol than rational analysis.

The second and third chapters contain short essays which offer a spiritual perspective on various challenges presented by our changing world. They were originally circulated privately (some were later published for parish use) to promote personal reflection on common spiritual concerns. Revised and collected here they will, I hope, serve that same function for a wider audience.

Chapter Two concentrates on love of self and the more personal aspects of the spiritual quest while Chapter Three deals more with love of neighbor and relationship questions. All the articles reflect the faith conviction that the gracious God remains present in our hearts and our relationships, even in the most complex and confusing times.

Chapter 1

Christian Spirituality in a Postmodern World

1. Overview

Our task is to bring this spiritual tradition into an open dialogue with the rapidly changing world.

As both scholars and the popular media have pointed out, we are experiencing a religious revival in the United States. A high percentage of our citizens participate in religious activities and many are involved in a quest for spiritual meaning. We need to understand this revival if we are going to tap its spiritual energy and play a constructive role in guiding its progress.

The United States has always been a remarkably religious country. The Puritans brought deep religious convictions to the New World which still influence the American imagination. In contrast to the anti-religious Enlightenment in 18th century Europe, our national enlightenment, well represented by Thomas Jefferson, maintained a sense of dependence on the Creator and a positive respect for religion. The 33 million Catholic immigrants who came to this country between 1820 and 1920 found personal strength and social cohesion in their faith. Despite the predictions of many sociologists and even some theologians, the modern secularization process has not destroyed the religious spirit in our country. At the very time that the press was trumpeting the death of God in the 1960's,

1

we were already beginning another of the many religious revivals that have punctuated our history since the time of Jonathan Edwards and the Great Awakening in the 1730's. During the past 30 years this revival has gradually picked up momentum and has now reached a point where it can no longer be ignored.

Recent scientific polls indicate that Americans today describe themselves as very religious. About 94% of our adult citizens say they believe in God, 90% pray regularly, 68% belong to a church or synagogue, 66% attend a religious service at least once a month and 42% are in attendance on a given weekend, 75% choose to have their marriages conducted by religious officials, 88% claim that religion is very or fairly important in their lives, 58% feel the need to experience spiritual growth, and 33% have had a religious or mystical experience.

These figures are even more remarkable when compared with other Western countries. To take an extreme example, a mere 15% of Swedish adults affirm belief in a personal God and 46% agree partially or completely with the statement that human beings consist only of body and matter.

The widespread religious interest in the United States has been noted with increasing frequency by our influential secular media. *Time* magazine picked Pope John Paul as the man of the year in 1994. ABC television hired Peggy Wehmeyer as a religion correspondent. *Time* and *Newsweek* carried cover stories on religious topics ranging from the historical Jesus to the existence of angels. *The New York Times* did a front page review of a book entitled *Encountering Mary* by Sandra Zimdars Swartz and later published a four-part series on the American Catholic Church under the title "Searching Its Soul." Raymond Brown's massive scholarly work *The Death of the Messiah* rated extensive coverage in *Newsweek, Time* and other popular magazines. *The Wall Street Journal* ran articles on Pope John Paul and his social teachings. Even prime time television has introduced a few programs with religious themes into its almost totally secularized version of American life.

The marketplace also reflects the current religious revival. Pope John Paul's *Crossing the Threshold of Hope* moved to the top of the best seller list immediately after publication. Scott Peck's spiritually oriented book *The Road Less Traveled* has been on the list for over 625 weeks. The Gregorian Chant CD by the Benedictine monks of Santo Domingo de Silos sold close to 3 million copies in less than a year.

In the world of scholarship almost all disciplines are showing an interest in religious matters. A growing number of psychologists recognize that finding spiritual meaning in life is crucial to healthy self-fulfillment. Sociologists are more aware of the role organized religion plays in providing a sense of integration and purpose. Even in the hard sciences such as physics, biology and astronomy researchers express feelings of awe and a sense of unity with the cosmos in language reminiscent of traditional mysticism.

Despite this bright portrayal of the current religious revival, it also has a darker side which bears examination. The spiritual revival has not been deep enough to overcome the consumerism and individualism which still dominate our culture. Too many people are using religion as an opiate to escape the complexity of our age and the demands of everyday life. Some Christian groups are dominated by an exclusive outlook which damns others to hell and makes genuine dialogue and collaboration impossible. When the spiritual search is disconnected from traditional wisdom, it often takes on a faddish and superficial character.

The Roy C. Blass Institute at the University of Akron conducted an in-depth random survey of 4,000 Americans on religious matters which highlights the ambivalence of the revival. Using criteria such as church attendance, membership, frequency of personal prayer and belief in life after death, the researchers concluded that only 19% of Americans are genuinely committed to their religion and regularly practice their faith. About 33% are totally secular in their outlook, 22% have only trace elements of religion in their daily lives, and 22% are moderately religious. These statistics help us draw a more accurate portrait of the way religion actually functions in the United States. We may be a country with the soul of a church, as Chesterton suggested, but our culture continues to show great resistance to spiritual wisdom and religious values.

Borrowing a distinction from John Henry Newman, we could say that the "notional assent" to religion in our country outweighs the "real assent." This means that many people say they believe, but do not act on faith convictions. Church attendance does not guarantee that worshipers appropriate the faith or try to spread the kingdom in the world. There is more lip service to religious values than genuine conviction. The essential connection between liturgy and life is often lost in practice. Augustine's dictum "God has many that the church does not have; and the church has many that God does not have" applies well to our day.

In our society the civil religion of nationalism often exercises more influence than Christianity. With the Gospel muted, church members are as prone to prejudice and intolerance as nonbelievers. Our culture tends to trivialize religion and thwart its liberating thrust by banning it from the public forum and confining it to the private realm.

All of this helps explain why our current religious revival is having so little effect in overcoming our social ills such as as apathy, violence, racism, sexism, nationalism, individualism and consumerism.

Nevertheless, it remains true that we are living through a significant spiritual revival with immense potential for good. The human spirit refuses to be contained in a one-dimensional world. Secularism does not give a full account of the human condition. A world without transcendence feels suffocating. We need our sacred places and times which enable us to breathe freely and prepare us to recognize the mystery dimension of ordinary life. An authentic spiritual revival must have social consequences. When religion is confined to the private realm the society as a whole is impoverished. A culture without spiritual moorings tends toward disintegration. A growing number of people within the church and without recognize that the spiritual resources found in the great religious traditions can play an important role in creating a more peaceful world and more harmonious society.

Christianity has rich resources which can guide and nourish the new quest for the sacred in the private and public realms. Our task is to bring this spiritual tradition into an open dialogue with the rapidly changing world. We can begin by examining the distinctive sense of spirituality found in Christianity.

Meaning of Spirituality

"Spirituality" is a rich and suggestive word which points to various aspects of lived experience. Traditionally, Christian spirituality has manifested a Trinitarian character. It has to do with responding to the call of our Creator to help humanize our culture, with putting on the mind of Christ in order to transform our world, with following the promptings of the Holy Spirit in order to bring unity to our fragmented society. Because spirituality is Trinitarian it always has a relational quality. Spiritually mature persons recognize a depth dimension in all their relationships: to themselves, others, nature, culture, society, church and, most fundamentally, to God. A genuine spirituality involves an imperative to improve these relationships and to make them more fruitful. We must learn to find God in and through all of the relationships which constitute our lives.

Spiritual growth involves a process of conversion in all aspects of our lives: physical, affective, imaginative, intellectual, moral and religious. Our conscience calls us to take good care of our bodies, to face and mobilize our emotions for personal growth and effective living, to cultivate healthy images of God and self, to seek truth, to opt for the good rather than expediency, and to be open to the mystery dimension of life. Binding all these tasks together is the call to Christian conversion in which we make Christ the center of our being and the guide for our actions. Jesus exemplifies fulfilled human life, the goal of the conversion process. He calls us to follow his example of complete surrender to gracious God. The conversion process in all its aspects enables us to be more faithful disciples of Christ.

Spirituality suggests vitality. The glory of God, as Irenaeus suggested, is the human person fully alive. The

Spirit dwells within us as a source of energy and strength. Christians should be energetic in pursuit of personal growth and passionate about the cause of peace and justice.

By emphasizing the universal call to holiness Vatican II invites all of us to take the spiritual quest seriously. By virtue of baptism all Christians are called to dedicate themselves totally to following Christ. The high ideals proclaimed by the Gospels are meant for every Christian and not just an elite few. We all have the task of responding more fully to the promptings of the Spirit within us. No baptized person can simply settle for mediocrity in the spiritual life. All of us must search for the best ways of relating our Christian faith to everyday life in the real world.

The spiritual life can also be described in more secular terms. It involves a search for meaning in the midst of absurdity, for integration that overcomes fragmentation, for depth in a culture which fosters superficiality, for purpose in an often directionless world. In our secularized society many people participate in this spiritual search without any direct relationship to a church. Some claim that institutionalized religion fails to nourish their spiritual growth or even impedes it. Much of the interest in spirituality is generated outside church circles. Deconstructionist scholars, for instance, are reviving interest in the Christian mystics. Twelve-step programs foster dependence on a higher power. Many people find inspiration and meaning from contemplating the beauty and power of nature or participating in support groups. Academic leaders want to create communities on campus which are more just, caring and celebrative.

As this brief summary suggests the spiritual quest in both its explicitly religious and secular version raises the most fundamental questions and plunges us to the depths of human existence.

2. An Age of Transition

We need a spirituality which will seize the opportunities and help guide our world in healthy directions.

We are called to pursue the spiritual quest in an age of transition when the old order is breaking up and new ways of relating are being formed. We need a spirituality which accepts the reality of change and seizes the opportunities for growth. A contemporary spirituality must maintain and preserve the values of the past so that we can live more effectively in our changing world. It is clear that we are living through a time of significant change, but the precise nature and full extent of these changes are not entirely clear. Scholars do not agree on the dynamics which are driving this period of transition. No one claims to know the precise shape of the new world that is being formed. Nevertheless, it is important to understand as much as we can about this age of transition, so that we can develop a spirituality which will be relevant to the times and effective in helping to humanize the world.

Historical Development of Modernity

Historically, the modern Western world developed from medieval Christendom centered in Europe and united by the traditional Catholic faith. Various developments in the 15th and 16th centuries called into question this unified worldview. Nicholas Copernicus challenged the common assumption that the earth was the center of the universe by proposing his heliocentric theory of planetary motion. The voyage of Columbus to the New World forced Europeans to expand their fundamental perceptions of the earth. The Protestant Reformation, led by Luther and Calvin, broke up the unity of Catholic Europe. The invention of printing eventually caused readers to think in a more linear and analytic fashion.

The collapse of the medieval worldview unleashed a new movement which we have come to call modernity. Modernity found its energy and direction from many sources. The modern emphasis on the importance of the individual was already suggested by the great medieval theologian Thomas Aquinas (1225-1274), who taught that human beings participate in the existence of God. By insisting on the inductive method of learning the English philosopher Francis Bacon (1561-1626) set the stage for the scientific method which has dominated the quest for knowledge in the modern period. The founder of modern philosophy Rene Descartes (1596-1650), initiated the enduring conviction that abstract reason provides the route to genuine human progress in all areas of life. The English philosopher John Locke (1632-1704) made major contributions to the political philosophy of modernity by stressing individual freedom and the right to pursue "life, health, liberty and possessions." Locke also proposed the system of checks and balances adopted by the United States Constitution.

The thought of these great 17th century pioneers established a foundation for the Enlightenment of the 18th century. This period, also known as the Age of Reason, insisted with great optimism that science and reason would bring about human progress. The European Enlightenment had a strongly anti-religious component. Voltaire (1694-1778) is representative of those who wanted to replace authoritarian religion with rational planning in order to improve the human condition. Referring to the institutional church, Voltaire and his followers desired to "crush the infamous thing" because it stood in the way of human progress. They wanted to create a new civil religion drawn from a rational analysis of the natural world. To symbolize this movement they changed the name of the Cathedral of Notre Dame in Paris to the Temple of Reason and set up a Torch of Truth which burned before the Altar of Reason. Even though this bizarre transformation of the Cathedral in 1793 did not last long, it does symbolize an important and enduring strain of the modern Enlightenment.

Enlightenment rationalism spawned the Romantic movement of the late 18th and 19th centuries which exalted the senses and emotions over reason and intellect. Romanticism called for a return to nature and believed in the innate goodness of human beings. It admired heroic individuals and celebrated the individuality of creative artists. Jean Jacques Rousseau (1712-1778) set the tone and direction of the Romantic movement by insisting that human beings are essentially good and equal in the state of nature, but are corrupted by modern science and commerce. The Romantic tradition was carried on by important poets including William Wordsworth, S.T. Coleridge, Lord Byron, John Keats and P.B. Shelley. The composer Richard Wagner synthesized many of the Romantic themes in his grand operas. The conflict between hard-headed scientific Rationalism and the softer nature-based approach of Romanticism has continued throughout the 20th century and into our own time. It is manifested in debates over many issues from curriculum reform in the schools to the direction of spiritual renewal in the churches.

Both Rationalism and Romanticism contributed to the tremendous optimism of modernity. The Enlightenment produced the general conviction that reason and science could bring solutions to our great problems. Despite Calvinistic teachings on the depravity of human nature, many people developed strong beliefs in the innate goodness of human beings. Establishing democratic governments and safeguarding human rights would enable human beings to flourish. Science and technology, energized by a growing sense of universal benevolence, would reduce suffering in the world. Liberated from grinding poverty and political oppression, individuals would be able to find significance in ordinary daily life.

The Collapse of Modernity in Europe

In Europe, World War I challenged the prevailing optimism of modernity. Science and technology had simply multiplied the destructive effects of military combat. The savagery of the conflict called into question the innate goodness of human nature. Democratic movements could not prevent war. After a few decades of peace, World War II once more dashed the dreams of human progress. The monstrous holocaust initiated by Hitler and the gulag established by

Stalin revealed the darkest side of human nature. Despite the Allied victory over Nazi Germany, the ensuing cold war between the Soviet Union and the Western Allies intensified the somber mood. The threat of a nuclear disaster brought a new sense of dread and foreboding to the human family. Hiroshima and Nagasaki function as enduring reminders of the destructive force of atomic weaponry. Grim revelations of the Cambodian killing fields forced us to face once again the senseless cruelty of tyrants. The heartless systematic repression of Communist regimes around the world reminded us that human reason can serve demonic ends. The increasing number of terrorist attacks and the threat of random violence have continued to undercut our sense of security. With extensive media coverage of disasters, violence and tragedies, it becomes increasingly difficult to maintain the naive optimism celebrated by Rationalism and Romanticism.

History of Modernity in the U.S.A.

It is important to note that the history of modernity in the United States has distinctive features. The people who came to these shores during the Colonial period had great dreams of founding a new world. They left a Europe that was ravaged by terrible plagues in the 14th and 15th centuries. Cities were overcrowded and suffered from poor sanitation. Life was violent and famine was a constant problem. The European explorers did not discover an unknown land but came to a place already occupied by Native Americans. With a few bright exceptions, the Europeans adopted repugnant strategies toward the native people: convert them to Christianity, enslave them or exterminate them. A huge number of Native Americans died as a result of violent conflicts and especially of new diseases brought by the Europeans. American Christians are still trying to come to terms with this dark history.

During the Colonial period, Puritanism became a dominate cultural influence. This Calvinistic tradition stressed the sovereignty of God and the need for a disciplined response to the divine call. The Puritans believed that God entered into a covenant with them which placed on their shoulders the responsibility of spreading the kingdom in the world. The Puritan emphasis on discipline and hard work, whether expressed in religious or secular terms, remains an important aspect of the American outlook on life.

Our political revolution in the late 18th century was rooted in a distinctively American version of the Enlightenment. The principal architect of our revolution, Thomas Jefferson, was greatly influenced by European rationalism. For him the greatest thinkers in history were Francis Bacon, the father of the modern scientific method; John Locke, the philosopher of modern democracy and individual rights; and finally, Isaac Newton, a great practitioner of modern science. But Jefferson's appropriation of these modern thinkers was distinctive. The United States did not have a premodern history. We never knew feudalism or Christendom. Our political revolution was not antireligious or anticlerical like the French revolution. Jefferson and most of the other Founding Fathers did not espouse atheism or feel the need to smash the church as an infamous institution which retards human progress. On the contrary they expressed belief in a Supreme Being, a Creator who endowed us with certain inalienable rights. Their God may have been remote, but was still worthy of trust. For Jefferson, God was the great architect or builder who wrote his law into nature. Jesus was the greatest of ethical teachers. Religion plays a positive role in the ordering of human life.

The founders also had a strong sense of the sinful side of human nature and thus devised a system of the separation of governmental powers in order to avoid the tyrannies which plagued Europe. They adopted the First Amendment to create a framework for religious peace. It was designed not to suppress religion, but to enable citizens to practice their own religious traditions without coercion and with complete freedom. The American Enlightenment was fundamentally open to the religious dimension of life and was positive about the role of religion in society. The Deism espoused by Jefferson has remained an important influence on the American spirit.

During the 19th century a strong strain of utilitarian individualism took hold in the United States. It represented the triumph of the thinking of John Locke over the more communal sense of life favored by the Puritans and upheld by the republican Deism of the Founding Fathers. At its extreme, utilitarianism celebrated the rights and freedoms of individuals to the detriment of the common good. As the sociologist Robert Bellah and others have pointed out, individualism remains a dominant feature of American life today (cf. *Habits of the Heart*). Its influence is pervasive: in economics as the desire for personal gain without regard for others; in politics as a selfish accumulation of power; in family life as an unwillingness to sacrifice; and in religion as a preoccupation with personal salvation. Contemporary spirituality has the difficult task of promoting a more communal sense of life and of fostering collaborative efforts on behalf of the common good.

The 19th century also witnessed the rise of the Transcendental Movement represented especially by Ralph Waldo Emerson (1803-1882). Emerson was convinced that we all possess an interior divine spark and that our inner experience can lead us to God. This theology, reminiscent of European Romanticism, was very individualistic, centering on the solitary individual who finds saving enlightenment from within. It had little sense of tragedy and not much room for the cross of Christ. This rather utopian religious outlook was not well suited to embrace and interpret the tragedy of the Civil War. That task was left to the encompassing vision of Abraham Lincoln who understood the redemptive power of suffering and the sovereign judgment of God on human sin. But Transcendentalism did contribute to the optimistic spirit which prevailed in the late 19th and early 20th century. The American dream rose again from the ashes of war. As God's chosen people we could still build that shining city on a hill which would be a beacon of hope for the whole world.

This optimistic mood continued in the United States right through World War I. This horrendous conflict, which shattered the utopian dreams of Europe, was considered more of a triumph than a tragedy in our country. The economic crash of 1929 and the Great Depression did place crushing burdens on the American spirit. But the victories achieved in World War II over Imperial Japan and Nazi Germany brought renewed hope to Americans. After World War II, the G.I. Bill enabled many veterans to go to college and eventually improve their soco-economic status. High hopes and dreams of Camelot accompanied the election of President John Kennedy in 1960.

A Somber Mood

With the assassination of President Kennedy in 1963, chaos invaded Camelot. And nothing since has been the same. A new somber mood took over the country. Since then numerous tragic events have darkened the American spirit: Vietnam, the assassinations of Robert Kennedy and Martin Luther King, Watergate, terrorist attacks, Iranian hostages, and the Oklahoma City bombing.

Although strains of traditional American optimism are still evident in our culture, the dominant mood seems to be more sober, pessimistic and even cynical. Ordinary people experience the precariousness of modern life with its violence, discontinuities and disruptions. Despite the recent decrease of violent crimes in the United States, the sensational cases continue to dominate the news, striking fear in the hearts of many. The threat of terrorist attacks, drive-by shootings and random violence undermines our sense of security. In addition, there is great frustration in the country over our inability to solve our social problems. Racial tensions persist and affirmative action has become a symbol which polarizes public opinion. The volatile topic of abortion divides the country and we have not yet found an acceptable way even to frame the question so that a civil argument can take place. Life today feels more fragmented. We are more realistic about the failures of science and technology to solve our problems. Concerned citizens worry about the power of interest groups to subvert the common good. The human desire for a smooth evolutionary development towards a better world is constantly thwarted by disruptions and destructive random events. It is difficult for us to find overarching goals or common stories which bring us together as a nation. Parents worry about their children growing up in a youth subculture which promotes sexual promiscuity and the use of drugs. They also must face the possibility that their children will abandon their religious heritage and family values in favor of different worldviews and lifestyles. Polls show that citizens have a growing distrust of government. Believers are often perplexed by pluralism and polarization in the churches. Most people are alarmed by the breakup of the family, the high divorce rate and the growing number of children born out of wedlock. Single parents feel overwhelmed by the burden of supporting and raising children. Many families with two wage earners still feel financial pressure as the buying power of their incomes has gone down over the last couple of decades. Corporate mergers, downsizing and plant closings often thrust middle class persons into the ranks of the unemployed or into jobs beneath their competency level. For various uncontrollable reasons individuals suddenly lose their health insurance. Job changes and opportunities cause many families to experience the emotional upheaval of leaving familiar surroundings and moving into a new world. Despite all the impressive advances of modernity, many persons in the United States today are feeling frustrated, worried, insecure, harried and anxious.

It is remarkable that positive events around the globe have done so little to lighten the heavy mood of average Americans. Imagine that someone in 1988 predicted the following events: the collapse of the Soviet Union, the end of the cold war, the liberation of Eastern Europe, the election of Nelson Mandela as president of South Africa, the destruction of the Berlin wall, the peace accords between Israel and both the PLO and Jordan. Back then almost no one saw any one of those events as a real possibility in the short term, and yet, they have all happened in less than a decade. In a brief period the world has made unprecedented progress towards peace, freedom, democracy and the establishment of human rights. It is true that most of these situations remain terribly ambiguous and fraught with danger. But real progress has been made and the potential for more progress still exists. Nevertheless, these liberating events have not lifted our col-

lective spirits. It is as though Americans have been anesthe-
tized so that we are unable to feel the joy of success and progress. We have a collective amnesia about past victories and
show little capacity for savoring the triumphs of the moment.

Managing Change

Much of our energy today goes into managing the tensions produced by our changing world. We have become
more aware of the ambiguities and contradictions built into
the modern project. The Enlightenment conviction that reason and science would bring us automatic progress and produce a better society has proven to be illusory. Autonomous
reason disconnected from religious moorings has created a
one-dimensional world which feels suffocating. Science mas-
querading as a religion has failed to provide an overarching
sense of meaning and purpose. Scientific technology has produced nuclear weapons with the potential to destroy civilization. Industrialization has polluted our earth. Urbanization
has created slums and ghettos. Colonialism destroyed native
cultures. The patriarchal bias fostered by modernity erased
the experience of women. Nationalism produced world wars.

Even the clear triumphs of modernity seem to produce
ambivalent results. Medical technology has prolonged life,
but created new problems of caring for the aged. Capitalism
has created more wealth, but the gap between rich and poor
grows steadily wider. Freedom has been extended to more
people, but has often led to license and irresponsibility. Democracy opens up the political process, but enables groups to
pursue their own interests while ignoring the common good.
Technology has given us labor saving devices, but also fosters a soft hedonistic lifestyle. Many countries have been liberated from Communist tyranny, but they are experiencing
increased street crime and black market economies.

In the realm of religion where people look for stability,
change has also challenged traditional securities. Modern biblical criticism developed by scholars during the 19th and 20th
centuries has gradually come to the attention of average
church members, calling into question the historical reliabil-
ity of the Scriptures. The general acceptance of evolutionary

theories has forced Christians to reinterpret traditional doctrines. As believers become more aware of multiple perspectives and diverse opinions on moral and doctrinal questions,
they find it harder to accept popular claims to absolute certitude on religious questions. The ecumenical movement has
made it difficult for members of one denomination to maintain a clear and distinct identity from Christians who belong
to other denominations. The contemporary feminist movement has fostered significant changes in congregational life,
including women pastors and inclusive liturgical language.

Catholics in the United States have lived through a half
century of disruptive changes. World War II enabled Catholic
young people in the military to get to know Protestants. The
GI Bill afforded Catholics the opportunity to go to college
and move up the socio-economic ladder. As a result these
more affluent Catholics moved from the cities to the suburbs,
where they established new parishes. As educated people
they related to their pastors in a more mature way and
looked for more enlightened preaching and teaching. The
election of John Kennedy in 1960 signaled the movement of
Catholics from a suspect minority in a predominantly Protestant society to active participants in the mainstream of
American life.

It was from this newly won position of power and acceptance that educated American Catholics experienced the
profound changes initiated by the Second Vatican Council.
Although some of the changes seemed disruptive from the
viewpoint of recent church practices, middle class American
Catholics generally accepted them as reasonable expressions
of their own culturally conditioned religious sensibilities.
Educated Catholics understood that the church must always
reform itself and applauded the call for greater lay participation in the life of the church. The call for more collegiality in
the church made sense to persons steeped in the democratic
process. Christians who flourished in the soil of religious
freedom could appreciate the affirmation of religious liberty
enunciated by the Council. The call for better ecumenical relationships made sense to citizens of a country which celebrates pluralism. Most of the liturgical changes were

welcomed by Catholics who wanted more participation and expected greater intelligibility in their worship.

Despite the congenial nature of the Vatican II reforms, Catholics still experienced them as part of a rapidly changing world which challenged traditional sources of stability and security. In the decades since the Council, an increased awareness of pluralism has called into question the essence of Catholic identity. Harsh debates on many church issues make it difficult to stake out the Catholic common ground. The polarized disputes between liberals and conservatives highlight the problem of maintaining religious identity in an age of transition.

Today's collegians, part of the large cohort known as Generation X, are heavily influenced by the changes and discontinuties of the contemporary world. Let us consider a composite example of a young man named David. He is from a Catholic family but his parents were divorced when he was 12 years old. At first he blamed himself for the breakup of the family, but his counselor helped him see the picture more clearly. Holidays are difficult for David as he struggles to balance his time between his mother and father. He even dreads his approaching graduation because his parents, who find it difficult to be in the same room together, will both demand his attention. David is very cautious about his other relationships, mostly hanging out with a small group of guys he first met at college. He has a girlfriend but is in no hurry to get married. Haunted by the trauma of his parents' divorce he is determined to make a successful permanent marriage himself, and plans to wait until he is in his late 20s.

David, a business major, is pessimistic about the nation's economy, which he expects to get worse during his lifetime. He joins most of his friends in the fatalistic conviction that the social security system will be bankrupt by the time he retires. At the same time David believes he himself will do quite well economically – an optimistic assessment shared by over 80% of collegians. Politically, David is cynical and turned off. He does not follow the election campaigns and has never voted. He does not read the weekly news magazines or even watch the nightly news, much to the bewilder-

ment of his father who likes to stay informed and would love
to discuss world affairs with his son. The great social issues
such as homelessness and racism strike David as intractable
and overwhelming so he chooses to ignore them. One exception is the environmental crisis which periodically attracts his
attention and efforts. It angers him that the previous generation left the earth so polluted. David goes to church about
twice a month and no longer feels guilty for missing Mass.
He likes the liturgies on campus and is more likely to go to
Mass at school than when he is home. He meets regularly
with a small group of collegians who pray together and talk
about their spiritual lives. By his own admission David
knows very little about Catholic doctrines and often feels
frustrated when he is unable to respond to the fundamentalist Christians who periodically accost him. The polarized debates in the church make almost no impact on him except for
one issue – women's ordination. Periodically his girlfriend
brings it up and often refuses to go to Mass with him because only men preside at the liturgy. David cannot understand why the church refuses to give equal opportunities to
women. Finally, David clearly inhabits the electronic world.
He watches a lot of television and does very little reading.
Computers are his friends and the Internet gives him access
to a whole world of information. The rapidly changing technology generally excites him, but at times he is apprehensive
about keeping up with the changes.

David is typical of young people who have grown up in
an unstable world. They have known the disruption of family
life, the corruption of government officials, the intractability
of social problems, the ambivalence of rapid technological
developments and the polarization in the church. Furthermore, the members of Generation X have come of age in a
world filled with images of death. Most of them have vivid
memories of the explosion of the space shuttle Challenger
which killed the teacher Christa McAuliff. They know young
people who died in car accidents or committed suicide. The
AIDS epidemic has shadowed their experience of growing
up.

All of these shaping experiences have helped produce a certain cynicism and even resentment among some young people. Spokespersons for Generation X have contrasted themselves with the previous generation: the Boomers shared in a flourishing economy; we have a massive debt. They enjoyed free love; we have AIDS. They had the successes of the civil rights movement; we have the problems connected with Affirmative Action. They had the victory over Communism; we have to contend with Bosnia. The experiences of young people today remind all of us of the discontinuities which characterize our age of transition. If we are going to develop a viable contemporary spirituality, we need a better understanding of our rapidly changing world and its effect on human consciousness.

Analysis of the Transition

Many scholars are convinced that we are living through a major paradigm shift in which the modern worldview is being gradually replaced by a new one. An American physicist and historian of science, Thomas S. Kuhn, developed the notion of paradigm changes in his classic work *The Structure of Scientific Revolution*, first published in 1962. Kuhn describes a paradigm as "an entire constellation of beliefs, values, techniques, etc. shared by the members of a given community." Fundamental paradigms begin to break down when they no longer serve as coherent explanations of reality or lose their power to inspire members of the community. Paradigms collapse because historical developments bring momentous changes to society and culture. The breakup of established paradigms generally produces a period of great uncertainty as new problems arise, creative hypotheses are tested and intimations of a new worldview gradually emerge. At times decisive thinkers perceive the direction of the transition and are able to provide conceptual explanations of the changes. There is a dialectical relationship between social-historical developments and early theories about them.

Paradigm changes also occur within particular disciplines when the dominant model is not able to explain new data, manage changing situations or account for developing aspects of human experience. The scientific world has experienced such a decisive transition in the shift from Newtonian physics to Einstein's theories of relativity.

The field of theology has also gone through important paradigm shifts throughout Christian history. We can identify these decisive changes by the influential thinkers who helped shape them: Paul and his preaching of the crucified Christ to the Gentile world; Origen (d. 254) and his reinterpretation of the Scriptures in a Hellenistic culture; Augustine (d. 430) and his defense of Christianity after the fall of Rome; Aquinas (d. 1274) and his synthesis of Christian theology and Aristotelian philosophy; Martin Luther (d. 1546) and his rereading of the Scriptures according to the principle of faith alone; Friedrich Schleiermacher (d. 1834) and his outreach to the modern cultured despisers of religion; Karl Barth (d. 1968) and his neo-orthodox return to Jesus as the unique revelation of the "wholly other" God; and finally Karl Rahner (d. 1984) and his reinterpretation of Christian doctrines for the contemporary world. Each of these thinkers has responded to changing situations in the world and church by articulating a new influential model for Christian theology.

Today, no genius or prophet has yet appeared to offer a comprehensive and coherent theory of our changing world which is able to gain general acceptance. Many commentators who recognize the disruptive character of our times speak of a fundamental shift from the modern to the postmodern world which is as yet unformed and undefined.

Frederich Nietzsche (d. 1900) was the great early prophet of the collapse of modernity. More than anyone else in the 19th century he understood the chaos lurking beneath the rational veneer of the Enlightenment project. He felt in his own soul the consequences of the effort to construct a humane world through science and reason divorced from religious belief. In his provocative parable of the madman found in *The Gay Science* first published in 1882, Nietzsche tells us that if God is dead then "the earth is unchained from the sun." We "feel the breath of empty space" and are "straying as through an infinite nothing" unable to determine up from down. Nietzsche describes well the instability and insecurity felt by many people today who experience the collapse of absolute truths and struggle with the absence of God.

The contemporary French philosopher Jean-Francois Lyotard has developed this theme of the collapse of absolutes in his book *The Postmodern Condition*. He argues that the postmodern world is characterized by "an incredulity towards mega-narratives." In other words the modern attempts to interpret and organize the world according to the great stories or universal paradigms of liberal democracy and Marxist ideology have failed. The French philosophers who share this view are also critical of the exclusive claims of the monotheistic religions, including Christianity which they accuse of supporting Western colonial domination. For these scholars the postmodern world can benefit from tribal religions, but must resist the exaggerated claims of biblical religion to have a universal message. The deconstructionist scholars, such as Jacques Derrida and Michel Foucault, insist that any attempt to impose a determined meaning on a text is a form of domination. This critique challenges the authority of the church hierarchy to interpret the Bible in an official way. Deconstructionist scholars offer us the helpful reminder that every analysis of spirituality must take into account cultural conditioning and multiple perspectives. But taken to its logical conclusion, deconstructionism becomes nihilism and undercuts the very foundation of shared spiritual discourse.

Alasdair MacIntyre, who teaches philosophy at Notre Dame, is representative of those who perceive the moral exhaustion of the modern project. In his important book *After Virtue*, he argues that we are in a great moral crisis because we continue to use the traditional language of morality, but have lost our sense of what morality is all about. According to this line of thought modernity carried the seeds of its own destruction because it lost the moral foundation of pursuing virtue and the common good. This analysis helps us understand the way a fundamental cultural change affects our efforts to live the Christian life today. It also suggests the importance of connecting spirituality with the cultivation of the traditional moral and theological virtues.

Stephen Toulmin argues in *Cosmopolis* that we are in the process of totally reversing modernity. Beginning with Descartes in the 17th century, modern thinkers attempted to ground all knowledge in the autonomous conscious self. Through reason, human beings would uncover the universal principles and the timeless truths which would make progress possible. Toulmin contends that today we are moving from the emphasis on the universal to the particular, from the general to the local, from the timeless to the timely, and from the domination of the written word to a renewed emphasis on oral communication. Toulmin joins other scholars in recognizing the limitations of Cartesian rationalism. Even scientific inquiry requires trust in the work of others, and is never merely a matter of objective observation and analysis. The pursuit of totally objective knowledge and value-free discourse has proven to be illusory and destructive. In the pursuit of truth we must often settle for converging probabilities and relatively adequate arguments. These challenges to modern rationalism set the stage for a postmodern spirituality which is more attuned to the mystery dimension of life. The scholars we have noted, as well as many other analysts of the contemporary scene are convinced that we are living through a major paradigm shift from the modern to the postmodern world. They are clear on the ambiguities, contradictions and limitations of modernity, but are far more vague on the shape of postmodernity. For them the term "postmodern" functions heuristically, focusing attention and inviting efforts to specify its content. The developing new world remains unpredictable and open to many options. From the viewpoint of spirituality such a fluid situation invites all believers to take an active role in creating a society which builds on the accomplishments of modernity while rejecting its destruction aspects.

Some authors give the word "postmodern" greater content. In his valuable book *The Condition of Post-Modernity* (Basil Blackwell, 1989), David Harvey claims that postmodernism emerged as a full-blown movement somewhere between 1968 and 1972. It had its roots in the new left politics of the 1960s and was often connected with universities and the cultural fringes of big city life. The movement insists that all particular groups should have their own voice and express their own ideas and needs. While the machine was the dominant model for modernity, Harvey identifies the collage as the primary form of postmodern discourse. Television puts the emphasis on collage approaches to communication rather than in-depth analysis. Typical postmodern philosophers, such as Richard Rorty, are convinced that there is no way to achieve a comprehensive explanation of reality, to uncover universal patterns in human existence, or to find totally satisfying answers to fundamental questions. We are really left with "chronic provisionality" and a plurality of perspectives. Ideologies such as Marxism are dead and the universal claims of religious traditions, including Christianity, are called into question. There is no overarching metaphysical language which all accept; we can communicate effectively only within particular language games and in very specific contexts. Harvey suggests that Los Angeles is the typical postmodern city because it has no clear center, involves great movement, has a diverse population, and cannot be reduced to a single principle. As Nietzsche foresaw, people today are very aware of the chaotic forces which threaten all efforts to construct a rational world.

According to Harvey postmodernity is characterized by the compression of space and time. It costs the same to communicate over 600 miles as it does 6,000 miles via satellite. Transnational corporations hold simultaneous meetings at offices across the world. Billions of people around the globe watched the Olympic games at the same time. In this compressed world it is hard to find a sense of rootedness. Postmodern novels, such as Anne Tyler's *The Accidental Tourist*, feature individuals wandering through a pluralistic world without a clear sense of location. Mobile people today sometimes wonder where they are and which personality they are to employ in changing situations. Such complexity produces an intense desire for a clear personal and collective identity and for secure moorings in a shifting world. Individuals want to spend time with kindred spirits. Ethnic groups develop a new sense of identity and seek autonomy. Special interest groups dominate national politics. In short, the postmodern compression of time and space has intensified the normal human desire for identity, security and stability. Although some of David Harvey's presuppositions are questionable, he identifies important postmodern trends that invite a Christian response. We must search for depth in a culture that trivializes religion, for roots in a transient society and for direction in a complex world.

Other Transitions

We can extend our understanding of the new world by examining significant transitions which contribute to the fundamental shift from modernity to postmodernity.

We are, for example, moving into a post-colonial period. The great modern empires established by European countries have been dismantled. The Soviet Union has collapsed. Countries all over the globe have gained their freedom. The dismantling of the apartheid system in South Africa and the election of Nelson Mandella symbolizes the demise of colonialism. In *Culture and Imperialism* (Knopf, 1993), Edward W. Said argues that despite great progress most people on the earth today are still influenced by colonial practices and attitudes. Many people in the West continue to see the East as exotic and inferior. Indigenous people still bear the scars of colonial domination. We need only look at the experience of Native Americans in the United States to realize the enduring destructive effects of the social sin known as colonialism. In the post-colonial period we have new opportunities for genuine dialogue among diverse cultures. In the global village, no culture, East or West, can claim to be normative for the whole of the world. When a society recognizes its own limitations, it is more open to learning from others. As Said points out, we still have the task of overcoming the colonial attitudes which prevent genuine dialogue and collaboration. The post-colonial world is filled with new possibilities for Christian spirituality. We have much to learn from the great mystical religions of India and the wisdom traditions of China as well as the indigenous religions of Africa.

Ever since Daniel Bell published his classic work, *The Coming of Post-Industrial Society*, in 1976, there has been a general recognition that the contemporary economy puts more emphasis on services than the productive work of agriculture and industry. Today there is a greater demand for services in transportation, health, education, training, research, trade and administration. We have been moving from a producer society to an information-based culture in which technical knowledge becomes a new form of capital. Today there is a greater awareness of the ecological crisis created by industrialization and the need to find more harmonious ways to live with nature. In our post-industrial society a credible spirituality must help people find meaning in their work and ways to use their knowledge for the common good. Already we have made strides toward an eco-spirituality which appreciates nature and promotes good stewardship of the earth.

Modernity carried on the patriarchal practices of the medieval world. White males dominated economic, political and social developments in Europe and the United States. Typically the activities of men in the public arena were divorced from any religious and spiritual roots. It was assumed that the marketplace had its own autonomous rules. Women dominated the domestic sphere and had the task of passing on the religious heritage within the setting of the home. In this way, modernity reduced religion to the private realm of personal piety. The feminist movement of the 20th century has raised consciousness on the destructive aspects of sexism. Progress has been made in constructing a post-patriarchal society, but gender bias continues to be a major problem. Women have to contend with the glass ceiling in the corporate world and continue to be paid less than men for comparable work. The Catholic Church denies them the opportunity to serve as ordained priests. Violence of all types directed against women continues to be a major problem: wife battering, harassment at the work site and date rape. Young couples these days speak about partnership and mutuality in marriage, but the reality seldom matches the ideal. Women generally continue to do more than their share of the domestic chores, even while holding down full time jobs outside the home.

It has been difficult to find acceptable theories of gender differences. For a period in the 1970s feminists did not want to discuss gender differences of any type. Publication of Carol Gilligan's book *In a Different Voice* (1982) signaled a new effort to talk about gender differences in a way that would not lead to domination and inequality. Unfortunately, popular theories of complementarity, whether based on the theology of Genesis or the psychology of Carl Jung, often work against the best interests of women because masculine characteristics are generally considered superior. Some authors today suggest we drop the notion of distinctive male and female characteristics, while admitting statistical variations. For example, all humans beings seek both autonomy and intimacy, but in the United States today more men seek success and fear failure and more women seek intimacy and fear aloneness. This approach avoids stereotyping and makes it easier for individuals to accept their own unique mix of human characteristics.

The strong feminist movement has created a reaction among men. Some men feel uncertain of their own role and feel constrained in their relationships with women at the work site and in other settings. The specter of being charged with sexual harassment is ever present. The best-selling book *Iron John* by poet Robert Bly represents the beginning of a movement among men to find new strength and vigor, especially by reconnecting with their fathers. Support groups for men provide a sense of solidarity for males who are trying to find their place in the post-patriarchal world. We already have a large and impressive body of work on feminine spirituality and spirituality for women. The literature on men and their distinctive issues is growing. We need a post-patriarchial spirituality which integrates the public and private realms of life and challenges the injustices created by sexist attitudes. This spirituality must enable men and women to relate on the basis of equality and mutuality, while respecting and fostering the unique potential of the other person.

In the United States believers have gradually moved into a post-denominational situation. In the early part of our national history citizens generally gathered with others of the same religious background. The Catholic immigrants of the 19th and 20th centuries tended to cluster together in the same neighborhoods, to build their own schools, and to marry within their own subculture. But as Robert Wuthnow has pointed out in his excellent study *The Restructuring of American Religion,* we now live in a post-confessional period in which believers relate more on the basis of fundamental worldviews than membership in historical denominations. Concretely, conservative Catholics are finding new common ground with evangelical Christians. Progressive Catholics often feel more at ease with liberal Protestants than with reactionary Catholics. This new situation is in a very fluid state. The political ramifications of the new alignments are not yet clear. Remnants of denominationalism are still evident. Geographically, Baptists still dominate the South and Catholics remain a strong presence in the large cities of the North. Individuals who grow up in a particular denomination tend to retain the religious sensibilities of their tradition. Believers today must be solidly rooted in their own tradition so that they can be open to truth and goodness in other traditions.

One of the most striking features of our world today is that we no longer live with the tensions of the Cold War. For decades after World War II our national policy was dictated by the threat of communism and the military might of the Soviet Union. With the collapse of the Soviet Union and the liberation of Eastern Europe, we now have a totally new situation. It is true that Russian nationalism still represents a threat, but we are gradually forging economic and cultural ties with the former Soviet states which make the resumption of the Cold War less likely. In the post-Cold War period, new ethnic rivalries and regional conflicts have become more prominent. The horrible conflict in Bosnia epitomizes the new problems that arise when a communist dictatorship breaks up. As the lone superpower, the United States is still exploring its proper role in the new world order. Some far-sighted leaders are calling for an expanded role for the United Nations. No one has easy answers to the tensions which are built into the post-Cold War period. Christian spirituality which is faithful to the social dimension of the Gospel cannot withdraw into a new isolationism, but must take an active role in creating a more just and peaceful world where nations can live in harmony.

Although individualism continues to be dominant in our culture, the postmodern era has produced a remarkable interest in small groups. The birth of the small group movement has been chronicled by Robert Wuthnow in his book *Sharing the Journey.* His statistical studies show that in a recent five-year period about half of American adults participated in some sort of small group. Such groups typically meet once a week for a couple of hours and command serious allegiance from the members of the group. Members tend to gather with others who are of like mind or are struggling with similar problems. The various types of twelve-step programs make up a large portion of this movement. Individuals seldom make lifelong commitments to these groups and easily move out of them if they no longer meet their needs. Many people today find their real spiritual nourishment in gathering with kindred spirits. The danger is that the groups turn in on themselves, failing to develop a proper concern for the common good and missing the enrichment of interactions with others who are different.

In one area the shape of the postmodern world is clearer and can be properly named. We have definitely moved into the electronic age. The invention of the printing press in the 15th century helped create the book culture and produced a linear form of consciousness which was crucial to the progress of modernity. The development of television and the spread of the audiovisual culture has changed the way people think and perceive the world. People who have grown up with television and live in a world of amplified music have fundamentally different ways of acquiring knowledge and viewing the world. In his book *The New Era in Religious Communication* (Fortress 1991), the religious educator Pierre Babin analyzes the new electronic civilization from the perspective of Christian formation. The sons and daughters of Guttenberg gained knowledge by reading books. In the book culture the eye is dominant. We look down on a printed page and decipher the meaning of printed symbols. Reading enables a person to step back, adopt a perspective and analyze the text. It creates a distinctive form of consciousness which is sequential, linear, logical, active and capable of penetrating reality. In the book culture the left hemisphere of the brain tends to dominate.

Following the lead of his mentor Marshall McLuhan, Babin argues that the new media technologies leave an imprint on the nervous system and activate the right brain. Today the average eighteen-year-old American has already spent 20,000 hours watching television and countless hours playing video games and listening to loud, pulsating music. People immersed in the audiovisual world develop a new mode of consciousness which is more symbolic, holistic, receptive, intuitive and simultaneous. In this aural culture, according to Babin, the ear is the dominant organ and vibrations are the dominant mode of communicating. At a rock concert young people are not observing an event but are resonating with the pulsating rhythms. Listening to loud music encloses an individual in a vibrating environment. The contrast between the book culture and the electronic civilization is evident at social gatherings where some people want soft music so they can talk while others desire to be encased in loud music. The aural culture also influences the way the eye functions. In reading the eye scans, composes and analyzes. Watching television, an individual is more passive, receiving the predigested image. MTV bombards the viewer with a rapid succession of images which enter consciousness without the possibility of analysis.

According to Babin, the new audiovisual world produces a sense of disintegration. Television brings violence into the home. The media report only spectacular or odd events which deviate from the norm. Computers offer us vast amounts of new information, but we have little time or ability to organize it into logical, coherent patterns. Under such bombardment it is difficult to maintain a sense of personal integration or to achieve a comprehensive view of reality.

The electronic culture also has a powerful effect on the affective life of those immersed in it. Advertisers use images to generate an emotional reaction. Amplified music draws listeners into a web of feeling. Videos often appeal to the instincts. Television is a powerful force in shaping the imagination. For Babin the most damaging effect of the electronic culture is the loss of interiority. Constant messages to conform to the standards set by the media produce a subtle form of self-alienation. It is difficult to get in touch with one's own thoughts and feelings when being bombarded by external stimuli. The constant drumbeat of amplified sound can drown out the whisperings of the Spirit in our hearts. An image-dominated culture puts more emphasis on making a good impression than being true to oneself.

Following some suggestions of Babin, a spirituality for the electronic age will try to cultivate the interior life through the practice of silence and meditation. People immersed in the audiovisual culture must learn to listen to their own hearts and be more attuned to the Spirit within. Retreats that incorporate silence will help young people separate themselves from the external stimuli which constantly bombard them. Reflective liturgies can provide the distance and perspective needed to keep alive the memory of Jesus. Regular meditation creates space for listening to the gracious God who calls us by name.

The computer is now an essential part of the electronic civilization. Computers perform complex tasks in seconds and enable us to store and retrieve amazing amounts of information. They have revolutionized the process of writing and the way research is done. The Internet connects people all over the world and enables collaborative efforts on projects. But there are dangers as well. The new technology can be used to invade an individual's privacy. Some commentators are afraid that computers will form an electronic moat which will isolate us from other people. Communication by E-mail lacks the depth and personal touch of face to face encounters. We will be able to buy things without leaving our homes or listen to sermons without going to church. Human memory and the mastery of specific knowledge will become less important. The new electronic technology has already affected the traditional relationship between children and the parental generation. It is not unusual for parents to ask their children, even younger ones, how to use a computer to program their VCR. We have to wonder if this role reversal undercuts the respect the young should have for their elders, or makes them less inclined to seek knowledge or wisdom from them. Computer technology is fundamentally ambivalent. The spiritual task is to help humanize this amazing technology and to check its destructive potential.

Together with television, computers have propelled us into a new audiovisual culture. This transition has created a new mode of consciousness as did the invention of the alphabet and the printing press in the past. The book culture fostered a spirituality which tends to be individualistic, rationalistic and active. The electronic age calls for a new spirituality which is more communal, intuitive and reflective.

Describing the contemporary situation as post-colonial, post-industrial, post-patriarchal, post-denominational, post-Cold War and, with greater specificity, electronic, is to emphasize the discontinuity between the modern Age of Reason and the new world that is being formed. A spirituality in tune with this analysis will put great emphasis on avoiding the mistakes of modernity and creating a very different world more reflective of Gospel values.

Continuities in the Age of Transition

We find an important alternative reading of the contemporary situation in the work of the Canadian Catholic philosopher Charles Taylor, especially in his large volume, *Sources of the Self: The Making of the Modern Identity* (Harvard University Press, 1989). In general, Taylor doubts that we are passing through a great paradigm shift. On the contrary, the dynamics of our time are still fueled by the energy flowing from the Enlightenment and Romanticism. Our culture's values, self-perceptions and moral outlook are still determined by these two great moments. We treasure the modern ideals of human rights and democracy and have made gradual progress in extending them to new nations and to new classes. Our society espouses the Enlightenment moral imperative to put an end to suffering, or at least to reduce it. We find significance in ordinary life and believe in the ideal of universal benevolence. Our culture celebrates the dignity and worth of the individual person. We respect the power of both logical reason and the creative imagination. Freedom is a central good which must be defended against all forms of coercion. We affirm justice for all and continue to work for its implementation.

Taylor discerns a continuing struggle between the 18th century Enlightenment which celebrated reason and 19th century Romanticism which emphasized the creative imagination. Enlightenment rationalism remains a powerful force in our culture today. Influential philosophers insist that only the empirically verifiable can be counted as true. Many still consider the scientific method to be the best vehicle for human progress. Our society celebrates cool logic as a mark of maturity. We pay efficient managers large salaries. Organizations make use of bureaucratic structures.

But Romantic criticisms of the Enlightenment project are also evident in our culture. Rationalism fragments human life by splitting reason and feeling and by dividing us from nature and one another. The Enlightenment has produced a rugged individualism which ultimately undermines concern for the common good and weakens participatory democracy. Industrialization has plundered the natural environment. Academic disciplines from physics to psychology have ignored the mystery dimension of life and neglected imaginative approaches in the search for truth. The combination of a utilitarian value system and a bureaucratic mode of existence impoverishes human existence by emptying life of its meaning, depriving us of a high sense of purpose, and diminishing our passion for truth and goodness. According to Charles Taylor, the romantic protest against rationalism which began early in the history of the Enlightenment continues to fuel the discussion today of how to produce a better world. Our challenging task is to integrate discursive reason and creative imagination in a holistic spirituality which propels persons toward greater maturity and more effective efforts to humanize the world.

Professor Taylor does recognize that we live in an age of transition. For him, the most significant change is that more people now think about the moral order apart from belief in God. This trend began in England and the United States in the latter part of the 19th century. Rationalistic critics of religion developed a new ethic of belief which contends that we ought not to believe in religious tenets unless we have sufficient evidence. In the contemporary world we continue to feel the moral demand for universal justice, equality, freedom, self-rule and the limitation of suffering. The real battle is over the moral source of these convictions. Christians continue to ground these moral ideals in their belief in God. Some humanists try to justify them on the basis of reason. Others with a more romantic bent root their convictions in the creative imagination and the general sense that it feels right. One of the great questions of our time is whether the high ideals of the Enlightenment can be maintained without the religious convictions which originally supported them. In other words, does modernity carry its own seeds of destruction? In the 19th and 20th centuries influential critics of religion such as Marx, Nietzsche, Freud and Sartre have claimed that Christianity is the enemy of human progress because it keeps believers in an infantile state and prevents them from wholehearted involvement in the world. A credible spirituality today must demonstrate that Christianity is a powerful liberating force which promotes the modern ideals of human growth and societal improvement.

Taylor remains very positive about the essential values of modernity. He celebrates reason and insists that we should not repudiate it because some individuals have used their rational powers for evil purposes. In our culture we must be careful to avoid all forms of subjectivism which effectively deny the claims of the objective world upon us. Taylor finds this danger in the human potential movement and the "triumph of the therapeutic" which some commentators have discerned in our culture. A healthy drive for self-fulfillment realizes that we have responsibilities for the common good. It is true that we are suffering from a deep-seated loss of meaning within our culture. The solution, however, is not to abandon reason, but to make sure that it is balanced by pursuing other goods in life. This means working for the general welfare and avoiding a subjectivism which searches for meaning and value only within. Taylor insists that we must find moral sources outside of ourselves. The world makes claims upon us. Our freedom is always situated in a particular setting which must be respected. Great prophets and poets call us to respond to the voice of reality. Realism demands that we face the ambiguities of life and find ways to work together for peace and justice even with those who do not share our religious convictions.

Charles Taylor is well aware that elements of the Enlightenment have fostered the worst kinds of violence, destruction and exploitation. Modernity gave us colonialism, patriarchy, pollution and nuclear weapons. But Taylor insists that we not make a blanket condemnation of the whole modern project. Quite the contrary, we need to celebrate and extend the impressive progress made in crucial areas such as human rights, democracy and religious liberty.

Jurgen Habermas of the Frankfurt school is another author who wants to extend rather than dismiss the ideals of the Enlightenment. According to him modernity moved in destructive directions because its understanding of human reason was too narrow. It generally thought of reason in instrumental terms as an isolated faculty which logically mobilizes means to achieve goals which remain largely unexamined. In response, Habermas argues that our very being is constituted by exchange with others and that we can overcome the ambiguities of modernity by improving interpersonal communication. In his terms we must rely on communicative reason and not simply instrumental reason. We should not reject reason in favor of a soft romanticism, but should employ communicative reason to serve the cause of human development. Thus Habermas joins Taylor and others who insist that we should not abandon the worthy ideals of modernity. Our high calling is to find better ways of achieving the modern goals of extending human rights, reducing suffering, achieving equality and finding personal fulfillment.

Scholars such as Taylor and Habermas direct our attention to the continuities which prevail in our age of transition. Even in the midst of major cultural changes many things remain the same. Some scholars estimate that 80% of the old still recurs in one way or another even after a great political or social revolution. Individuals living through a paradigm shift are still able to read texts from the previous age and appreciate its art. Human beings continue to experience both joys and sorrows. Families still rejoice over the birth of a baby and grieve over the death of a loved one. We carry memories of the past and plan for the future. Fads come and go quickly. Social movements develop over decades. Cultures usually change only gradually over centuries. Even great paradigm shifts are the result of a long period of preparation and lead into another lengthy period of assimilation. Persons who experience the trauma of sharp transition periods usually retain significant traditions from the past as they gradually adapt themselves to the changing world. Many people today can find in themselves traces of premodern, modern and postmodern characteristics.

A spirituality which takes seriously the account of Charles Taylor and Jurgen Habermas will be attentive to the continuities in our changing culture and the family resemblances in diverse approaches to the spiritual life. It will retrieve the valuable aspects of premodern and modern spiritualities. Such a spirituality will continue the task of integrating head and heart in a holistic Christian approach to personal growth and social transformation.

Summary and Assessment of the Transition

Despite the impressive work of Charles Taylor, it seems to me that we are indeed living through a major paradigm shift. Only a profound transition in worldview can explain the confusion, tension and frustration so prevalent in the United States today. Only a fundamental shift in consciousness can account for the new ways young people learn and experience the world. Only massive institutional changes could cause the kind of personal insecurity and future shock that people are experiencing today.

At this stage of the transition process it is still helpful to describe it as a shift from modernity to postmodernity. The word "postmodern" is useful precisely because it is vague and acknowledges that we are in a fluid situation. Discussion of a postmodern world contains an implicit invitation to participate in shaping a more humane, just and peaceful world.

In our rapidly changing world certain trends are already clear. It is possible to discern distinctively postmodern dynamics if not a defined movement. We now have an expanded global awareness of our common destiny on spaceship earth, but this is accompanied by a new tribalism which celebrates ethnicity and seeks community with kindred spirits. Our greater awareness of pluralism has fostered a new search for roots and identity. The rapid development of communications technology needs to be balanced by greater attention to personal interactions and face-to-face encounters. People constantly traumatized by amplified sound need time for silence and reflection. The breakdown of institutional authority calls for greater personal commitment as well as a healthy balance of freedom and responsibility. With a greater appreciation of other cultures comes the need to understand our own culture in greater depth. Successful interfaith collaboration for world peace demands that religions reappropriate the teachings and spirit of their founders. Individuals and groups who are especially hurt by the disruptions of our world need compassion and spiritual care. As the lone superpower the United States has to develop new global strategies for achieving justice and peace in the world. The dark mood in our culture calls for a renewed sense of hope.

The disruptions and discontinuities of the postmodern world render it fundamentally open to religious teachings and inspiration. We need a spirituality which will seize the opportunity and help guide our world in healthy directions.

3. Developing a Spirituality for an Age of Transition

We need to face all the ambiguities and darkness of our disrupted age without escaping into a fantasy world of cheap grace. We must stay open to the hidden God who joins us in the struggle against human suffering.

Throughout the centuries Christian spirituality has shown a remarkable capacity to adapt to changing times. Christians have always found ways of relating their faith to particular cultural situations. From the early centuries pluralism has always been a characteristic of Christian spirituality. Distinct pieties developed in the East and the West. Even among Western Christians, Catholics and Protestants responded to modernity in diverse ways. Furthermore, Christians in the United States have developed spiritualities different from believers in Europe.

Protestant Response

In 1799 the Protestant theologian Friedrich Schleiermacher published a book entitled *On Religion: Speeches to its Cultured Despisers.* This important work signaled the beginning of a long effort within the Protestant community to enter into dialogue with the modern world. Schleiermacher felt that he could speak as a Christian theologian to the enlightened nonbelievers of his time by beginning in common human experiences, especially the feeling of absolute dependency and the taste for the infinite. By adopting this methodology, Schleiermacher became the father of all modern theology, as Karl Barth later recognized. The followers of Schleiermacher, often referred to as liberal Protestants, made many accommodations to the spirit of the modern world throughout the 19th century. Critics of this liberal movement commonly contend that it sold out to modernity by emptying Christianity of its traditional belief in the miracles, the resurrection and the divinity of Christ. Left only with the "fatherhood of God and the brotherhood of man," liberal Protestants could not challenge the ambiguities of modernity. Although this blanket criticism misses the richness and nuance of the

liberal tradition, it does remind us that 19th century Protestant theology took seriously important trends in the modern
world.

In 1919 the great neo-Orthodox theologian Karl Barth
first published his famous *The Epistle to the Romans,* which
blasted liberal Protestant theology for capitulating to modernity and insisted on a return to orthodox belief in Jesus
Christ, revealed in the Scriptures. With remarkable vigor
Barth insisted that God was the Wholly Other and could not
be found by human reason or modern philosophy. Barth's
neo-Orthodox theology set the stage for a biblically based
spirituality which drew its nourishment entirely from the
Christ revealed in the Scriptures. Throughout the 20th century this spirituality has provided a clear alternative to the
piety of liberal theology which was far more open to the various currents of modern thought.

Barth's theological project must be distinguished from
the approach of the Fundamentalist movement which developed in the United States in the early part of the 20th century. Like Barth, some American Evangelical Christians
became very aware of the shortcomings of modernity and the
dangers it posed for Christianity. Returning to a premodern
theology, they repudiated the modern scientific theory of evolution in favor of the creationism taught by the book of Genesis. They also rejected modern critical approaches to
interpreting the Bible, while insisting on the absolute inerrancy of the scriptures. In order to defend themselves and
their faith against the attacks of modernity, these Christians
vigorously affirmed certain fundamental truths including the
virgin birth, the divinity of Jesus, the atonement for sins
through the blood of the cross and the bodily resurrection of
Christ. They did not attempt a comprehensive reinterpretation of the Christian tradition as Barth did, but selectively
retrieved certain truths as weapons in the life and death
struggle against the demonic forces of the modern world.
While Barth's theology preserves the ultimately mysterious
character of the transcendent God, Fundamentalists tend to
domesticate God and to exclude from salvation all who do
not share their theology and piety.

Catholic Response in Europe

In Europe the Catholic response to modernity was primarily negative all the way into the middle of the 20th century. The Syllabus of Errors, disseminated by Pope Pius IX in 1864, harshly condemned many elements of the modern project, including democracy, freedom of speech and religious liberty. This stance effectively precluded the Catholic Church from dialogue with the world and fostered a spirituality which was isolated and defensive. The famous encyclical of Pope Leo XIII, *Rerum Novarum,* published in 1891, brought the church back into dialogue with the modern world, at least on the question of capital and labor. At the same time Leo XIII rejected much of modern philosophy and opted instead for a return to the premodern thought of Thomas Aquinas. This sparked a revival of neo-scholastic philosophy and theology which gained momentum during the first half of the 20th century. Working out of this framework, the most influential of the neo-scholastics, Jacques Maritain, was able to open up some constructive conversations with the modern world on a variety of topics including art, politics, economics and human rights. Out of these discussions he fashioned a Christian humanism which strengthened many Catholics to be self-confident participants in modern culture.

It was Pope John XXIII who opened the door to a genuine dialogue with modernity in which the Church would be both teacher and learner. In his amazingly influential encyclical, *Pacem in Terris,* the Pope embraced for the first time the whole tradition of human rights which had been developing since the time of the Enlightenment. The Second Vatican Council, called by Pope John, went a step further by affirming the positive values of religious liberty for all people. The Pastoral Constitution, *Gaudium et Spes,* explicitly addressed many topics arising from the position of the Church in the modern world, ranging from politics to family life. The Council promoted a Christocentric spirituality concerned with spreading the Gospel in the world. It also reminded us of the universal call to holiness and fostered a lay spirituality nourished by the liturgy and dedicated to the work of peace and justice.

Catholic Responses in the United States

In the United States, Catholics generally were pleased with the Council's openness to the modern world. After all, they had benefited greatly from the achievements of modernity including democracy, freedom of the press, cultural pluralism, religious liberty, human rights, a market economy and the separation of church and state. Historically, Catholics were divided in their assessment of American culture and society. Influenced by European thinking, the Romanists were very critical of the individualism, relativism and indifference spawned by American modernity. This outlook created a closed, defensive spirituality which prompted some Catholics to withhold involvement in the dominant culture. On the other hand, the Americanists celebrated the ideals of democracy, freedom, religious liberty and the separation of church and state because they enabled individuals and the church as a whole to flourish. Their position lead to a more open and engaged spirituality which propelled Catholics into an active role in society. With the bishops leading the way, Catholics played a major role in establishing the rights of workers. The Catholic hierarchy proposed and fought for social legislation to aid the poor and unemployed. By the 1960s most American Catholics had benefited from the system and were in the social, political and economic mainstream. The spirituality espoused by the Americanists had generally prevailed. Indeed the distinctive American approach to religious liberty was adopted by the Council and became the official teaching of the universal church. American Catholics accepted the Council's approach to the modern world because it resonated with their own experience.

Challenges to Modernity

But while the church was adopting a more open outlook on modernity, influential secular scholars were already pointing out its ambiguities and contradictions. Feminists challenged the inequality and exploitation built into modern patriarchy. Economists identified the destructive effects of global capitalism on local economies. Peace activists proclaimed the folly of the arms race. World leaders with a broad vision attacked the narrowness of nationalism. Sociologists warned about the fragmentation of society and the weakening of institutions including the family. Environmentalists called attention to industrial pollution. Cultural critics discerned a new somber mood gaining momentum in the United States. Philosophers spoke of inherent contradictions in the Enlightenment project. In short, modernity was unraveling just as many Catholics were embracing it.

Contemporary spirituality must take seriously these criticisms of modernity as well as the opportunities presented by the still malleable postmodern world. We need a dialectical approach to the modern world which affirms its accomplishments and challenges its destructive tendencies.

Continuities in Spirituality

In our rapidly changing situation, it is important to recall the continuities in Christian spirituality. There are certain family resemblances in all the spiritualities which have developed in diverse cultures throughout Christian history. In general terms Christians have always drawn their inner strength from Jesus Christ who reveals the Father and sends the Spirit to guide the task of spreading the kingdom. More specifically, Christians in all ages have understood themselves as graced but sinful. Human existence is incomplete and flawed but touched by God's healing power. Authentic Christian spirituality has always been Trinitarian. We are called by the Father who guides us with maternal care along the path. Our task is to put on the mind of Christ and become better disciples of the Lord. We are temples of the Holy Spirit who enlightens and empowers us. Healthy forms of Christian piety have been essentially Christocentric. Jesus Christ is the Son of God, the definitive prophet, the universal savior. Spirituality in the past and today has an ecclesial dimension. God calls us into the church and saves us as members of a people. Divine grace seeks visibility in the community of faith. The church keeps alive for us the memory of Jesus. Christian morality has always centered on the law of love of God and neighbor as the highest ideal which calls for a generous response. Prayer, both public and private, is the way all Christians worship God and nourish their souls. Christians from all historical periods have found motivation in the hope that God will bring the divine plan to completion and will grant everlasting happiness to faithful people. An authentic postmodern spirituality will incorporate these elements, maintaining family ties with all traditional pieties.

We can also identify a common Catholic imagination which has influenced very diverse spiritualities in the past and continues to do so today. The Catholic imagination is incarnational. It tends to see the infinite revealed in the finite, grace present in matter, the Spirit at work in ordinary life. We live and move in one graced world. All things are potentially revelatory. This Catholic sensibility is engendered and nourished by the sacramental life of the church, especially the Eucharist. We remember First Communions and Christmas midnight Masses. Liturgy frames and interprets important events such as weddings, funerals, graduations and anniversaries. Catholicism is a heavily sacramental religion. Attending Mass regularly has an influence on how we interpret reality. At its best, liturgy attunes us to the presence of Christ in our world. Mother Theresa stated the point simply: "If we can see Jesus in the consecrated bread we ought to be able to see him in the faces of the poor and the outcasts."

For the Catholic imagination, the world is so organic and connected that to grasp one part of it accurately is to know something of the whole. Reality has an intelligible structure which reflects the wisdom of the Creater. Following this insight, Catholic theology has traditionally accepted natural law approaches to morality and made use of reason and philosophy in explaining and defining the faith. The Catholic imagination has a both/and character which tends to be inclusive and comprehensive. Thus we hold both scripture and tradition, both faith and reason, both grace and works. In contrast, the traditional Protestant imagination is more dialectical. It has less room for reason and philosophy and tends to an either/or approach which insists on scripture alone, faith alone and grace alone. The existence of a distinctive Catholic imagination helps explain the family resemblances we find among Catholic spiritualities. It also provides common ground for Catholics who espouse very diverse pieties.

In addition to recognizing a Catholic common ground, a postmodern spirituality must retrieve elements from previous periods which accord with the Gospel and can guide us today. We do not want to lose valuable insights from the fathers, the medieval theologians, and the modern spiritual masters. This is a dialectical process which also calls for rejecting destructive trends from the past which are opposed to the thrust of the teaching of Jesus. We should retain, for example, the modern emphasis on the dignity of persons while rejecting the sexist bias found in many modern spiritual authors.

A viable spirituality today will respond to the distinctive needs of people living through a paradigm shift. We need spiritual resources to cope with rapid change, bewildering complexity and frightening disruptions. Our souls need reflective silence to counter the noisy confusion of life. In a fragmented world we need supportive communities of faith. In our constricted world we need to hear the voices of those silenced by modernity. In a culture threatened by cynicism we need a large measure of Christian hope.

A spirituality which hopes to influence the postmodern world must be explicitly relational. We must relate in healthy ways to ourselves, others, nature, society, church and most fundamentally to God. Relationships constitute our very being and engage both our minds and hearts. They provide a privileged place for hearing a revelatory word. Improving our relationships is crucial to creating a postmodern world that is less exploitative and more humane. As Jesus taught us, love is the key. We must love ourselves, other persons and God.

Love of Self

Achieving a proper love of self is a difficult task in our post-Enlightenment culture. In working out a healthy relationship to ourselves, we must retain the traditional Christian understanding that we are graced but sinful creatures. Divine grace permeates our whole being. This positive but realistic outlook is helpful in countering the cynicism threatening our culture. Many insights from the modern period are also helpful. We can reinterpret the Enlightenment ideal of self-fulfillment as a call by God to develop and use our gifts for the good of others. The romantic emphasis on creative imagination encourages us to explore the terrain of our own religious imaginations and to seek ways of reconfiguring the postmodern world. We should build on the modern conviction that ordinary life is important by developing a spirituality attuned to the divine presence in everyday activities. Catholic spirituality still resonates with the insight of Emerson and the Transcendentalists that inner experience is an important pathway to God. Freud's discovery of the unconscious, which questioned the Enlightenment ideal of rational adulthood, must remain part of a Christian spirituality prepared to deal with interior dark forces. Finally, we must never lose sight of the fundamental conviction shared by Augustine, Aquinas and Karl Rahner that our restless hearts are driven by an innate desire for the gracious Mystery called God.

In addition to these insights from the tradition, a postmodern spirituality will remember that every individual with a restless heart is situated in a particular social, political and economic context, which influences the way he or she hears the Gospel and appropriates the tradition. In Europe, spiritual writers have often addressed their fellow citizens as nonbelievers heavily influenced by secular culture. Gustavo Gutierrez and other liberation theologians in Latin America have taught us that poor people in their countries are not nonbelievers but are often treated as non-persons. Most middle class citizens of the United States hear the Gospel neither as nonbelievers or non-persons. We live in a free, democratic, affluent, and in some ways highly religious society which at the same time tends to privatize and trivialize religion. Our spiritual challenge is to deepen our commitments and to extend the influence of our faith to all dimensions of life including the public.

Postmodern spirituality is necessarily pluralistic. Nonbelievers, non-persons and the uncommitted all hear the Christian message in a distinct way. Individuals in diverse cultural subgroups must appropriate aspects of the Gospel which will help them move toward greater wholeness. The process of becoming adult Christians is highly personal. God calls each one of us by name to become our better self. In this task it helps to find kindred spirits to share the journey. It is also important to recognize and respect others following a different path. We cannot relate properly to ourselves when the only feedback we get is from soulmates. We all are impoverished when some of our sisters and brothers are treated as non-persons. A postmodern spirituality faithful to the Gospel will foster a great conversation which includes the voices of all those silenced by modernity.

In order to relate well to ourselves we need a spirituality that combines acceptance and protest. Our challenge is to accept without excessive pride or undue anxiety all the factors which constitute our existence, including strengths and weaknesses, achievements and failures, health and sickness, life and death. We have to accept that we live in a transitional period filled with ambiguity and confusion and not in a simpler bygone era. Acceptance today may mean persevering even when God seems absent and worthwhile causes seem doomed. Acceptance which overcomes anger, frustration and self-pity is rooted in the conviction that we are loved by a God who remains faithful even when hidden. At the same time we must protest against and work to overcome all that stifles human growth, ranging from personal sin and cultural prejudice to institutional violence and international strife. As the great Protestant theologian Reinhold Niebuhr taught us, we should pray for the grace to accept with serenity the things that cannot be changed, for the courage to change the things that should be changed and for the wisdom to distinguish one from the other. In trying to attain this wisdom, Christians look to Jesus, the model of full humanity, who challenged the hypocrisy and legalism of his day and ultimately accepted the death occasioned by his provocative actions and subversive teaching.

Love of Others

In a society prone to false dichotomies we must maintain the essential connection between love of self and love of others. We need a spirituality today which challenges and empowers us to transform selfishness and the will to power into love and respect for other persons.

In this task, Christians will find their primary motivation and guidance from the command of Jesus to love our neighbor as ourselves. The wisdom of rooting love for others in a healthy self-love is more apparent in our postmodern age which understands that relationship problems are often caused by low self-esteem and personality disorders. The Gospel ideal of loving enemies and forgiving those who harm us remains essential to overcoming the hatred and violence which poison human relationships. We must also maintain and extend the achievements of modernity which have helped humanize personal relationships, such as the reduction of suffering and the establishment of human rights. Spirituality today still draws on the personalism of Martin Buber and other modern scholars who insist that self-fulfillment occurs only in loving relationships based on mutual respect. Finally, contemporary spirituality must build on the crucial insight, shared by authors from diverse ages ranging from the prophet Hosea to modern romantics, that human love has a special power to reveal the divine to us.

In the postmodern world we are more aware of the impact of social and cultural factors on personal relationships. Liberation theologians have directed our attention to the New Testament image of Jesus the liberator of captives and the remarkable teaching of Matthew 25 that Christ is identified with suffering people. Modernity did make progress in reducing suffering, establishing human rights, and moving toward greater equality. But it understood this progress almost exclusively from the viewpoint of white males. This meant that the dominant culture consistently ignored the experience of women and people of color, thereby effectively erasing their distinctive experience from history. Furthermore, modernity assumed that persons on the fringes could make it in the dominant society only by conforming to the rules of those in charge. Those with power controlled the only pathway into the network of relationships which provide status and power.

An effective contemporary spirituality must challenge this systemic evil. Theologian David Tracy has argued that postmodernity contains a helpful, if often unrecognized, ethical principle: let the other be other. Do not force other persons into predetermined roles or stereotypical patterns. Do not manipulate relationships. Do not demand that lovers be clones or friends meet arbitrary expectations. Respect the uniqueness of individuals. Allow others to make their own distinctive contributions to the common good. Write inclusive histories. Recognize multiple perspectives. Respect diverse pathways to spiritual growth. Celebrate the Mystery present in every individual.

This ethical imperative has special application to relationships between men and women. The modern patriarchal system harmed both men and women by pressuring them to conform to arbitrary patterns of being and behavior. Placing men in a totally secularized work environment and confining women to the private world of home and religion had a deadening effect on both sexes. Joseph Holland proposes the image of the "fertile embrace" to describe a more energetic pattern of interaction between men and women in our society. This image suggests that men and women work together both to bring religious resources into the public arena and to enrich the spiritual life of the family. Such collaboration promises to generate a new energy for the task of improving personal relationships and humanizing the world.

Developing a mature sense of interdependence which combines autonomy and dependency is crucial to improving our personal relationships and living out the law of love of neighbor. We need a confident sense of our own identity, dignity and worth which enables us to think for ourselves and take responsibility for our own lives. We also must recognize that we are social creatures who need each other in order to achieve personal fulfillment and to contribute to the larger society. When we feel loved and respected our self-confidence solidifies. When we feel good about ourselves we are able to reach out to others and form solid relationships. It is within a vibrant community life that personal development can occur. Small communities of faith which offer support and challenge based on Gospel values can make a great contribution to healing our fragmented world.

For us Christians, Jesus shows the way in forming community and establishing mature relationships. Radiating the Spirit, he made a tremendous impact on all those he encountered. With complete assurance he challenged the complacent and strengthened the weak. With uncommon freedom he loved others and allowed others to love him. Individuals felt liberated simply by being in his presence. Jesus understood the importance of community for personal growth and spreading the kingdom. He called God's people to repentance, gathered the Twelve, healed the sick and brought them back into the community. With great compassion he reconciled differences, broke down social barriers, treated women with respect, associated with sinners and gathered people for shared meals. Through his death and resurrection Christ sent the Spirit to strengthen and instruct the community of disciples.

Love of God

Love of self and neighbor always draws its power from love of God. A contemporary spirituality, which faces the collapse of modernity, has to rethink its most fundamental convictions including the doctrine of God. The disruptive events of the 20th century have forced theologians to reexamine the rationalistic approach of modern theology to the God question. Personal tragedies often make it difficult for ordinary Christians to accept the sentimental God of popular piety. Some people continue to find comfort and challenge in the modern notions of God, including Karl Barth's "Wholly Other," Paul Tillich's "Ground of Being" and Karl Rahner's "Holy Mystery." But important theologians have argued that we must now rethink our whole approach to the question of God. In recent lectures David Tracy has suggested that we move beyond the modern efforts to name God by a single concept and reinstitute the older tradition of naming the Deity through a great variety of symbols, myths, images and stories. The modern approach which cast the discussion about God in terms of various "isms" such as deism, atheism, agnosticism, theism and pantheism is too abstract and rational. It is difficult to pray to the Ground of Being. The truth is that no abstract theory is ever adequate for talking about God. Tracy reminds us that the Bible does not try to define the divine nature through rational concepts, but rather points to the divine presence through marvelous stories and diverse symbols. We come to know something of the always mysterious God by reading the story of the Exodus in the Hebrew scriptures and the passion narratives in the Gospels. Biblical images of God such as shepherd and king have a surplus of meaning which touches the mind and heart. By overwhelming us with stories and symbols of God, the Bible teaches us that God is always greater than any human concepts. Tracy discerns two fundamental ways of naming God in the New Testament: John's more mystical approach which culminates in the affirmation that God is Love, and the more prophetic approach of Paul which emphasizes the God of judgment revealed in the sufferings and death of Jesus. Tracy sees these two strains reappearing in postmodern thinkers who are interested in various forms of mysticism and are determined to overcome the injustices created by modernity.

A contemporary spirituality reflecting Tracy's analysis will avoid easy answers and glib talk about God. It will take seriously the traditional teaching that the great God is ultimately incomprehensible. Postmodern searchers will turn to the Scriptures not for clear definitions, but for its grand narrative structure and marvelous individual stories which offer intimations of the Mystery. They will draw inspiration from the numerous biblical symbols of the Diety which suggest the abiding presence of God, even in the midst of suffering and confusion.

Guided by the example of holy people, they will recognize the importance of combining the mystical and prophet aspects of spirituality in their own lives. Prayer will lead to the works of justice, and involvement in the world will send individuals back to reflective solitude. Spirituality will find new energy by listening to the God-talk of those silenced by modernity.

In a culture tempted to discouragement and cynicism, the dialectical virtue of "hopeful realism" is especially important. We need to face all the ambiguities and darkness of our disrupted age without escaping into a fantasy world of cheap grace. We must stay open to the hidden God who joins us in the struggle against human suffering. It is imperative for believers today to distinguish optimism based on human effort from Christian hope which trusts that the God who suffers with us will one day triumph over all the dark forces. The virtue of "hopeful realism" enables Christians to discern God's power revealed in the cross of Christ and the suffering of oppressed people today. It empowers us to join the struggle against the injustices of modernity and to collaborate with others in the exciting task of creating a more humane postmodern world.

Chapter 2

Love of Self: Facilitating Personal Development

1. The Christian Call to Conversion

Consciously entering into a systematic process of conversion is a great way to transform stagnation into spiritual growth.

Sometimes we make progress in the spiritual life without much apparent effort and prayers of gratitude are clearly in order. But we also know the problem of stagnation. We find ourselves falling into the same destructive patterns. Our sins repeat like a television rerun. The content of our yearly examination of conscience can be depressingly familiar. Vices get entrenched, blocking our spiritual progress.

Such stagnation calls for a more structured and systematic approach to our spiritual development. One way of organizing this effort is around the traditional notion of a call to conversion. Some Christians are not comfortable with the word "conversion" because they associate it with emotional revival meetings and sudden rebirth experiences. But the idea of conversion has roots in the Bible and admits of more contemporary interpretations. The Hebrew Scriptures speak of God calling his people to turn from idolatry and injustice to a life of righteousness. The New Testament uses the Greek word "metanoia" to describe a total change of direction in which a person turns from a self-centered, superficial way of living to a deeper life of dedication to God.

Contemporary theology understands conversion as more of a process than a once-for-all event. Many people experience growth in their lives as a gradual, never-ending process of closing the gap between their ideals and their actual behavior. Even individuals who report sudden conversion experiences have already gone through a period of preparation and are called to an ongoing process of growth. Furthermore, conversions are never merely private events. They are nourished in community life and invite continuing contributions to the common good. Finally, conversions can occur in various dimensions of the human personality. We are multidimensional creatures who have diverse capacities: to feel sad over suffering and enjoy blessings; to ask questions and solve problems; to commit sins and act virtuously; to search for meaning and utter prayers of gratitude; to believe in the Gospel and follow Christ. In all these dimensions – emotional, intellectual, moral and religious – it is possible to turn our lives around and to decide for growth over stagnation. We can set out on the journey of conversion by trying to improve in any one of these dimensions.

An affective conversion enables us to face, understand and criticize our emotions so that we can mobilize them for effectively living the Gospel message. Hidden, unexamined emotions can lead to destructive consequences including insensitivity, fatigue, self-deception and compulsive behavior. A systematic effort to achieve emotional maturity begins with recognizing and naming precisely what we are actually feeling in a particular situation and not what we think we are supposed to feel. Contrary to the popular advice simply to accept all our feelings and to express them freely, it is important to distinguish appropriate from inappropriate emotional responses as a first step in managing and transforming those that are excessive or disproportionate. From a Christian perspective, the decision to disclose emotions should be governed more by charity than frankness. Our goal is to achieve affective integration so that our emotions help us to evaluate persons and things in the light of the Gospel and to focus our energies in spreading the kingdom. The whole process of affective conversion is well illustrated by the case of a middle-aged man suffering from anxiety and fatigue who consistently repressed his anger. Recognizing the destructive effects of this approach, he purposely confronted a co-worker who often angered him with his overbearing attitude. The encounter helped clear the air and convinced him of the wisdom of this more open approach. He now regularly discusses his feelings with his wife and finds this practice liberating and energizing.

Intellectually converted persons are wholehearted and resolute in pursuing the life of wisdom. They overcome inattention and boredom by cultivating their mental faculties. Rejecting the diverse forms of anti-intellectualism found in our culture, they cherish the power of intelligence to foster human development by probing, understanding and judging all aspects of experience. Wise persons transform intolerance and arrogance into a healthy sense of pluralism which is open to the valid insights of others. The life of wisdom demands that we stay alert though tempted by indifference, ask probing questions though prone to complacency, and admit mistakes though fearful of embarrassment.

We can cultivate the life of wisdom through systematic efforts. Keeping a journal, reading good books, engaging in serious conversations, taking a course, all provide intellectual stimulation and make us more attentive to our experience. We can sharpen our ability to understand by a careful reading of a classic work and by trying to comprehend rather than refute what others are saying in a serious discussion. We can learn to make better judgments by carefully analyzing one of our significant mistakes and by checking our important decisions with a confidant. Joining with others in responsible action for the common good helps to solidify our insights and to test the accuracy of our judgments.

Intellectual conversions can happen to persons of any age or background. A priest in his middle sixties, who had not read a theology book in 40 years and was by his own admission an authoritarian pastor and a moralistic preacher, took a summer course on the theology of Karl Rahner, which completely changed his life. He became convinced of the value of theology for his pastoral work and continued to read and study regularly. He learned to work more collaboratively with his people and his teaching, preaching and counseling improved dramatically.

Through moral conversion individuals decide to pursue goodness and virtue rather than expediency and selfishness. They strive to give generously of themselves out of a spirit of love, rather than merely observing the law out of fear. They reject the ethical relativism rampant in our culture in favor of a life of responsible freedom which takes into account the wisdom of the past, the current teachings of the church, the personal call of God and the example of Jesus. Given our contemporary awareness of social sin and the oppressive power of unjust institutions, responsible believers today join with the oppressed and needy in the common task of promoting justice and peace.

Moral conversion requires the cultivation of virtues which are like a second nature that gives us the assured capacity to respond constructively in changing circumstances. Through well-chosen disciplines and the repetition of fitting behavior we can gradually replace vices with virtues which enable us to choose the good with delight and relative ease.

Recognizing that his marriage was in trouble, a husband who often spoke harshly to his wife made a conscious decision to change his behavior by paying her honest compliments each day and by apologizing every time he hurt her. On the way home from work he regularly stopped in a church to ask God's blessings on his efforts to improve the marriage. After about six months he found himself naturally and spontaneously treating his wife with greater respect and care.

Religious conversion involves a movement from a false sense of self-sufficiency to a greater dependence on God. Through this process we put aside idols and make God our ultimate concern. We surrender ourselves to the gracious Mystery who alone can satisfy the longings of our hearts. Our center of gravity shifts from ourselves to the God who, paradoxically, inhabits the very center of our being. To be converted religiously is to fall more deeply in love with God.

Surrendering to God has the power to transform and liberate us. We find new energy and courage in the conviction that God is in charge and will ultimately satisfy the longings of our hearts. Entrusting ourselves to the merciful God, we have the strength to rise above our sins and to continue on the path of spiritual growth. By accepting God's enduring love for us, we discover a new motivation to share that love with others.

For us Christians, the process of religious conversion is focused and mediated by Jesus Christ. As the living parable of divine love, he reminds us that self-surrender places us in the arms of the God who is totally trustworthy. As the exemplar of fulfilled humanity, he demonstrates that complete dependence on God leads to greater freedom and growth. Commitment to Christ means that we accept him as the final prophet and dedicate ourselves to following his example and teaching in our daily lives.

A religious conversion focused on Christ affects all the other dimensions. A Catholic women in her late 50s who led a good life and went to Mass regularly made a three-day retreat at a Trappist monastery which brought her much closer to Christ. Her deeper personal relationship to the Lord made her feel more integrated and less in need of affirmation. She found new stimulation in reading the Bible and was more attentive to the Scripture readings at Mass. She treated her husband with greater kindness and started regular visits to a few elderly people in a nursing home. On a few occasions she surprised herself by responding to friends in need not only with her time, but also with some simple words about her own faith in Christ.

Consciously entering into a systematic process of conversion is a great way to transform stagnation into spiritual growth. If we do indeed make progress, we must thank the gracious God who sustains and guides all our efforts.

2. How to Get More Out of the Gospels

We come to know something of the power of this Paraclete, the divine teacher within us, when we bring our concerns to the Gospels and find that the text does indeed speak to our minds and hearts.

Those of us who worship regularly with mainline Christian communities hear most of the material in the four Gospels proclaimed over a three-year period. Recent advances in biblical studies which draw on scholarly disciplines such as narrative criticism, reception theory and reader-response criticism can help us get more out of our frequent encounters with the Gospels (cf. *Mark and Method*, ed. by Janice Anderson and Stephen Moore).

One simple approach gleaned from the new studies is to relate our own personal concerns to the distinctive teachings of one of the four Gospels. In other words, we can think of every opportunity to read a Gospel privately or to hear it proclaimed in church as a conversation in which we bring our own needs and concerns to the discussion with the expectation that we will hear something insightful or inspirational in return. A person, for example, who is suffering from guilt feelings would benefit from reading the Gospel of Luke straight through, with extra attention to the many passages on mercy and forgiveness. An individual struggling with questions about the divinity of Christ could pay special attenion at Mass when the reading is from the Gospel of John which presents an exalted view of Jesus.

This simple idea of a conversation between ourselves and a particular Gospel demands further explanation and concrete application. As we approach a particular Gospel, we should be aware of our own worldview and dominant self-understanding. It helps to have a sense of the deepest sources of our joys and satisfactions as well as our anxieties and fears. We need to know our strengths and weaknesses, virtues and vices, goals and motivations. We must be ready to receive from the text both affirmation and challenge. Reading a particular Gospel might confirm our current conduct, but it also might call us to broaden our perspective, change our worldview, adjust our attitudes or reform our behavior.

For a fruitful dialogue, we also need to know more about the Gospels in general and each one in particular. The Gospels are our best sources for coming to know Jesus of Nazareth and the great cause which consumed his energy and brought him to his death. Written in the light of the Resurrection, they reveal the enduring significance and power of the risen Christ.

All four Gospels can be considered as classic texts. They are highly particular portrayals of Jesus of Nazareth which contain a universal message. Each of the Gospels has a permanent core of meaning which is fixed by the intent of the author and the structure of the text, but each also contains a surplus of meaning which can speak to the mind and heart of every honest inquirer in any historical period or cultural milieu. The Gospels have a message for us today just as surely as they did for Christians in the early centuries.

We enter into dialogue with a particular Gospel text and not with Gospels in general. Since most of us know the Gospels by hearing short segments of them proclaimed in the liturgy, we end up with an amalgamated story of Jesus, often without recognizing the precise source of the various parts. For example, most Christians carry in their memory the story of the birth of Jesus, which includes an annunciation to Mary and Joseph's dream, a census and a long journey to Bethlehem, the visit of the Magi and the shepherds, the perfidy of Herod and the flight into Egypt. It would be difficult for many, however, to determine which of these elements in the story came from Matthew, and which from Luke. When such an amalgamation occurs, our conversation with a particular Gospel is impaired because we miss the distinctive accents and insights of the evangelist.

The four Gospels have a great deal in common, especially the Synoptics Mark, Matthew and Luke which often agree word for word. But each one also has a distinctive structure (John organizes his material around seven great signs or miracles of Jesus), a characteristic theology (Matthew presents Jesus as Son of David and the new Moses), a personalized style (Mark offers a vivid, disconnected, fast-paced narrative), and a particular worldview (Luke views all of history as a story of salvation). These differences in structure, theology, style and worldview account for the fact that individuals and communities are attracted to one or the other of the four Gospels.

A good way of discovering the distinctive power of each Gospel to touch our imagination is to read one of the four straight through. In choosing a Gospel to read, it is important to match our own interests, concerns and questions with the distinctive characteristics of a particular Gospel. A few clues might guide this process and help us to get more out of the Gospel segments read at Mass.

Traditionally, Matthew's Gospel has appealed to those interested in the life of the church and the formation of faith communities. The text speaks a great deal about the call to discipleship and has a special message for those discerning their vocations or making career decisions and lifestyle changes. Matthew often writes in exaggerated terms and employs a "rhetoric of excess." Thus he calls upon us to turn the other cheek, to go the extra mile, to love even our enemies. He teaches us that the last shall be first and the first last and that we should give alms in secret. This language of excess represents a stern challenge to those of us tempted to self-righteousness or in danger of settling for mediocrity.

Individuals who are struggling to live effectively in the postmodern world with all of its disruptions, contradictions, and absurdities may find the Gospel of Mark remarkably relevant. This Gospel does not read very smoothly. The style is rough and there are very few good transitions. It is like a collage of disparate memories of Jesus. Scholars tell us that the original Gospel ended at 16:8 – a very abrupt conclusion in which the women flee from the tomb, shaking with terror and saying nothing to anyone because they are so afraid. This strange ending suggests to the reader that the real action is beyond the text, that we are the ones that must gather our courage and proclaim the message of the Risen Lord. In Mark the demons and the outsiders recognize the deepest truths about Jesus, while the disciples remain confused. The identity of certain characters is also confusing: for instance, John the Baptist is seen as Elijah, and Herod thinks Jesus is John the Baptist come back to life. Fear, astonishment and amazement are frequent reactions to encountering Jesus. At the baptism of Jesus the sky is split, and at his death the temple veil is torn. The reader of the Gospel, however, realizes throughout that this disjointed narrative is really the story of the Son of God. This is a striking reminder, especially to those wrestling with displacement, confusion and complexity, that God's hidden plan is unfolding in our own lives.

Historically, Luke's Gospel has attracted activists committed to social justice and charismatics fascinated by the gifts of the Spirit. Individuals struggling to be more compassionate and forgiving can profitably linger on Luke's stories of the Good Samaritan and the Prodigal Son, which suggest that conversion of heart is possible right here and now. As a master storyteller with a good sense of the dramatic, Luke invites us to identify with his characters. Persons who are introspective or are seeking to deepen their interior life should notice Luke's interest in the personal psychology of his characters. Those struggling to make sense of everyday life will be taken by his emphasis on finding God in all aspects of daily experience. Individuals suffering from guilt feelings will want to spend a lot of time on the 15th chapter which includes the Prodigal Son story and other marvelous reminders of God's forgiveness. There is a great deal of joy in Luke's Gospel which can appeal to those struggling with depression and sadness. Feminists will find attractive Luke's intriguing pattern of drawing on the experiences of both men and women: for example, the twin prophecies of Simeon and Anna and the parallel stories of a shepherd finding a lost sheep and a woman a lost coin.

John's Gospel has traditionally appealed to mystics and theologians because of its lofty rhetoric and profound insights. Participation in the divine life is a major theme for John. Christ is the vine and we are the branches. To be united with Jesus is to be close to the Father and other believers – a comforting thought for those dealing with loneliness and estrangement. The Gospel continually summons us to deepen our awareness, to see beneath the surface. John gives us the Doubting Thomas story, which calls upon us to believe even if we have not seen. In reading John we are struck by his great emphasis on the divinity of Jesus. In many passages Jesus makes himself equal with God as in the classic verse: "The Father and I are one." And yet, in another place Jesus clearly says "the Father is greater than I." John's acceptance of this paradox is instructive for those struggling with questions about the identity of Jesus Christ. John says nothing about apostles but does speak a great deal about the disciples, especially the Beloved Disciple, the unnamed founder and ongoing inspiration of the community which produced the Gospel. Among the disciples a fundamental equality prevailed. Women played prominent roles. In John, Jesus first appears to Mary Magdalene and not to Peter. The woman at the well becomes the founder of the church in Samaria. Those struggling for women's rights in the church will find valuable support in these passages. Someone has said that John's Gospel is "an inbuilt conscience against the abuses of authoritarianism" because it places greater emphasis on the Paraclete, the divine teacher within us, than on church laws and structures.

We come to know something of the power of this Paraclete when we bring our concerns to the Gospels and find that the text does indeed speak to our minds and hearts.

3. The Gospel of Mark and the Age of Transition

In our complex, rapidly changing world filled with insecurity and pessimism, we are called to tell anew the hopeful story of the isolated and abandoned Jesus who was raised to a new and glorious life by the ever-faithful God.

Some individuals thrive on the complexity of the postmodern world and are energized by the continually changing scene. But many others find that the rapid changes challenge their faith, making life seem less trustworthy and God more remote. It is easy to feel isolated and insecure in today's world.

The Gospel of Mark, with its odd mix of discontinuity, misunderstanding and incompleteness, now appears to be a surprisingly helpful resource for coping with the challenges of postmodernity. This is especially true of Mark's dramatic account of the passion and death of Jesus. In his monumental two-volume study *The Death of the Messiah* (Doubleday 1993), the great Catholic New Testament scholar Raymond Brown organizes his meticulous commentary on the passion stories found in all the Gospels into four Acts: Jesus prays and is arrested in Gethsemane, Jesus before the Jewish authorities, Jesus before Pilate, and Jesus crucified and buried. In each Act, Fr. Brown's analysis of Mark highlights the increasing isolation of Jesus. He is betrayed by his disciples, condemned by the Jewish leaders, rejected by the crowds, sentenced unjustly by the Roman governor, and mocked by passersby as he hangs on the cross. In contrast to the triumphal Jesus described in John's Gospel and the compassionate Jesus of Luke who always remains in communion with his Father, Mark portrays Jesus as completely abandoned and badly shaken.

In the first Act of the passion drama in Gethsemane, Mark's Jesus tells Peter, James and John about the profound horror and intense anguish troubling his soul and asks them to watch and pray with him. Overwhelmed by deep sorrow, Jesus prays that his Father spare him the sufferings of the horrible death which he anticipates will be part of the final showdown between God's kingdom and the power of evil. Ironically, Jesus, who previously challenged his disciples to drink the cup of suffering, is now praying to God to be spared the cup himself.

Without any mention of the comforting angel found in Luke's Gospel, Mark continues to stress the abandonment of Jesus. On three separate occasions, he returns to the disciples seeking their support, only to find them sleeping. In the hour of the great trial, they yield to the weakness of the flesh and fail to support their Master when he needs them most.

Immediately, Judas, one of the Twelve, as Mark pointedly reminds us, arrives with a crowd armed with swords and wooden clubs. According to a prearranged signal, he identifies Jesus by kissing him warmly. In Luke's Gospel, Jesus says, "Judas, would you betray the Son of man with a kiss?" Mark's Jesus says absolutely nothing to Judas, leaving us to ponder his emotional response to such treachery.

In Mark, Jesus does address the armed crowd in a tone of injured innocence: "Day after day I was with you in the Temple teaching, and you did not seize me." Sadly, Jesus is rejected by a group of people who are well aware of his passion for God's kingdom of justice and love. While we are still contemplating the growing isolation of Jesus, Mark hits us with the next line: "And having left him, they all fled." All of his closest disciples now abandon him. Jesus must face his passion and death deprived of the comforting presence of the ones he called his friends.

Mark alone closes the first Act with the story of the disciple clothed with a linen cloth who flees naked when the authorities try to seize him. Mark's irony is instructive. Disciples should leave all things to follow the Lord. This last disciple, too fearful to face the great trial, has literally left all things to *flee from the Lord!* Now there is no one left to support Jesus in his hour of suffering.

In the second Act of the passion narrative, Mark places Jesus before the Jewish authorities in a full-scale trial. The chief priests and the scribes seek testimony against Jesus, but when it proves to be inconsistent, they condemn him for blasphemy based on his own words. Jesus makes no attempt to explain his teachings, limiting his response to an affirmation that he is indeed the Messiah. After all the members of the Sanhedrin judge him guilty punishable by death, some individuals begin to mock him by physically abusing him and calling on him to prophesy. Abandoned by friends, Jesus must endure misunderstanding and rejection by the religious leaders who should have been his allies in the great cause of making Israel a genuine light to the nations.

At this point, Mark takes us back to Peter. Perhaps the impetuous leader of the Twelve will overcome his fears and support the Lord. After all, he did follow Jesus at a distance to the courtyard of the high priest. But he has not yet learned that a disciple must suffer with the Master. Precisely at the moment Jesus affirms his Messiahship, Peter repudiates his previous confession of Jesus as the Messiah by denying him three times with progressively greater vehemence. The disciple who had been most confident of his fidelity now curses and swears that he does not even know the man. Suddenly recalling the prediction of Jesus, he goes out and weeps bitterly. Jesus is bound and taken to Pilate, burdened by another anticipated, but still painful, betrayal.

In the third Act, Jesus stands alone before the procurator of Judea, who represents the vast power of the Roman Empire. Asked if he is the King of the Jews, Jesus responds simply, "You say so." When Pilate persists, Jesus refuses to say another word. Mark tells us that Pilate was not convinced of Jesus' guilt and, in fact, knew that the Jewish leaders handed him over out of envy.

Mark places Pilate's response to this perplexing situation in the context of a custom of releasing a prisoner during the Passover feast. He asks the crowd if they want him to release Jesus the King of the Jews. Incited by the chief priests, they demand that he release Barabbas instead, a man imprisoned for murder during the riot. Pilate keeps pressing the crowd about what he should do with the one they call "the King of the Jews" and they keep shouting "Crucify him." The crowd, who cheered his triumphal entry into Jerusalem, suddenly turns against him. They now prefer a common criminal to the one who went about doing good. Not one voice is raised in defense of Jesus. Neither Mark nor any of the other Evangelists offer us an adequate explanation for this deeply distressing change in public opinion. Without any guilt on his part, Jesus has lost his base of support among the people. Acceding to the wishes of the crowd, Pilate has Jesus scourged and hands him over to be crucified by the Roman soldiers. Still smarting from the psychological abuse inflicted by his own people, Jesus now endures physical abuse at the hands of the Roman soldiers who mock him with the taunt, "Hail King of the Jews."

In the final Act, Mark paints a dark and foreboding picture of the crucifixion and death of Jesus. He hangs on the cross for six hours. People passing by blaspheme him. The chief priests and scribes mock him. The two bandits crucified with him revile him. Mark makes no mention of Luke's good thief, who offers Jesus words of affirmation and support.

For Mark the progressively greater isolation of Jesus culminates in his final anguished cry, "My God, my God, for what reason have you forsaken me?" Already rejected by his disciples, the religious authorities and the crowds, Mark's Jesus now quotes the opening line of Psalm 22 to express the worst abandonment of all – his sense of being forsaken by the One he called Abba. We are left to reflect on that final self-emptying of Jesus. The Lord has experienced the depths of the dark night of the soul. He has seen the abyss created by the absence of God. He has known the terror of absolute aloneness. The only response to his prayer is total silence. Mark does not even offer us the comfort of a final trusting word from the lips of Jesus. It is only in Luke that Jesus prays, "Father, into your hands I commend my Spirit." Mark's Jesus simply utters a loud cry and expires.

It is only after the death of Jesus that Mark allows the light of hope to enter the dark picture. The Roman centurion becomes the first human being to express the full truth about Jesus when he proclaims, "Truly this man was the Son of God." Mark also informs us for the first time that Mary Magdalene and some women disciples were observing from a distance. They see Joseph of Arimathea, a respected member of the Sanhedrin, place the body of Jesus in a burial place hewn out of a rock. They return early Sunday morning to anoint the body only to find the tomb empty. A young man tells them to go and tell Peter and the other disciples that Jesus is risen, but they are so frightened that they say nothing to anyone. Thus the Gospel of Mark originally ended.

Borrowing a phrase from Raymond Brown, we can say that Mark's somber drama contains a "pedagogy of hope" for the postmodern world. No contemporary experience of isolation and insecurity is completely foreign to Jesus, who remained faithful despite his terror. None of our failures or betrayals are greater than that of Peter, who still became the rock on which the Lord built the church. Mark's odd conclusion, which highlights Mary Magdalene's silence, suggests that the task of proclaiming the good news of the Resurrection has fallen to us. In our complex, rapidly changing world filled with insecurity and pessimism, we are called to tell anew the hopeful story of the isolated and abandoned Jesus who was raised to a new and glorious life by the ever-faithful God. Authentic hope today rests not on simple solutions to complex problems, but on the risen Lord who continues to encourage and guide us.

4. How to Listen to the Parables

Jesus was a master teacher. His parables deserve greater study and reflection. Ultimately they point back to their author who is himself the parable of the Gracious Mystery.

The parables of Jesus are familiar fare for Christians. On numerous occasions we have heard the stories of the Good Samaritan, the Prodigal Son, the Pharisee and the Tax Collector, the Lost Sheep, the Rich Man and Lazarus and the many other parables found in the Synoptic Gospels. But the parables are difficult to interpret. They do not easily yield their deeper meaning. They are deliberately enigmatic, designed to challenge common assumptions and to promote deeper reflection. They reflect a time and culture which is foreign to us. It is impossible to extract one precise meaning from them because they are open to various legitimate interpretations. Moreover, our very familiarity with the parables makes it more difficult to derive new insights from them. When we hear the opening lines of a well-known parable, it is easy to shut down mentally, assuming that we already know the story and what it signifies. It takes a conscious effort to get more out of the parables of Jesus. Here are some suggestions.

1. *Try to hear the parables in a fresh way, as though for the first time.* Specific strategies can help: be attentive to all the details; determine the main character in the dramatic stories; speculate on the motivations of the various characters and try to identify with one of them; imagine how the unresolved aspects of the story turn out. For example, concentrate on the older son in the Prodigal Son story, with various questions in mind. How does he relate to his father?

Why does he not want to go to the party for his brother? Does he end up going or not? How am I like him? Retelling a parable in our own words can also suggest new interpretations and surprising insights.

2. *Feel free to make allegorical interpretations of the parables by applying the details of the stories to our current situation, but do so within the framework of Christian teaching.* It is helpful to think of Lazarus as representing poor people in the world today, but it is not legitimate to compare the self-righteous Pharisee to all those who happen to disagree with us. In 1888 Adolf Julicher published a seminal, two-volume work in German which argued that the original parables of Jesus were not allegories and that he did not intend the details of the stories to refer to some future reality. This generally accepted analysis warns us against bizarre and arbitrary applications of the parables. But the church has always made use of allegorical interpretations. The evangelist Mark offered a detailed allegorical explanation of the Sower and the Seed parable by comparing the seed to the word of the Lord and using the details of the story (for example, seed falling among thorns) to explain why some people reject the teaching of Jesus. In the fifth century Augustine proposed this allegorical interpretation of the Good Samaritan parable: the man who was beaten and robbed is Adam; Jerusalem from whence he came is the state of original happiness while Jericho represents human mortality; the Samaritan is Christ; the wounded man is the church and the innkeeper is the apostle Paul. We can get more out of the parables by concentrating on how they illumine our current efforts to be authentic disciples. Allegorical interpretations which are faithful to the thrust of the Gospel can help.

3. *Extract from a parable the one major teaching which arises from the primary point of comparison.* Thus, in the Prodigal Son story the reconciling gesture of the father to his wayward son teaches us that God has unbounded mercy for sinners. This method of interpretation, which was proposed by Julicher before the turn of the century, was dominant

among scholars until the 1960s. Even though it has been superseded by new approaches, it remains a helpful way of reading the parables without getting lost in unimportant details or strained comparisons. The parable about the Wise and Foolish Virgins teaches us that we should always be alert for the coming of the Lord. The story of the Pharisee and Tax Collector praying in the temple warns us against self-righteousness. The Lost Sheep parable reminds us that the merciful God will seek us out even if we stray. We can appropriate these essential teachings without understanding all of the background or applying all of the details of the story.

4. *Read the parables as poetic narratives rich in metaphor which convey fundamental assumptions about human existence.* In the middle 1960s Amos Wilder, a poet as well as a theologian, challenged the well-established approach of Julicher by insisting that the parables of Jesus are not pedagogical devices to teach a lesson. They are rather stories with odd twists which force us to rethink our common assumptions about life as a whole. They convey a vision of reality that cannot be reduced to logical analysis or conceptual categories. The parables function metaphorically, shocking our imaginations with the strangeness of the comparisons made. When Jesus originally told the story of the Good Samaritan, his Jewish audience would have been totally shocked that the hated foreigner was the one to assist their half-dead countryman. The shock prompts a reexamination of the whole question of who is the insider and who is the outsider and, more radically, whether such a distinction makes any sense at all. A similar imaginative shock occurs when we hear that workers who labored only an hour are paid the same amount as those who worked all day. Reflection on this parable could lead to a radical reassessment of God's dealings with the human family. The philosopher Paul Ricoeur, who has had tremendous influence on biblical interpretation, explains the shocking character of the parables in terms of their metaphoric power to orient, disorient and reorient us. In other words, they begin with a familiar pattern and then introduce a strange or

surprising twist which disorients us and calls us to a new way of thinking and acting. Luke's story of the Wily Steward makes sense when the fired manager tries to ingratiate himself with his master's debtors by reducing their debts. But the disorienting shock occurs when the owner praises the fired manager for his behavior. Luke supplies us with one possible reorienting key when he suggests that we must be astute like the manager in pursuing the goals of the Kingdom.

In order to appreciate the shocking character of the parables we need to know more about Jewish life in first century Palestine. Jesus talked about situations well known to his audience. It was dangerous to travel from Jerusalem to Jericho. Owners of vineyards had to hire extra day-laborers at harvest time. Young Jewish men did take their inheritance and migrate to other countries. He used stock characters very familiar to his audience: prodigal sons, greedy land owners, insistent widows and dishonest tax collectors. But Jesus usually injected material that was odd, strange and unfamiliar. Owners of vineyards did not negotiate directly with workers, but did it through their stewards. Jewish fathers did not run out to greet their returning sons, whether wayward or not. Samaritans did not help wounded Jews. Shepherds did not leave the whole flock to search for one stray. Mustard seeds did not grow into large trees. A master going on a journey did not give his servants money equivalent to 150 years wages. Sometimes a careful reading of a parable can reveal these oddities. We can figure out for ourselves that an owner of a vineyard would not send his son to negotiate with his tenants after they already abused and killed his servants. In other stories we need a scholarly commentary to point out the strange twists. Especially helpful in this regard is John Donahue's *The Gospel in Parable* (Fortress 1988), with helpful background material also found in John Dominic Crossan's *In Parable* (Polebridge Press 1992) and Bernard Brandon Scott's *Hear Then the Parables* (Fortress 1989). In any case the surprising elements invite us to rethink our fundamental assumptions about life.

5. *Read the parables in context.* Be attentive to what immediately precedes and follows them and how each of the evangelists uses them for his own distinct purpose. Mark highlights the difficulty of understanding the parables. Even the disciples do not really grasp their deepest significance. This suggests that we must continue to probe the meaning of these enigmatic stories, allowing them to challenge our established perspectives and attitudes. Matthew's parables call us to discipleship and remind us that we stand under the judgment of God. This is most evident in his parable of the Last Judgment in which individuals are saved or dammed depending on whether they helped or ignored those in need. Reading Matthew today challenges our complacency and gives urgency to the task of following Christ. Luke often provides clues to his understanding of a particular parable. For instance, he introduces the story of the Pharisee and Tax Collector with the note that it is for the benefit of those "who believed in their own-self righteousness while holding everyone else in contempt" (18:9). The realism of Luke's distinctive parables, such as the Good Samaritan and the Prodigal Son, invite us to participate in the story and to identify with the characters.

6. *Allow the parables to illumine and guide our internal struggle to become more mature Christians.* In his book *The Kingdom Within,* John Sanford, who has served an an Episcopal pastor and Jungian analyst, argues that the kingdom symbol points to the Spirit of God in our minds and hearts calling us to a greater integrity and authenticity. Interpreting the Prodigal Son parable from this perspective, he suggests that the two brothers symbolize two aspects of one whole personality. The elder brother represents a strong sense of duty and the desire to conform and please, while the younger represents a spontaneous and adventurous spirit. If the older brother dominates, a person becomes rigid and self-righteous. If the younger takes over, all discipline and restraint are lost. The father in the story represents the reconciling power of the kingdom. He attempts to reunite

both sons by getting each one to face his one-sidedness and to incorporate the opposite characteristics. In the same way the reign of God within us calls us to unite the more disciplined and the more spontaneous aspects of our own personalities in a fruitful and energizing synthesis. Following Sanford's lead, we could interpret all the parables as road maps for the inner journey. They call us to move toward greater integrity by bringing the unrecognized shadow side of our personalities into the light of consciousness.

Jesus was a master teacher. His parables are endlessly fascinating and supremely instructive. They deserve greater study and reflection. Ultimately they point back to their author who is himself the parable of the Gracious Mystery.

5. Catholic Identity and the Catholic Imagination

In our age of transition the question of Catholic identity is both important and complex. By approaching it through the Catholic imagination we can focus on the primary stories, images and rituals that bind us together.

The question of Catholic identity has become increasingly prominent both inside and outside the church. In the spring of 1994 *The New York Times* ran an excellent four-part series entitled "Searching Its Soul: the American Catholic Church" which explored this theme. In the final article the religion editor, Peter Steinfels, noted that some observers perceive a "hollowing out" of Catholicism which is putting the church at risk of losing its distinctive identity. What was once primarily a conservative concern over the loss of Catholic identity has become, according to Steinfels, a concern of liberals and centrists as well. Today Catholics of very diverse outlooks are searching for the common bonds which hold us together as a people.

From a historical perspective this new quest for identity among American Catholics is not surprising. The 33 million Catholic immigrants who came to the United States between 1820 and 1920 had to form a monolithic block in order to survive in a predominantly Calvinistic country. Establishing and maintaining a viable Catholic subculture demanded that the church place great emphasis on uniformity in doctrine and practice.

With the major social changes brought about by World War II, Catholics moved into the mainstream of American life. This momentous shift, signaled most clearly by the election of President John Kennedy, enabled Catholics to move beyond a defensive posture and to deal more directly with internal problems and differences. The Second Vatican Council furthered this process and brought the notion of pluralism into the consciousness of many Catholics. The church no longer appeared as a monolithic institution. Bishops disagreed publicly on church policy, theologians held various opinions on questions of doctrine and morals, and lay people manifested diverse pieties. An American Catholic church which was no longer on the defensive could openly manifest its newly recognized diversity.

The age of pluralism, which exhilarated some and frightened others, eventually produced a backlash, a new quest for unity. Given the great diversity among Catholics, what holds us together? What do we have in common that can keep us from splintering into polarized groups?

One way of responding to these questions is by exploring the Catholic imagination. This approach highlights the stories, images and symbols which create a distinctive Catholic way of perceiving the world. Without denying the crucial importance of doctrinal orthodoxy, it examines the more amorphous area of general sensibilities and dominant metaphors. This approach broadens out the search for common ground and emphasizes the factors that unite rather than divide us.

The word "imagination" points to a variety of significant human functions. Through imagination we can revisit past events and make them present to consciousness once more. We can also envision a future different from the present which frees us to remake ourselves and to reconfigure our world. Imagination includes the root power to compare and illustrate through images, metaphors, symbols and par-

ables. We are able to appreciate myths which illumine fundamental questions of life and to form paradigms which serve
as models of reality as a whole. Imagination enables us to
penetrate beneath the surface of things and to gain an organic feel for the depth dimension of reality. Through our
imaginations we pass over into the different worlds created
by classic texts and works of art and then return to ourselves
enriched. We tell stories which interpret and order our experience; we also share common stories with others which draw
us together in community. Finally, imagination provides a basis for hope by assembling positive images drawn from our
experience and putting us in touch with the symbols of our
religious tradition.

The importance of the imagination is suggested by the
often quoted aphorism of the contemporary philosopher Paul
Ricoeur: "the symbol gives rise to thought." First we appropriate the fundamental stories of our faith and only later do
we analyze them. Religious symbolism shapes our consciousness even before we are able to understand doctrinal formu-
lations. By participating in religious ritual we prepare
ourselves to accept the dogmas of our faith.

The Catholic imagination shares common stories and
images with other religious traditions. With Hindus and Buddhists we sense the existence of a deeper world of the spirit
which is revealed through prayer and meditation. With Jews
and Muslims we find guidance and inspiration in the story of
Abraham, our father in faith. With Orthodox and Protestant
Christians we recognize Jesus as the primary image or icon of
the great God.

Religious imagination is always influenced by culture.
Catholics in the United States share common sensibilities
with other Catholics around the world, for example, an appreciation of the long and rich Christian tradition. But we are
also influenced by the distinctive strands woven into our national culture such as Puritanism, deism, pragmatism and
consumerism. American Catholics, for instance, share with
their fellow citizens a commitment to religious liberty and a
conviction that religious beliefs should have practical consequences. We also value hard work, maintain a certain distrust

of institutions and are influenced by the individualism rampant in our country.

In conjunction with family life, Eucharistic celebrations play a major role in shaping the Catholic imagination. Most Catholics have special memories of their First Communion, whether positive or negative. Going to Mass regularly has a cumulative effect in determining the Catholic outlook on the world. Special liturgies such as Christmas midnight Masses, weddings, funerals and home Masses supply an emotional tone to this general sense of reality. The Eucharist provides the setting for hearing large portions of the Bible, including the familiar stories and striking images which are crucial components of the Catholic imagination. The changes in the liturgy mandated by the Second Vatican Council have had a profound effect on the religious sensibilities of Catholics by placing greater emphasis on the immanence of God, the humanity of Christ and the priestly role of the whole assembly.

But even with these changes the Catholic imagination continues to have at its core a sacramental or incarnational sense of reality. This means that "the world is charged with the grandeur of God," as the Jesuit poet Gerard Manley Hopkins put it so well. The great God can be found in all the ordinary things of life. We live and move in one graced world. All things are potentially revelatory. Exploring the finite in depth reveals the infinite. The beautiful things of this world point to the Source of all beauty. The Christ present in the Eucharist is also present in all human beings, especially those who are suffering and in need.

David Tracy has pointed out that the Catholic imagination is analogical, rather than dialectical (cf. *The Analogical Imagination*). This means that Catholics tend to see the world as a coherent, intelligible whole which can be known through a central focus or image. By knowing the love that is in our own hearts, for instance, we grasp something true about the energy which vivifies the entire universe and about the ultimate Source of love which we call God. This analogical sense is the basis for confidence in reason, trust in the process of life and hope for a successful outcome to the human adventure. On the other hand, persons with a dialectical imagination, such as the early Protestant reformers and many evangelical Christians today, are attuned to the discontinuity between our own limited perceptions and the world as a whole. As a modern representative of this dialectical outlook, the great Protestant theologian Karl Barth spoke of God as the "Wholly Other," who is inaccessible through reason or philosophy and is known only through faith in Christ revealed in the Scriptures. This is in sharp contrast to the Catholic sensibility represented by Thomas Aquinas who insisted that reason and faith could work together in harmony to recognize the God revealed in and through all created reality.

In his book *The Catholic Myth*, Andrew Greeley draws on his empirical research to show that the Catholic analogical imagination views God as a comforting presence who can be imagined as mother, lover, friend and spouse. Catholics generally assume that human nature is fundamentally good despite its flaws, although this positive assessment often breaks down in the area of sexuality. We human beings are essentially communal and find our home in society. We expect to learn important truths about reality through open dialogue with philosophy, science and other disciplines. The church plays a positive role in producing and proclaiming the Scriptures, in keeping alive the traditional memory of Jesus and in mediating God's grace to us. The church needs a focal point of unity which is provided by the bishop of Rome. Mary continues to play a prominent role in the Catholic imagination even among younger members of the church. Saints serve as role models and intercessors. Catholics tend to value loyalty, obedience and patience as well as other virtues which protect family and community life. American Catholics have a sense that prayer and the prophetic task of working for justice should go together. The outstanding representative Catholics of our century, Thomas Merton and Dorothy Day, earned the respect of many by living out this ideal.

In our age of transition the question of Catholic identity is both important and complex. By approaching it through the Catholic imagination we can focus on the primary stories, images and rituals that bind us together. We find solidarity in our sacramental sense that the Lord present in the Eucharist is found in all other human beings including our fellow Catholics.

6. World Youth Day and Catholic Identity

United in essential matters, the Catholic community will be better prepared to join with other people of good will in the task of humanizing our world.

The celebration of the eighth World Youth Day in Denver during the summer of 1993 was by all accounts a spectacular event. The presence of Pope John Paul II attracted huge crowds, including an estimated 400,000 people for the concluding Mass at Cherry Creek State Park. Around 186,000 young Catholics from over 70 countries officially registered for the convocation. Some 3,000 journalists covered the event. President Clinton was on hand to greet the Pope and the two spoke privately for over an hour. Exemplifying the spirit of the convocation, young people ranging in age from 13 to 39 joined together in a variety of service and educational activities. Many worked on community projects, which included cleaning up the city's parks and recreation areas, visiting nursing homes and gathering food for the needy. About 200 participants joined Habitat for Humanity volunteers in building four homes in a Denver neighborhood. Large numbers attended structured catechetical sessions organized according to age and language groups and taught by cardinals, archbishops and bishops from around the world.

How are we to interpret this striking World Youth Day celebration and what can we learn from it? The national media generally cast the whole event in terms of a struggle between a conservative Pope and a more liberal American Catholic Church. They reported recent scientific polls indicating that the majority of Catholics in the United States disagree with well-known papal positions on certain controversial issues: for example, 70% of Catholics think married men should be allowed to be priests; 62% are in favor of the ordination of women; and 84% reject the ban on artificial birth control. Some reports noted the activities of representatives of Catholic Organizations for Renewal, a national coalition of 22 church reform groups, espousing causes such as women's ordination, abortion rights, and respect for lesbian and gay Catholics. Many commentators interpreted the Pope's addresses within the framework of his opposition to abortion, highlighting the conflict between his teaching and the pro-choice position of many Americans, including President Clinton. Images of protesters with messages such as "I Vote Pro-Choice," "Keep Abortion Legal," and "Colorado is not a Papal State" often accompanied stories with a conflictual slant.

Other reports presented World Youth Day as a Catholic Woodstock, a jamboree featuring the Pope as the superstar. This interpretation, which evokes memories of the famous 1969 rock music festival, emphasized the charisma of the 73-year-old Pope, an intellectual, a poet and a moral leader who has survived an assassination attempt and has traveled the world, drawing large crowds wherever he goes. At the first major event of the convocation, the Pope entered Mile-High Stadium in his Popemobile as 85,000 people, who had been exuberantly awaiting him for over an hour, greeted him with cheers, stomping, dancing and handkerchief waving. During the four days, the whole city of Denver was transformed. Huge numbers of students walked the streets, enjoying the companionship of kindred spirits. Groups gathered to pray, to discuss spiritual matters and to have fun. Youths from around the world exchanged small gifts and addresses to keep in touch in the future. Observers of the scene marveled at the contagious exuberance of the youth which developed spontaneously without drugs or sexual promiscuity. One T-shirt spotted in the crowd read, "I Got a Mile High With the Pope." This reading of the jamboree suggests an intriguing paradox: an elderly Pope with a strict moral message expressed in traditional language enables a large number of young Catholics today to enjoy their own Woodstock-type experience.

Guided by some revealing interviews with participants, I see a deeper, more significant dynamism at work in this remarkable World Youth Day. Simply stated, it was for the young people present a much needed and genuinely inspiring celebration of Catholic identity. The huge gathering gave them a sense of belonging to a church which transcends national boundaries and encompasses diverse cultures. They felt affirmed in their fundamental beliefs and values. Some who had felt vaguely embarrassed by their faith found a new and a liberating sense of pride in their heritage. Other more self-confident Catholics heard a challenge to give greater public witness to their religious identity. One collegian told me that her pilgrimage to Denver was the "most amazing week in her life." She now feels even more pride in her faith and is eager to share it with others.

This affirmation of Catholic identity is especially important to young people today because they have not known the type of common experiences which bind older Catholics together. Their memories are not filled with stories about strict nuns, meatless Fridays and midnight fasts before Communion. They have not had to fight overt prejudice or argue that a Catholic could function as president. Their religious imaginations are shaped more by the tolerant attitudes of contemporary ecumenism then by the demanding struggle to maintain Catholic identity in a predominantly Protestant country. They have not known the exhilaration of Vatican II or the challenge of implementing its reforms. These young people need their own set of common experiences as a solid base for their Catholic identity.

In his various addresses, Pope John Paul II gave expression to this quest for an authentic Catholic identity. He invited the young people to reflect seriously on the words of Jesus: "I came that they may have life, and have it abundantly" (Jn. 10:10). He reminded them that their experiences of unity and friendship at the convocation were genuine intimations of the abundant life which Christ promised. His homily at the closing Mass put this message in the context of a challenge to spread their faith and to transform the world. He pointed out that there is "a culture of death which impedes the life-giving power of the message of Christ." The Pope challenged the young people to make their "yes" to life concrete and effective. Indicating that this involves a long and difficult struggle, he exhorted the young people: "Place your intelligence, your talents, your enthusiasm, your compassion and your fortitude at the service of life!"

The collegians I talked to embraced this part of the Pope's message. The core of Catholic identity is to be committed to Christ, who gives us a more abundant life. They were excited by the challenge of it all. They felt a sense of solidarity in all the joys and hardships of the conference: meeting new friends, seeing the Pope, walking the 15 miles to the Mass, sleeping on the ground, and enduring the heat of the day. They seemed to absorb the message that we must die to self in order to share in this richer life of Christ. The challenge is to choose service and commitment over expediency and convenience. To be a member of the Catholic people is to know that the cross is a part of life, and that discipline is necessary for growth. When the Pope enunciated this message, he touched the hearts of the young people. They viewed him as a powerful symbol of their aspirations, a forceful spokesman for Gospel ideals and a living example of the core values of their faith. This helps to explain the immense popularity of the Pope with young people who disagree with him on particular issues. I asked a bright, progressive collegian if the Pope's position on controversial issues such as the ordination of women influenced the way she experienced World Youth Day. She said she remained committed to women's rights in the church, but that during the celebration, other factors seemed more important, especially the challenge to dedicate herself to Christ and the task of transforming the world. She was moved intellectually and emotionally by her realization that she was an integral part of a large community of believers. She feels a kinship with the Pope on the most important matters and has great respect for his personal holiness. Her identity as a Catholic is not threatened by her disagreements with the Pope. She likes being Catholic and sees no reason for people to leave the church because of disputes over Vatican policies.

I believe that this woman represents the viewpoint of a sizable segment of young Catholics in the United States. They are not particularly interested in the controversies of the past.

Having grown up in a pluralistic democracy, they accept dissent in the church as normal and commonplace. They make their own decisions on moral matters and do not feel much guilt if they violate official church teaching. Their religious commitments are more to personal development and serving others than to all the doctrines and laws of the church. The Pope is popular with this group of young persons because he represents the core of Catholic identity and not because all his teachings seem reasonable and acceptable.

At the all-night prayer vigil on Saturday, a young woman representing the youth of the United States told the Pope and the vast assembly: "We, the youth, are not just the future of the Catholic church. We are the present – with a future. We are the Catholic Church." Young people want their distinctive experiences to be taken seriously within the Church and indeed their voices must be heard. They deserve to be part of the discussion on Catholic identity which currently engages members of the church with very diverse mindsets, histories and interests. From one another we can learn more about the common sensibilities and fundamental convictions which bind us together. United in essential matters, the Catholic community will be better prepared to join with other people of good will in the task of humanizing our world.

7. The Potential Impact of the *Catechism of the Catholic Church*

The initial stage in the process of reception suggests that many Catholics are going to use this text selectively in accord with their own theological outlook and spiritual needs.

The new *Catechism of the Catholic Church* is now part of the ongoing life of the universal church. In the United States alone, over two million copies of the English translation were sold within a few months of its publication in November of 1994. Most dioceses have been sponsoring programs to introduce the book to the clergy and laity. Publishers are including material from the *Catechism* in their new and revised religion textbooks. Some parishes are basing their religious education programs on it. Many Catholics have read sections on particular topics of interest, if not all 803 pages of the massive text.

It is difficult to predict how the *Catechism* will be received by the whole church over the long haul and what impact it will make on Catholic spirituality. But initial reactions are instructive. Writing in the January 1995 issue of *First Things*, Jesuit theologian Avery Dulles praised it as "the boldest challenge yet offered to the cultural relativism which threatens to erode the contents of the faith." He is taken by the beauty and admirable proportion of the book which "rises like a basilica over the ground it covers." It is a "serene and comprehensive presentation" of the Catholic tradition which is packed with information essential to a wide public. It "speaks to the heart eliciting prayer and devotion." The tone is appropriately "calm and irenic" in presenting the "deposit of faith," the truths entrusted to the apostles which we must defend and pass on. With its clear focus on the mystery of the Trinity, "it manifests and evokes heartfelt praise, which at times rises almost to the pitch of ecstasy." After defending the unhistorial way the *Catechism* uses scripture and church teaching, Dulles concludes his glowing review: "As a reliable compendium of Catholic doctrine, the *Catechism* brings together the wisdom of the centuries in an appealing synthesis. By virtue of its consistency, beauty and spiritual power, it offers a veritable feast of faith."

Avery Dulles speaks for those who applaud the new *Catechism* as a powerful weapon in the war against the relativism which threatens society and church. They find support in its conservative theology, confident tone, authoritative style and traditional teaching. For them the absolute moral prohibitions, especially in the area of sexuality, provide needed ammunition in the battle against moral relativism. Moreover, they are pleased that the text does not try to relate Christian doctrines to personal experience and cultural trends. Some view this as a victory for the methodology of the Swiss theologian Hans Urs von Balthasar, who argued against Karl Rahner that the best strategy for evangelizing the modern world is simply to present the Catholic faith in all its beauty and integrity without attempting to relate the message to contemporary concerns.

Not all reactions to the *Catechism* have been so favorable. When the first draft of the text was sent to the bishops in November 1989, a number of progressive theologians criticized it harshly, calling for a total rewrite and suggesting that the whole project be abandoned as unnecessary. Most everyone agrees that the final text made a number of improvements: a clearer focus on the trinitarian character of Christian faith; more concern for ecumenical and interfaith relations; greater emphasis on the call of all the faithful to holiness; a more explicit connection between the Ten Commandments and the law of love; a more extensive treatment of the Church's social teaching; and a fuller explanation of Christian prayer as a context for discussing the Lord's Prayer in detail.

Despite these improvements many liberal Catholics are still critical of the *Catechism*. The most vehement reactions have come from those who are upset with the non-inclusive, sexist language consistently used throughout the book. Some registered their protest by refusing to buy or use the *Catechism* in any way. Another general criticism is that the division of the text into the "four pillars of the faith," creed, sacraments, commandments and prayer, does not provide the kind of organic sense of the Catholic faith which is needed in the postmodern world. This structure, developed in the Middle Ages and employed by the 16th century Roman *Catechism*, fails to provide a comprehensive treatment of individual topics which is pastorally and catechetically useful. For example, the *Catechism* discusses the problem of atheism in the section on the commandments and not under the first article of the Creed where it could have been presented as a contemporary challenge to belief in God the creator of heaven and earth. Elements of major Christian doctrines such as grace and revelation are scattered throughout the text. It is difficult to discern the essential connections and dynamic flow between Christ, the church, the liturgy and the Christian

moral life. This structural weakness of the *Catechism* is highlighted by a comparison with Karl Rahner's *Foundations of
Christian Faith*, a classic summary work of contemporary theology. Rahner begins with an experience based discussion of
human existence and then treats in succession God, grace,
revelation, Christ, church, morality, liturgy and the last
things. Throughout, *Foundations* offers a comprehensive organic sense of the Christian faith as a whole which responds
to the deepest longings of the human heart. In comparison,
the new *Catechism* appears more like an encyclopedia containing a vast amount of disparate information.

Scripture scholars noted that the *Catechism* almost entirely ignores the results of modern biblical scholarship.
There is no effort to understand the scripture passages according to historical context, literary form, parallel passages
or intent of the author. For instance, it draws lessons from
the miracles, parables and sayings of Jesus without discussing the theology of the evangelist who edited them. Furthermore, the *Catechism* fails to reflect the modern insight that the
Bible teaches more through stories with multiple layers of
meaning than through abstract general truths. It uses scriptural passages primarily to defend or explain church teaching. Although a few scripture scholars support this uncritical
approach as proper for a catechism, most are convinced it
weakens the credibility of the text.

Liberal critics expressed many other reservations. The
text makes no mention of the work of the great 20th century
theologians such as Karl Rahner, Bernard Lonergan and Yves
Congar. The section on social justice does not utilize the insights of liberation theology. The part on morality does not
clearly and consistently connect the material on the beatitudes with the extensive treatment of the commandments.
With only a couple of exceptions, there is no admission of
sinfulness and failing on the part of the church. The text seldom recognizes or taps the experience of ordinary believers.
In general, many progressive Catholics fear that reactionaries
will use the *Catechism* as a weapon to force preachers and
teachers into a more rigid mold.

But liberal commentators also found positive things in the *Catechism.* The Prologue insists that catechists must adapt the material to the experience of their students. Much of the progressive teaching of Vatican II is maintained, including ideas on human existence and social relationships from the Pastoral Constitution. The material on Mary is balanced and keeps the modern appearances in perspective. There are many references to the Greek Fathers which should promote understanding with the Orthodox Churches. The treatment of human sexuality is more positive than some earlier church documents. The last section on prayer is beautiful and contains rich resources for personal reflection. The text includes hundreds of insightful and inspiring quotes from great theologians, saints and mystics.

As Pope John Paul has indicated, the *Catechism of the Catholic Church* is a "reference text." The initial stage in the process of reception suggests that many Catholics are going to use this text selectively in accord with their own theological outlook and spiritual needs.

8. The *Catechism* and Christian Anthropology

The Catechism of the Catholic Church *contains valuable information for teaching and reflecting on the mystery of human existence.*

Let us imagine that we have to teach a course on Christian anthropology to young people and that the only book we can use for preparation is the *Catechism of the Catholic Church.* Or, to get at the same point from a different angle, we could imagine that we are on a retreat meditating on the mystery of our own existence with only the new *Catechism* to guide our reflections. In these situations, will the *Catechism* prove to be helpful? In general, my answer is that used properly it will serve as a valuable resource on this topic of human existence.

This is not to ignore its limitations. Given a choice, I can think of other books I would rather have at my disposal, for example, *The Summa Theologiae* of Thomas Aquinas, *Foundations of Christian Faith* by Karl Rahner, *Systematic Theology* by

Paul Tillich, *Principles of Christian Theology* by John Macquarrie, *On Being a Christian* by Hans Kung and *Catholicism* by Richard McBrien. In contrast to these other books, the *Catechism of the Catholic Church* does not offer a comprehensive treatment of Christian anthropology or a sustained reflection on human existence. Furthermore, it does not explicitly cite any of the great theologians of the 20th century or make extensive use of liberation theology. Finally, the new *Catechism* makes only an initial passing attempt to relate its teaching on human nature to the experience of people today, thus rendering itself ineffective as a textbook for classroom use. Despite these limitations, the new *Catechism* remains a rich resource for teaching and reflection on the question of human existence. Throughout the text we find useful material from a wide variety of sources, including the Scriptures; the fathers of the Church; the great mystics; the Second Vatican Council, especially the Pastoral Constitution (*Gaudium et Spes*); and the personalist philosophy of Pope John Paul II. The pastoral and catechetical task is to order this material and relate it to our contemporary situation.

We reflect on the mystery of our being in a culture heavily influenced by secular humanism which sees human nature as a self-contained and self-sufficient reality with no need of God. The *Catechism* provides a radical response to all secularist philosophies: "The desire for God is written in the human heart, because we are created by God and for God; and God never ceases to draw us into the divine life. Only in God will we find the truth and happiness we never stop searching for" (N 27 – here and in the following citations I have made the language more inclusive). Throughout history human beings "have given expression to their quest for God in their religious beliefs and behavior; in their prayers, sacrifices, rituals, meditations, and so forth." The universal character of these expressions indicates that we are indeed "religious beings" (N 28). The *Catechism* cites one of the best-known statements of this truth from the beginning of Augustine's *Confessions*: "You are great, O Lord, and greatly to be praised; great is your power and your wisdom is without measure. . . . You yourself encourage us to delight in your praise, for you have made us for yourself, and our heart is restless until it rests in you" (N 30). We do not find in the *Catechism* a detailed refutation of secular humanism, but it does suggest an alternative vision of human beings as essentially religious creatures.

In the Western world we generally celebrate the dignity and worth of persons, but over the last two centuries influential philosophers have questioned the religious basis for this conviction. Calling on traditional teaching, the *Catechism* clearly roots human dignity in our relationship to God. Reflecting on the source of human dignity, the 14th century mystic and Doctor of the Church Catherine of Siena was moved to address the gracious God: "You are taken with love for her; for by love indeed you created her, by love you have given her a being capable of tasting your eternal Good" (N 356). The Pastoral Constitution of Vatican II reminds us that God has endowed us with dignity as unified creatures composed of body and soul. "For this reason we may not despise our bodily life. Rather we are obliged to regard our bodies as good and to hold them in honor since God has created them and will raise them up on the last day" (N 364). We possess our dignity as sexual beings: "Men and woman were made for each other – not that God left them half-made and incomplete: God created them to be a communion of persons in which each can be a helpmate to the other, for they are equal as persons" (N 372). This notion that men and women are not incomplete in themselves helps us avoid some traditional gender stereotyping and reminds us that marriage at its best is a partnership of mature persons. The *Catechism* indicates that the baptized faithful as a whole have preserved a "Christian humanism that radically affirms the dignity of every person as a child of God, establishes a basic fraternity, teaches people to encounter nature and understand work, provides reasons for joy and humor even in the midst of a very hard life" (N 1676). For Christians, human worth is solidly rooted in the conviction that all people are created in the image of God and thus possess "the dignity of a person, who is not just something, but someone" (N 357).

In addition to its solid teaching on human dignity, the *Catechism* offers a realistic portrayal of the way human existence is threatened by sin and guilt. As the Pastoral Constitution describes it, "The whole of human history has been the story of dour combat with the powers of evil. . . . Finding ourselves in the midst of the battlefield we have to struggle to do what is right, and it is at great cost to ourselves, and aided by God's grace, that we succeed in achieving our own inner integrity" (N 409). Because of original sin "the control of the soul's spiritual faculties over the body is shattered; the union of man and woman becomes subject to tensions. . . . Harmony with creation is broken. . . . Death makes its entrance into human history" (N 400). While realistically recognizing these tensions built into the human condition, the *Catechism* maintains the traditional Catholic sense of the essential goodness of human nature. "Human nature has not been totally corrupted; it is wounded in the natural powers proper to it . . . (N 405). Echoing the apostle Paul, the text offers the fundamental reason for a positive outlook on human existence: "The victory that Christ won over sin has given us greater blessings than those which sin had taken from us" (N 420).

Throughout the 19th and 20th centuries influential critics such as Marx, Nietzsche, Freud, and Sartre have joined together in contending that Christianity is fundamentally dehumanizing. The *Catechism* does not provide a specific response to the objections of each of these critics, but it does offer a global claim that Christian teachings accord with human nature and call us to develop our God-given potential. As Vatican II taught, "Christ . . . makes us fully manifest to ourselves and brings to light our exalted vocation" (N 1701). In Jesus of Nazareth we see the full flowering of humanity and the supreme model for a mature and effective life. We find our perfection not in a will to power but "in seeking and loving what is true and great" (N 1704). Striving for autonomous freedom is not the path to fulfillment and happiness. On the contrary it is "through the exchange with others, mutual service and dialogue, we develop our potential" (N 1879). "Human freedom is a force for growth and maturity in truth and goodness; it attains its perfection when directed toward God, our beatitude" (N 1731). "The more one does what is good, the freer one becomes. There is no true freedom except in the service of what is good and just" (N 1733).

As this brief summary suggests, the *Catechism of the Catholic Church* contains valuable information for teaching and reflecting on the mystery of human existence. If the vast material in the text is properly selected, adapted and related to contemporary experience, the *Catechism* can also serve as a useful resource on other theological topics.

9. The Incarnation: Hope in a Disrupted World

The story of the birth of Jesus with its realistic portrayal of expectation, anguish and hope places the disruptions and distortions built into the whole of human existence into a larger context of meaning.

No doubt, T.S. Eliot had his reasons for calling April the cruelest month of the year. In our society today, however, the more obvious choice for this distinction is December. The month which brings us the joys of Christmas also spawns an amazing amount of consternation, anxiety and depression. Some of this tension is generated by clear and unavoidable dislocations. Families dealing with a recent death of a loved one experience a heightened sense of loss during the holiday season. Individuals who are unemployed or suffering from the economic crunch may be dismayed that they cannot give presents as they once did. Spouses recently divorced and their children know the pain of finding new patterns for celebrating Christmas.

In addition to these obvious disruptions, the cruelty of December takes more subtle forms. It is a time when customs and events conspire to upset the psychic balance we need for solid spiritual growth. The busyness of the season makes it even more difficult to keep a healthy balance between activity and reflection. Intense advertising campaigns encourage consumerism and threaten traditional Christian priorities. But December is most cruel when it upsets the balance between expectation and fulfillment. This loss of equilibrium takes many forms. The season generates an increasing excitement as it moves toward a one-day celebration which cannot possibly bear the weight of all the expectations. Adults who hope to relive exuberant childhood celebrations of Christmas are doomed to frustration. The constant message of advertising that material goods will satisfy the longings of our hearts always proves to be illusory. The prevailing assumption that an increased round of parties will ward off loneliness never gets to the root of the problem. A piety which expects the sentimental mood surrounding Christmas to continue indefinitely is out of touch with the harsh realities of life. December is cruel when it promises more than it can deliver. It is disruptive when it fosters unrealistic expectations which lead to painful and paralyzing letdowns.

Of course, December is not only cruel; it is also festive, exhilarating, joyous, expansive and religious. This month carries some of our best memories, leads to some of our most unselfish acts and brings some of our deepest joys. It instructs us in the meaning of the incarnation and offers rich liturgical experiences. In order to make the most of these positive opportunities, we need to manage the distortions which threaten our equilibrium during the Christmas season.

We can find enlightenment and encouragement for this task through an imaginative reflection on the infancy account in Matthew's Gospel. In this story, which has its share of strange twists and odd disruptions, we encounter a perplexed young man as he agonizes over his dashed hopes for a simple and happy married life. His fiancee, whom he trusts completely, is pregnant and he is not the father. He is a just man who takes his religious traditions seriously, but he is also a loving man who cares deeply for his girlfriend. He decides to break the engagement informally in order to shield her from the full rigors of the law which calls for the stoning of unmarried mothers. But as soon as he arrives at this decision, a new flash of inspiration and enlightenment occurs. This pregnancy, which defies mere logic and rational explanation, is the work of the Spirit. He must put aside his fears, rekindle his positive expectations and proceed with the marriage. And so with renewed confidence, he takes his fiancee to his home. In due course a son is born and they name him Jesus which means Yahweh saves. In this way Mary and Joseph manifest their convicton that in some mysterious way their son carries the hopes and expectations of the Jewish people. He is the fulfillment of the promises made to Abraham, Isaac and Jacob. He is the long-awaited heir to the throne of David and Solomon. His birth is connected with the prophecy offered by Isaiah that a virgin would conceive and that her son would be a sign that God is with us. Centuries of expectation and oft-repeated promises are now suddenly gathered in this new born babe.

Not long after the birth of Jesus, wise men from the East arrive quite unexpectedly bringing gifts for the infant king of the Jews. They speak of a mysterious star which guided them and of an alarming conversation with King Herod. The surprising and unexpected meaning of this visit is clear. The saving presence of Yahweh is not restricted to the Jewish people alone, but extends to the Gentiles as well. Yahweh shatters familiar expectations and does surprising things.

However, in the midst of this joyful realization, the darkness of evil casts its shadow. The devious King Herod fears the newborn king and wants to eliminate him. When his plan to find Jesus through the wise men is foiled, he orders all the male children two years and under in Bethlehem and the surrounding district to be killed. Fortunately, Joseph receives a warning in a dream and escapes by taking Mary and Jesus to Egypt. The fulfillment of the promises is not going to be achieved without price. The grieving mothers of the slain are not easily comforted. Yahweh will indeed bring salvation to his people through Jesus, but he will be a suffering messiah.

This familiar story has an inherent power to illumine the postmodern situation. It speaks to us as we struggle with the disruptions and imbalances that threaten our spiritual equilibrium. Advent prepares us to assimilate this message, but only if this liturgical season of preparation is properly understood. We are not preparing for the historical birth of Jesus which already occured 2,000 years ago. Nor are we simply preparing for the coming again in glory of Christ who departed from us at the Ascension and will return again at the end of the world. More precisely, Advent calls us to celebrate the historical birth of Jesus and to prepare for the completion of his work at the end of time while sharpening our awareness of the presence of the Lord in our lives today. Within this framework, Advent prepares us to assimilate the real meaning of the Christmas story. The Word has become flesh and continues to participate totally in our humanity. God the Son has pitched his tent in our midst and continues to share the human condition. Thus the Lord can be found in the busyness and confusion of life as a power which calms and comforts. He is present in the midst of frustration and anxiety as a surprising secret source of hope and serenity. He is the inner meaning of our daily routine no matter how chaotic and disrupted. If we learn the Advent lesson of finding Christ in the daily and the ordinary, then we can reduce the unreasonable expectations which abound during the Christmas season. Christmas is not merely a brief peak experience whose exuberance and joy quickly fades; it is rather a powerful reminder of what God is doing for us always and everywhere. The story of the birth of Jesus with its realistic portrayal of expectation, anguish and hope places the disruptions and distortions built into the whole of human existence into a larger context of meaning. We are strengthened in the struggle to maintain our spiritual equilibrium by our belief in the ultimate triumph of God's kingdom of justice and peace.

10. Christmas and the Spirit of Joy

Christmas as a feast of joy attunes us to the presence of the Lord and nourishes our hope that Christ will complete his saving work.

For the evangelist Luke, the birth of Jesus is a joyful event with universal significance. The angel of the Lord appears to a poor, uneducated group of shepherds keeping night watch over their flocks in the fields near Bethlehem. The angel immediately sets the joyous tone for this momentous occurrence: "I come to proclaim good news to you – tidings of great joy to be shared by the whole people. This day in David's city, a savior has been born to you, the Messiah and Lord." Indeed this messenger from God proclaims the most joyful news of all. The whole human family can rejoice because the long-awaited messianic age has finally been inaugurated.

As confirmation of this history-changing event, the angel offers the shepherds a simple sign: "In a manger you will find an infant wrapped in swaddling clothes." Intrigued, the shepherds go in haste to Bethlehem where they find Mary and Joseph, with the baby lying in a manger. Having seen for themselves, they now understand the message of the angel and begin glorifying and praising God for all they have been privileged to experience. They echo the joyful proclamation of the multitude of the heavenly host: "Glory to God in high heaven, peace on earth to those on whom his favor rests." The prophecy of Isaiah is fulfilled. The people who walked in darkness have seen a great light. They rejoice in the birth of the Prince of Peace. Luke's infancy account is indeed a masterful summary of the good news. It has an enduring power to touch our hearts with tidings of great joy.

In our culture today there are strong pressures to celebrate Christmas more as a holiday of happiness than a feast of joy. In many ways Christmas really is a happy time. Presents given and received often produce spontaneous smiles. The round of parties can be fun. The special meals and abundant desserts are delightful. The lights and decorations provide a visual treat. Our traditional greeting, "Merry Christmas," names something important about the season. But Christmas as a holiday of happiness has its limitations. Some try too hard to make it happy and end up spoiling it. Nostalgic efforts to recapture childhood bliss often end with disappointment and emptiness. With all of its inherent pressures, the Christmas season can easily produce a good deal of unhappiness. Christmas Day itself can never fulfill its promise of bringing happiness to all.

Christmas is a far different experience when celebrated in its deeper meaning as a feast of joy. Christian joy is not the same as happiness or pleasure or merriment or fun. Joy is a fundamental disposition rooted deep in our souls. It is a basic frame of mind which results from being in proper relationship with God. Being attuned to God's will enables us to know the joy of inner peace and harmonious relationships. This kind of joy involves spiritual delight, a feeling of inner confidence in the right order of things, a serene sense that the universe is ultimately hospitable, a hopeful conviction that God has redeemed us through Christ.

Christian joy can endure even in the midst of personal suffering. A former student once wrote me a letter describing her horrible life situation which included an abusive husband, chronic fatigue, real poverty and a rebellious son. After a graphic portrayal of these woes, she asserted, "Even with all of these trials, I have never felt so peaceful. I have found an inner joy because I am learning to rely totally upon God." This seems to be the secret of joyful people. They have developed a proper sense of reliance on God. They live in harmony with the Mystery that surrounds them. They are at peace with themselves and with other people.

By these standards many of us find our joy limited and incomplete. Nevertheless, we all know something of the power and beauty of a joyful spirit. We have moments of inner peace, flashes of spiritual delight, times of quiet confidence, or periods of trusting faith which remind us that a joyful spirit is a great blessing indeed. Tasting a bit of genuine joy triggers our appetite for more.

The Advent and Christmas liturgies invite us to reflect more deeply on the nature of Christian joy and how to attain it. On the third Sunday of Advent, Paul tells us to rejoice, and in case we miss the point, he insists, "Again I say rejoice." It is almost as if he is saying that we have a choice about being joyful. You can be glum, disordered, selfish and out of tune with God's will or you can live more harmoniously by following the promptings of the Spirit. Some joyful people do claim that they deliberately chose to change their fundamental disposition from negative to positive. They decided to quit acting like a victim of the fates and to start trusting in the power of God.

There is another side to this quest for joy. God is the source of all good gifts – joy included. Joy directly sought eludes us. Striving to be joyful can be as misguided as trying to be happy. We experience genuine joy as a gift. It comes as a by-product of healthy attitudes and proper behavior. In his book *Surprised by Joy*, C.S. Lewis tells the story of his consuming, but vain, search for joy. Only after years of heartbreaking failure did he recognize that the experience of joy was connected with his ability to forget about himself. When he set aside his own needs and desires, he was more likely to feel joyful. On the other hand, when he attempted to grab hold of joy or to analyze the feeling, it disappeared. Through a gradual process of conversion he came to see that he should concentrate on the object or source of his desire rather then the subjective experiences of joy. By cultivating a sense of awe before what he called the "Naked Other" or "The Desirable," he found that his compulsive search for joy dissipated. Thus liberated, Lewis now recognized his periodic experiences of joy as gifts which point to God, the source of all blessings.

The Christmas liturgies connect Christian joy with the threefold coming of the Lord, in the past, present and future. We can rejoice because during the reign of Caesar Augustus, the Word of God became flesh and dwelt among us. Luke's beautiful story of the birth of Jesus in Bethlehem 2,000 years ago continues to gladden our souls. Even though the infancy account is already shadowed by the cross, it brings us a sense of hope and confidence. Christian joy flourishes when the memory of Jesus guides and enriches our lives.

We also rejoice because the Lord comes to us in and through our daily activities. We can think of times when we rose above our selfishness and reached out to help someone in need, or occasions when we worked hard and met our responsibilities even when we did not feel like it, or situations when we treated family and friends with kindness even through they showed little appreciation. In all such activities the eyes of faith discern the presence of the Lord. Our Christian celebration of the Incarnation insists that God is in the world, that the infinite is revealed by the finite, that the extraordinary is found in the ordinary, that eternity is present in time. Enlightened by this faith conviction, Christians can rejoice in all the clues which suggest that Christ is present in our daily lives.

Finally, joyful Christians trust that the Lord will come again to mark the completion of his work. An adult celebration of Christmas has a future orientation. The reign of God announced by Jesus will one day reach its fulfillment. Joy is rooted in the conviction that the process of life can be trusted because it is encompassed and guided by the loving God. History will reach its goal and there will be a new heaven and a new earth. We rejoice because the birth of Jesus holds the promise of the final victory of good over evil.

Joyful Christians, attuned to the threefold coming of the Lord, can discern signs of hope in a world often dominated by bad news. On the domestic scene, during 1994 unemployment dropped from 6.4% to 5.8%, while inflation stayed below the 1993 level of 2.7%. Teenage pregnancy rates continued to go down, having fallen 19% in two decades. The rate of highway fatalities fell to 1.8 per million vehicle miles, continuing a 26-year downward trend. The infant mortality rate went down slightly. Overall, crime decreased 3% in the first half of 1994. Scientists made spectacular progress in diagnosing and treating specific diseases. It is now possible to produce synthetically the cancer fighting drug toxal without cutting down a huge amount of trees.

In the international arena, Russia is still a democracy, Eastern Europe is still free, and Nelson Mandela is still president of South Africa. During this past year, we avoided a military confrontation with North Korea over nuclear weapons and with Iraq over its renewed threat to Kuwait. Haiti returned to democratic rule. Israel and Jordan signed a peace treaty after nearly 50 years of hostilities. The Irish Republican Army announced a cease-fire which spawned new hope for peace in Northern Ireland.

Joyful Christians can discern these and many other signs of hope without denying the terrible problems which plague us at home and abroad. Christmas as a feast of joy attunes us to the presence of the Lord and nourishes our hope that Christ will complete his saving work.

11. Christianity and Self-Esteem

In short, our self-esteem is not based merely on an illusory type of positive thinking, but on the reality that we are personally loved by the Gracious Mystery.

In order to cope effectively with the challenges of the postmodern world we need a solid sense of self-esteem. Spiritual growth is dependent on a healthy love of self. And yet achieving and maintaining such a fundamental self-respect is not an easy task. Unfortunately some unhappy individuals walk the path of life burdened by a prevailing mood of self-loathing. "I hate myself" is the ever-so-sad expression of an abiding sense of unworthiness and a constant preoccupation with limitations and faults. Other people experience such self-doubts only periodically. Many days they feel capable of managing the challenges and responsibilities of life, confident that their best efforts will be sufficient and well received. But on other occasions they find themselves anxious about small matters, doubtful about their ability to cope, and insecure about interacting with people. Even those persons who enjoy a more abiding sense of self-worth often report how fragile this gift is. A failure can bring on a flash of self-doubt; a personal rejection can chop away at self-confidence; a mediocre performance can produce self-questioning. Even when everything is going well for them, a mysterious attack of anxiety may suddenly interrupt the positive flow and threaten their self-confidence. Clearly some people struggle more intensely with the demon of self-doubt than others. Few would claim, however, that the search for a deeper and stronger sense of self-worth is totally foreign to them. The effort to achieve and maintain a healthy self-esteem is indeed an essential part of the human adventure.

Unfortunately, distorted forms of religion can impede the quest for self-esteem. Christian formation, for example, which places more emphasis on sin than grace has a tendency to produce people preoccupied with guilt and personal unworthiness. Since our image of God is intimately correlated with our self image, the transmission of harsh and repressive images of the Deity is especially damaging. Scrupulous Catholics often connect scary notions of a wrathful God with their First Communion or going to Confession. Individuals who perceive God as angry or capricious have a difficult time recognizing their own dignity and maintaining a sense of self-worth. So do those who believe in a demanding God who tests people through suffering or a passive God who allows evil to befall innocent persons. A woman who gives birth to a defective child finds it hard to maintain her self-esteem, if she feels abandoned by God.

Popular preaching and teaching in the Catholic community has often reflected the traditional scholastic teaching that goodness results from having all aspects of our existence in order, while evil results from any defect whatsoever. Without analyzing the metaphysical truth of this axiom, we can recognize its harmful psychological effects. It suggests that a single moral fault can vitiate an individual's fundamentally good character. It puts the emphasis on a few defects while neglecting a person's many positive virtues and actions. It reinforces the common tendency to focus on what is wrong with ourselves rather than the things we do well. To accept the idea that evil results from any defect whatsoever is to condemn ourselves to an abiding sense of unworthiness, since no one is perfect and all of us are aware of failings and limitations. Unfortunately, many believers have appropriated these and other negative messages from their Christian tradition, making it difficult to achieve a healthy sense of self-esteem.

Individuals who become aware of the repressive elements in their Christian formation are often tempted to jettison their whole religious tradition in favor of a more enlightened outlook which emphasizes that human nature is essentially and unambiguously good. Influential modern critics of religion, including Karl Marx, have advocated precisely this strategy. Much of contemporary pop psychology preaches the same message by insisting that we are all OK, that we should think only positive thoughts and that our negative perceptions are the result of religious or societal hangups. In enlightened circles, talk of sin and guilt is replaced by the psychological categories of neurosis or false consciousness. We can achieve self-esteem by emphasizing positive thinking and rejecting religious moralizing.

There is no doubt that many have found this enlightened modern approach useful in moving beyond negative self-images toward a greater sense of self-worth. From a postmodern perspective, however, we can detect fundamental deficiencies in this whole approach. The main problem is that it denies the common human experience that we are all flawed creatures. We are not simply and unambiguously good persons; rather we are a mysterious mixture of good and evil. We cannot take our feelings and intuitions as our only guide because sometimes they take us in destructive directions. In the center of our being we know a certain emptiness, a lack of integration, a battle between conflicting tendencies. When we hear talk of the restless heart, or unfulfilled longings, or the unanswered question which dominates our journey, it resonates with our deepest experience. We cannot achieve a genuine self-esteem by denying this essential aspect of our experience. To tell someone wrestling with the mysterious gap at the core of their being that they are OK is to trivialize a fundamental aspect of our common experience. The power of positive thinking is limited, and an analysis of human nature which neglects its essential flaws is finally insufficient.

This brings us back to the Christian tradition and its positive potential for aiding us in the quest for greater self-esteem in the postmodern world. Christianity has the advantage of beginning with a realistic assessment of human nature which recognizes the ambivalence of the human heart. Christians in tune with the authentic tradition know that the human situation is flawed, that cultural distortions are powerful, that total personal integration is never achieved and that sin is an ever-present threat. At the same time, we believe that all dark and destructive forces are always encompassed by the greater power of good. For us, the ultimate power is benign and loves us unconditionally despite our unworthiness. We are called to accept that we are accepted even when we feel unacceptable. We read in our Scriptures that even if a mother should forget her child our God will not forget us. The all powerful One is more forgiving than the best of fathers and more loving than the best of mothers. We are worthwhile because the Spirit lives within us. We possess a dignity beyond belief because Jesus Christ has died and been raised for us. We are called to use our gifts and talents in order to cooperate in building the community of love. In short, our self-esteem is not based merely on an illusory type of positive thinking, but on the reality that we are personally loved by the Gracious Mystery.

We all need to find our own ways of assimilating and maintaining these fundamental Christian insights. It is helpful to meditate on positive biblical stories, quotes and images. When doing an examination of conscience or a daily assessment, individuals with a poor self-image should spend at least as much time reflecting on virtues and accomplishments as vices and sins. We should all try to assimilate honest compliments and positive feedback from others. From cognitive therapists we can learn the importance of recognizing and transforming fallacious thinking which undercuts our self-esteem, for example, the common over-generalization that one is a bad person because of a single transgression or a few failures. Reading uplifting spiritual books can provide us with guidance and motivation for the journey toward a deeper sense of self-worth. Taking an inventory of our talents and gifts and how they can be used effectively for the cause of God and humanity forces us into more positive thought patterns. Persons who need a more structured approach to developing self-esteem can do an imaginative meditation each day in which they prayerfully reflect on positive events from the past when they felt good or acted virtuously. Finally, we should all thank God for any sense of self-esteem we do enjoy and pray that we use it in the service of others.

12. Self-Actualization and Self-Forgetfulness

A viable postmodern spirituality must keep the cultural ideal of self-actualization and the biblical teaching on self-forgetfulness in a fruitful tension.

Developing a postmodern spirituality demands that we adopt a mutually critical stance toward both religion and culture. This involves discerning positive values as well as destructive tendencies in our Christian faith and our national culture. This framework enables us to analyze some of our important and enduring cultural values often clustered under the heading of "self-actualization." According to humanistic psychologists such as Abraham Maslow, self-actualizing persons have satisfied their fundamental needs and therefore are less dependent on others and act more out of their own inner resources. They are motivated less by the demands of their environment and more by their own wishes and plans. For them, dedication to personal growth demands that they gradually learn more about their own talents and gifts and how to develop them. They sense an inner call to move toward greater personal integration and are able to deal better with the obstacles to such development.

These aspects of the self-actualization ideal are a great corrective for Christians who experience their religion as heavy, negative and moralistic. Believers who are plagued by guilt feelings are reminded of their essential goodness which is waiting to be tapped. Those who think that humility means denying their talents hear about the value of recognizing and developing their God-given gifts. Individuals who were taught that good Christians are passive and dependent are challenged by a philosophy which stresses active and intelligent involvement in the world. Persons who picked up the notion that morality is merely a slavish conformity to external laws learn that we are all called to respond out of inner conviction to the unique call of God echoing in our hearts. Christians who have routinely practiced their religion without much thought can find great excitement in personally appropriating their faith and exploring its implications for daily life. Members who have identified the church with the hierarchy may find a new sense of self-importance in assuming personal responsibility for the well-being of the community of faith. In sum, the diverse values connected with the term "self-actualization" can lead Christians to appropriate the good news that Jesus came to give life and to give it more abundantly.

Unfortunately, the cultural ideal of self-actualization can itself become distorted. It can lead to a narcissistic preoccupation with self and can be used to rationalize insensitivity to others. It can engender an egocentricity which effectively denies the communal and social character of human existence. Self-actualization can be reduced to pulling one's own strings and looking out for number one. It can induce good persons to undertake the journey of self-growth without regard for the needs and feelings of others.

Where do we find a corrective for such self-centered and individualistic tendencies? For the most radical solutions, we can look to the world's great religious traditions. Hinduism teaches that the true self is really identified with ultimate reality. Progress in life is achieved by a process of self-realization in which an individual puts aside ego and brings excessive desires under control. The goal is the oceanic experience in which the self is completely lost in the all. Buddhism goes further and denies that there is any "self" at all. Human suffering is caused by craving, by desiring of all types. Such craving is eliminated in the enlightenment experience which reveals that the very notion of a distinct self is illusory. Chinese humanism moves in the same direction. Chuang Tzu, representing the Taoist tradition in the third century B.C., claimed that people will never find happiness until they stop looking for it. Contentment and peace become possible only when a person ceases to seek them directly.

Our Christian tradition offers pointed and concrete teachings along this same line. Jesus taught that we must die to self in order to rise to new life. We must lose our life to gain it. In baptism, followers of Christ are buried with him in order to share in his resurrection. The apostle Paul insists that we put on the mind of Christ and offers personal witness to this truth: "I live now not I but Christ lives in me."

This dying-to-self theme informs the Christian mystical tradition. In the early church the Desert Fathers spoke of achieving a purity of heart which involves an emptying of all desires and self-interest. The 14th century mystic Meister Eckhart insisted that we should have nothing and want nothing so that God could create his own space within us and act through us. Teresa of Avila in the 16th century heard the Lord say, "Don't try to hold Me within yourself, but try to hold yourself within Me." In our century Thomas Merton has written, "The self is not its own center and does not orbit around itself; it is centered on God, the one center of all." Thus Christianity joins other religious traditions in reminding us of the dangers of egocentricity and the power of self-surrender which allows the higher power to take over.

These teachings are a helpful corrective to the cultural versions of self-actualization which tend toward egoism. They suggest the need for a dialectical counterpoint to self-actualization which could be called "self-forgetfulness." This corrective enables us to maintain the much needed emphasis on life-affirming Gospel values while avoiding the tendency toward a destructive narcissism.

The temptations toward self-centeredness are diverse and often subtle. At times our personal projects blind us to the needs of others. The ideal of self-forgetfulness reminds us that our own interests cannot be made into an idol; it also challenges us to submerge our own ego in the larger project of humanizing our world and caring for others. Some people feel as though they are on center stage performing for some imagined audience. A successful performance increases their sense of self-importance and may lead to pride, while a poor performance diminishes their self-esteem and may cause unwarranted guilt feelings. A healthy dose of self-forgetfulness enables us to get off center stage and to play a more modest role. When we remember that God is really at the center of the whole universe of persons and things, we become freer to be ourselves and to make our limited but significant contribution to the spreading of the reign of God.

Another temptation fostered by our postmodern, media-dominated culture is an excessive concern about personal image. Worry about what people think of us and whether we made a good impression can sap our energy and can deaden our spirits. Preoccupation with our public image obscures our true identity and leads to an inauthentic and superficial lifestyle. The ideal of self-forgetfulness encourages us to put aside the masks we wear in public, allowing more of our true selves to appear. It reminds us to act out of genuine conviction and to be confident of our inherent goodness. To renounce the false self of contrived images enables us to encounter the Spirit who inhabits the center of our being. Empowered by this Spirit, we can relate to others in more honest and authentic ways.

Self-forgetfulness is not just a technique for getting along with people. It is rather a core Christian ideal based on the fact that we are totally dependent on the Invisible Power in rule over our lives. A viable postmodern spirituality must keep the cultural ideal of self-actualization and the biblical teaching on self-forgetfulness in a fruitful tension. The Christian tradition, with its emphasis on self-denial, places the drive for personal fulfillment in a larger context which challenges any tendencies to selfishness. The cultural emphasis on self-fulfullment has encouraged Christians to rediscover the Gospel ideal of living a full and abundant life in Christ. In turn, the Christian tradition consistently challenges us to develop our potential so that we can better serve others and the cause of the kingdom.

13. Aging and the Healing Power of the Eucharist

At a recent reunion of the class of 1954, we succeeded in uniting once more around the familiar rituals and common stories which keep us in touch with our roots and provide us with hope as we experience the joys and pains of advancing years.

When did personal health problems become the major topic of conversation? For the Toledo Central Catholic High School class of 1954, it seemed to happen somewhere between our 30th and 40th class reunion. Perhaps we slid into it gradually as major operations multiplied and daily aches and pains became more troublesome. It is hardly worth having a quadruple bypass heart surgery if you cannot tell someone about it afterwards. The answer to a question about whether one still plays tennis has to include some commentary on the limitations imposed by arthritic knees. Of course, at the 40th reunion we talked about many things: politics, economics, sports, careers, children and grandchildren. Our conversations included the stories of the past which bind us together and dreams for the future, including retirement, which a surprising number of our classmates already enjoy. But people in their late fifties have a hard time remaining silent about health problems. The bodies we are and have know too much about pain, weakness and fatigue.

This is not to say that the aging process functions with absolute impartiality. Some of our classmates are amazingly healthy. Time has been kind to the brunette without an apparent trace of gray who looks ten years younger than she is. On the other hand, the years have dealt harshly with the thin, stooped, bald man who passed by some former good friends without being recognized. Individuals take very different approaches to bodily health. One man who weighs less than he did in high school eats very little fat and does 45 minutes of aerobic exercises at least four times a week. Another who is overweight and has suffered two heart attacks was observed smoking and drinking at the reunion. Chided by some friends for his destructive habits, he proclaimed, with expletives for emphasis, that he would outlive all those health nuts.

Much of the talk about health during our 40th reunion reflected the faith nourished by our Catholic heritage. More than one person asked me as a priest to pray for them as they battled serious illnesses. A doctor, who had himself undergone four surgeries and six months of radiation in the past year, finds that he is now extremely grateful to God for the gift of each new day. A corporate executive who was remarkably lucky that his cancer was detected and successfully treated remarked, "I guess God is not finished with me yet."

The subject of death could not be avoided at the reunion. During the Mass which began the evening, a woman solemnly recited the names of 43 of our deceased classmates, almost 10% of the class. The moment was precious and evoked various responses. One person who has survived serious health problems thanked God he was not on the list. Another suffering from a rare form of cancer was overwhelmed with the thought that her name would be included at the next reunion. A man currently enjoying good health noted that he no longer fears death since he buried his parents and lost his son in a tragic accident.

In my homily at the Mass I explored the deepest roots of the Catholic identity which encourages us to approach both suffering and death with faith and hope. Forty years ago, we had a pretty clear idea of who we were as Catholics. The rules were clear: go to Mass on Sunday; do not eat meat on Friday; accept the teachings of the Pope. The challenge was to keep them. Today there is a public debate about the nature and characteristics of Catholic identity. The secular and religious media bombard us with stories of dissent and disagreement within the church. Theologians strive to delineate the broad mainstream of Catholic thought but cannot achieve consensus. Educated Catholics disagree on the significance and interpretation of some church teachings. Given this great pluralism, we are forced to ask what holds us together as Catholic people.

The Emmaus story (Luke 24), read as the Gospel for the reunion Mass, suggests an answer. The disillusioned disciples fleeing Jerusalem after the death of Jesus came to recognize the Lord in the breaking of the bread. This is the clue to the deepest level of Catholic identity. We are a people bound together by the formative power of the Eucharist. Our faith is nourished by gathering in church, telling the biblical stories and breaking the bread of life. Our religious sensibilities are colored by a whole series of liturgical experiences. We can all recall some story about our First Communion. Christmas midnight Mass has traditionally been an especially joyful aspect of Catholic life. Most of our classmates celebrated their marriage vows at Mass. Many have buried their loved ones in the same familiar and comforting liturgical setting. Some have known the spiritual power of the Eucharist celebrated in their homes or on retreats. We have begun all of our reunions with a Mass. Catholic identity is essentially tied to recognizing Jesus in the breaking of the bread.

Because we are programmed to recognize the Lord in the Eucharist, we can discern his presence in all of reality. Our fundamental outlook on life bears the stamp of the liturgy. Going to Mass regularly produces a sacramental sense which recognizes that the whole world pulsates with the power of the gracious God. Belief in the real presence of Christ in the Eucharist prepares us to see the infinite God in the beauties of nature and in other people. The proclamation of the biblical stories of God's activity in history reminds us that the Lord remains active in our lives today. We who recognize Christ in the breaking of the bread can also find his Spirit in family meals, neighborhood parties, national celebrations and international relief efforts. The Catholic imagination is comfortable with blessing food, cars and pregnant women. We see divine grace at work in the lives of the official saints and in the good people we know. Mary retains special prominence for us because the Word took flesh in her womb.

Growing up as Catholics, we first heard the Bible stories and participated in the liturgy before we learned the dogmas and doctrines of the faith. This repeats the pattern of Christian history. Jesus told stories about the reign of God; the early community recounted the story of the life, death and resurrection of Jesus in their liturgical celebrations; only later in the fourth century did the church begin to meet in General Councils to formulate the dogmas of the faith. The fundamental stories and symbols have an enduring power to form us into a distinctive people. We Catholics might disagree about some church teachings and policies, but we all recognize Jesus when we gather to tell the scriptural stories and share the bread and wine.

Through the stories and rituals we ingest the Catholic symbols into our bones and blood. They are tenacious and not easily discarded. In my homily, I told the story of a man who tried for many years through travel, education and career to rid himself of his ethnic background and Catholic heritage because he found them embarrassing. After a long fruitless effort, he decided the only solution for him was to befriend his Catholic tradition through further study and renewed participation in the church. The Catholic imagination resists dismantling and restructuring. This may explain the conclusion of the research of Professor Michael Hout, of the University of California at Berkeley, that the defection rate from Catholicism has remained steady at 15% over the last 30 years. Catholics stay in the church because they continue to recognize Jesus in the breaking of the bread. Despite the evident problems in our church, we stay because we still find meaning, comfort and strength in the fundamental stories of our faith. Doctrines are essential and theology is important, but the real power of our heritage is rooted in the stories and rituals which shape our imaginations.

This analysis provides hope for my classmates who are distressed because their offspring do not practice their faith. Perhaps these young people have retained ties to Catholicism which are not immediately evident. Despite their indifference or anger, it is likely that they still have a Catholic imagination which may one day reassert itself. No doubt many have maintained a sacramental sense of life which grounds a genuine spirituality. Studies suggest most of them continue to pray to the God revealed in the stories of Jesus.

To reinforce the point, I told the story of an ardent feminist collegian who had a deeply moving religious experience at the 1993 Papal Mass in Denver, despite the exclusion of women from major liturgical roles. Rather than leave the church, she now intends to fight for women's rights from within the community of faith. This decision is rooted in her new appreciation of the deep sacramental bonds which unite Catholics, despite their disagreements on church policies. Some classmates told me after the reunion that they had encouraging conversations with their sons and daughters about the enduring power of the Catholic symbols.

I concluded the homily with the hope that during the Mass we would all once more recognize Jesus in the breaking of the bread and thus strengthen our bonds with one another and the whole church. Reactions to the liturgy reinforced my convictions about the unifying power of the Eucharist. Both liberals and conservatives reported they found meaning and inspiration in the Mass. Persons who disagree on most issues said they felt a surprising sense of solidarity during and after the celebration. We succeeded in uniting once more around the familiar rituals and common stories which keep us in touch with our roots and provide us with hope as we experience the joys and pains of advancing years.

14. The Popularity of Pope John Paul II

Pope John Paul II has produced highly polarized responses. Most of us can locate ourselves somewhere within this broad spectrum of responses. It is more difficult and more revealing to articulate with precision the emotional and intellectual reasons for our positions.

Around the world, Pope John Paul II is an immensely popular public person. On his 62 trips abroad to various countries he has consistently drawn large throngs. On January 15, 1995 in Manila, he broke his own record by attracting an estimated four million people to the Mass concluding the 10th World Youth Day. His book *Crossing the Threshold of Hope* reached the best seller lists in 12 countries, including the United States. Recognizing his vast influence, *Time* magazine picked him as Man of the Year for 1994.

What accounts for the Pope's astounding popularity and what does this tell us about the spiritual quest today? The *Time* article honoring John Paul gives a good sense of what the secular world admires in the Pope. The authors are taken by his charisma: "His appearances generate an electricity unmatched by anyone else on earth." They admire him for proclaiming his ideals to a world suffering from moral confusion. "In a year when so many people lamented the decline in moral values or made excuses for bad behavior, Pope John Paul II forcefully set forth his vision of the good life and urged the world to follow it." The article notes many of his accomplishments. Under his leadership, the *Catechism of the Catholic Church* was published and diplomatic relationships between the Vatican and Israel were established. John Paul supported the trade union Solidarity in Poland which many believe was "a precipitating event in the collapse of the Soviet bloc." But *Time* is most impressed with his role as "a moral compass for believers and nonbelievers alike." The Pope spreads "a message not of expediency or compromise but of right and wrong." In a world filled with fear, he speaks a strong message of hope.

It seems the secular world, dominated by moral relativism and shadowed by a somber mood, is hungering for moral guidance and a hopeful vision. At least some secularized opinion-makers have come to respect John Paul for his moral rectitude and courageous stands, even though they disagree with him on particular issues such as abortion. They are impressed with his unwavering vision and his untiring efforts to implement it.

In addition to this praise from the secular world, John Paul enjoys a good deal of support from evangelical Christians who are not encumbered by anti-Catholic bias. They like his uncompromising stand on abortion and the strong statements of the Vatican condemning the homosexual lifestyle. They share his approach to scriptural interpretation which concentrates on the clear religious meaning of a particular text, while generally ignoring modern biblical criticism. Many evangelicals in the United States have great admiration for the Pope's implacable and effective opposition to Communism. They also appreciate his frequent exhortations on family life which accord with their own efforts to place family values at the center of the American political debate. The popular preacher Billy Graham is representative of evangelicals who respect the Pope as a powerful spokesman for their moral values. According to Graham, John Paul is "the greatest of our modern Popes" and "the strong conscience of the whole Christian world."

Michael Novak, a neo-conservative Catholic who cofounded *Crisis* magazine, represents those who are pleased not only with John Paul's moral leadership in the world but also with his defense of orthodox teachings and traditional Catholic practices. Novak praises the Pope for his "fierce integrity" and his "rocklike determination to preach the truth," especially unpopular truth. Novak admires John Paul as an intellectual giant possessing the "most finely honed philosophical mind in the history of the modern papacy." He has produced a truly remarkable philosophical and theological synthesis, a "massive and solid body of work, of such high quality as to have no precedent in modern history." In discussing John Paul's encyclical *Veritatis Splendor*, Novak says, "Few works on conscience equal it in depth, thoroughness, subtlety, and beauty of expression." In the political realm he is convinced that the Pope's moral leadership was the decisive factor in the fall of Communism. He discerns a progressive growth in John Paul's appreciation of the values fostered by the capitalistic system. The Pope's consistent opposition to abortion especially at the 1994 Cairo Conference on Population and Development wins the admiration of Novak.

John Paul also gets high marks from Novak and other neo-conservatives for his internal church policies. They support his opposition to women's ordination, optional celibacy and birth control. They applaud the new *Catechism of the Catholic Church* and Vatican crackdowns on dissident theologians. The Pope's many statements about the traditional role of women are generally well received by the neo-conservative journals.

Finally, large numbers of ordinary Catholics throughout the world love and respect the Pope as head of the church. They appreciate his pastoral visits and his personal holiness. For them John Paul represents the solid rock of tradition and the guiding light of the Catholic faith.

Of course John Paul does not enjoy universal support. Militant secularists often resent his interference in worldly affairs. Some fundamentalist Christians consider him to be the anti-Christ. Buddhist groups are upset with his portrayal of Buddhism as "an atheistic system." The strongest opposition comes from progressive Catholics who are convinced that the authoritarian policies of John Paul have undercut the credibility of the church and stifled the spirit of Vatican II. According to Hans Kung, this Pope "is a disaster for our church." John Paul has pursued his own conservative agenda without really listening to various segments of the church. By appointing conservative bishops and silencing progressive theologians, he has set back the cause of church reform for decades to come. By maintaining the strict prohibition of birth control he has alienated many Catholics and weakened the church's voice in the important discussion of worldwide population control. His insistence on mandatory celibacy for priests has prevented the church in many countries from resolving the priest shortage problem and has, in some cases, deprived Catholics of the opportunity to celebrate the Eucharist. His refusal to soften the official position on the status of divorced and remarried Catholics has forced many to leave the church. John Paul's patriarchal attitudes toward women are especially devastating. He limits opportunities for women by defining them in terms of motherhood, while recognizing the importance of careers for men. His lofty language about respect for women does not include granting them full equality in the church. In the United States papal policies have made it increasingly difficult to defend the church against charges of sexism. These complaints enunciated by Kung and others resonate with many pastoral leaders who serve disgruntled parishioners chaffing under strict papal policies.

Some progressives have formed a more nuanced assessment of John Paul. Sharing the Pope's concern about militant secularism and moral relativism, they appreciate his steadfast defense of Gospel values and Christian principles. They admire his deep spirituality and his courageous witness to the cause of justice, peace and respect for life. For them the Pope's remarkable popularity is a salutary reminder that the world hungers for leaders who are consistent and authentic in the pursuit of the truth. His vast writings do constitute an important contribution to contemporary thought and deserve serious consideration.

At the same time these moderate progressives recognize an obligation to challenge papal policies which are opposed to the thrust of the Gospel and the spirit of Vatican II. This moral imperative creates a broad agenda. Hard questions must be asked about the scriptural and theological bases for restrictive policies on controversial issues such as mandatory celibacy, women's ordination and birth control. It is important to support liberal and moderate church leaders who are constantly pressured by reactionary Catholics emboldened by Vatican policies. Catholic people have a right to know about various opinions and legitimate dissent within the church. Charity demands practical efforts to serve those who feel excluded from the church, such as divorced persons and members of the gay community. Parishes should be inclusive communities which offer as much scope as possible to women who have the desire and talent to be church leaders.

By force of his charismatic personality and strongly held views, Pope John Paul has produced highly polarized responses, ranging from Novak's unstinting praise to Kung's blanket condemnation. Most of us can locate ourselves rather easily somewhere within this broad spectrum of responses. It is more difficult and more revealing to articulate with precision the emotional and intellectual reasons for our positions. Greater clarity on this question could be a helpful step toward a more effective contemporary spirituality.

15. The Spiritual Significance of John Paul's *Crossing the Threshold of Hope*

With the help of the Spirit we can "cross the threshold of hope," which places us in the hands of the loving God.

Pope John Paul's book *Crossing the Threshold of Hope* (Knopf 1994) deserves attention for a number of reasons. The author is the head of a church with around a billion members and is the most visible religious leader in the world. Millions of people around the globe have already purchased the book. Many reviews have been positive. Fr. F.X. Murphy (a.k.a. Xavier Rynne) called it "a masterpiece of spiritual awareness that may take its place beside Augustine's *Confessions*." Finally, the book is of general interest because of its content. The text contains intriguing glimpses into the soul of John Paul II. It presents valuable perspectives and insights which illumine the human adventure. We also find scriptural meditations which offer hope and encouragement to Christians struggling to relate their faith to everyday life. It is not necessary to agree with all the Pope's policies or share his particular piety in order to benefit from this volume.

The book contains written answers to 20 questions posed by a journalist, ranging from how does the Pope pray to does eternal life exist. John Paul's answers combine dense summaries of modern intellectual history, inspirational reflections on scriptural passages, insightful analyses of human existence and some revealing personal references. We get the picture of a highly intelligent, self-assured, Polish romantic who is convinced that he has a divinely appointed mission to prepare the church for the next millennium. With absolutely no trace of ethnic embarrassment, the Pope celebrates his Polish roots which gave him a clear Catholic identity and a strong faith. According to him, his heritage also fostered an openness to other religions, tolerance for diversity and a special fondness for the Jewish people.

John Paul manifests many characteristics of classic romanticism: a feeling for the poetic; love of nature; an appreciation of mysticism (as a teenager he learned Spanish so he could read *John of the Cross*); and respect for heroic individuals. His romantic spirit is most evident in his attitude toward human love and women. With obvious delight he tells the story of a friend trying to discern his vocation, who found the love of his life by getting down on his knees in prayer. Reflecting on the love between husbands and wives, he writes, "As a young priest I learned to love human love." He grew up in a time "of great respect and consideration for women, especially those who were mothers." Although the "rich tradition of customs and practices" that supported respect for women has eroded, we are seeing the birth of an "authentic theology of woman" which maintains an "amazement at the mystery of womanhood" and rediscovers "the spiritual beauty" and "the particular genius of women." In order to counter the "pro-choice" advocates of abortion, the Pope proposes a "pro-woman" policy which protects them from selfish men and offers them "radical solidarity" during and after pregnancy.

John Paul's romantic nature also finds expression in his devotion to Mary. As a youngster he regularly stopped to pray before the image of Our Lady of Perpetual Help in his parish church. He wore a Carmelite scapular and made pilgrimages to Marian shrines, including the site of the famous Black Madonna, the Queen of Poland. While working in a factory during the Second World War, he read St. Louis of Montfort and came to a deeper understanding of Mary as the Mother of God. After his election as Pope, John Paul chose as his motto *Totus Tuus*, which means "I am completely yours, O Mary." During his whole pontificate, he has maintained an "attitude of total abandonment to Mary." The Pope remains convinced that Christ will eventually conquer through Mary. He even sees significance in the fact that he survived the assassin's bullet on May 13, 1981, the exact anniversary of Mary's appearance at Fatima. The implication is that God saved him through the intercession of Mary, thus providing John Paul with the opportunity to prepare the church and the world for the third millennium of Christianity.

In framing his responses to the questions, it is remarkable how often John Paul refers to the teachings of the Second Vatican Council. He calls the Council the "seminary of the Holy Spirit," and sees it as a marvelous gift to the church and the entire human family. John Paul participated in the Council from beginning to end and was an active member of the group which prepared the Pastoral Constitution, *Gaudium et Spes*. Noting that we must always refer back to the Council in addressing problems today, the Pope feels a personal need "to interpret it correctly and defend it from tendentious interpretations."

In answering a question about the usefulness of believing in the Gospel, John Paul quotes extensively from article 16 of *Lumen Gentium* which says in part, "Nor will Divine Providence deny the help necessary for salvation to those who have not yet arrived at a clear knowledge and recognition of God, and who attempt, not without divine grace, to conduct a good life." This suggests to the Pope that these people have "an implicit faith" and thus "the necessary condition for salvation is already satisfied." The Gospel is "already at work in the depths of the person who searches for the truth with honest effort." The Pope insists this interpretation is necessary to avoid the Pelagian error that people can lead a good and happy life even without divine grace. Ultimately, only God can save us, but we must cooperate with divine grace.

Although John Paul's comments on youth reflect a European context, they contain valuable insights applicable to our situation in the United States. Young people today "live in freedom, which others have won for them, and have yielded in large part to the consumer culture." They grow up in a secular atmosphere and tend to express their innate idealism more by criticizing society than by simply doing their duty. For many of them, the church no longer provides a clear "point of reference" which helps them "focus their inner strength." And yet young people continue to search for meaning and a concrete way of leading useful lives. They want to discover their own identity and find goals worth pursuing. In the process they need guides, authority figures, who will set clear boundaries while walking the path of life with them. The older generation must show that "life has meaning to the extent that it becomes a free gift for others." Young people are searching for the beauty of love. They need to know that only God can give this love. We must call on them "to follow Christ, without caring about the sacrifice this may entail." They can accept this great challenge, with confidence that Christ walks alongside them as a friend who is always reliable and never disappoints. The Pope finds confirmation of his approach in the various World Youth Days where over a million young people have reacted enthusiastically to his message.

John Paul's reflections on the words of Jesus, "Be not afraid," found near the beginning and end of his book, are a rich source of inspiration and hope. With penetrating insight, the Pope points out that our deepest fears flow from our sense of unworthiness before the infinite God. Peter recognized this when he said to Jesus, "Depart from me, Lord, for I am a sinful man" (Lk 5:8). A genuine encounter with the Holy is always awesome; an honest self-examination can be frightening. In addition, we may fear the moral demands that the Christian life makes upon us. The demonic forces in the

world sometimes terrify us. The Pope believes the redemp-
tion is the solid basis for the courage we need to overcome
all these fears. "The power of Christ's cross and resurrection
is greater than any evil which a person could or should fear."
The Word made flesh, "Love crucified and risen," continues
to hold "in His hand the destiny of this passing world."
God's demands never exceed our capacity to respond. With
the help of the Spirit we can "cross the threshold of hope,"
which places us in the hands of the loving God.

16. Stories of Doubt: Thomas and Others

*The story of Thomas encourages us to believe what we
desperately hope is true: despite all absurdities and
contradictions, life has meaning; despite failures, our good
efforts are worthwhile and have lasting validity; and despite
doubts, faith eventually prevails.*

Believers attuned to the confusion and complexity of
contemporary life often find their personal convictions and
religious beliefs challenged by nagging doubts as the following disguised stories suggest. Pat, an attractive woman and
bright lawyer, often feels inferior and experiences an overwhelming sense of her personal limitations. As a consequence, she is constantly plagued by self-doubts which
threaten both her personal relationships and her career. Rick,
who became a fundamentalist Christian during his under-
graduate years, is now working on a master's degree in geol-
ogy. His studies have forced him to confront scientific
explanations of evolution, causing doubts about the inerrancy
of the Bible which describes a six-day creation. Sam's wife
left him after 22 years of marriage without any explanation.
Since the divorce was final two years ago, he has been struggling mightily to gather himself and get on with his life but
with very little success. Given his current distrust of women,
Sam has grave doubts whether he can ever again open himself up to an intimate relationship. Sarah, a practicing Catholic, decided to take a philosophy of religion course at the
beginning of her junior year. The graduate assistant teaching
the course was obviously bright, but sometimes struck her as

a bit overbearing. He was an avowed atheist who delighted in pointing out the flaws in the traditional proofs for the existence of God. When he expressed his negative views on religion, Sarah often felt bewildered and overwhelmed. Since she could not refute his arguments, she began to doubt her own faith. She now considers herself an agnostic but is still searching.

Bill, a liberal Protestant theologian, had a dream in which the atheistic existentialist Jean Paul Sartre definitively refuted the theistic position of Paul Tillich in a public debate. In his waking moments he ponders the significance of the terrifying nightmare. Every now and then a fleeting doubt flashes through his consciousness causing him to question whether he really believes all the things he preaches and writes about God. Mildred, a happily married woman with three very successful adult children, was extremely moved by a graphic portrayal of the Jewish Holocaust on TV. She began reading some books on it and found herself pondering all types of monstrous evils including the bombing of Hiroshima. An abiding sense of dread now inhabits her heart which surfaces as both utter rage and a radical doubt about how a loving God could allow such suffering. Roy, a sports fanatic, sat down one Sunday afternoon with a beer to watch his favorite Browns battle the Steelers and suddenly realized he was not all that interested. Ever since, strange doubts about the meaning and purpose of life have periodically threatened his usual happy-go-lucky outlook.

Doubts are part of life. No one escapes them entirely. The certitude and security we crave is never complete. We can all tell our own stories of doubt, whether highly dramatic or extremely simple. When our faith is challenged, it is healthy to seek a deeper understanding and more effective ways of coping. Perhaps an imaginative reflection on a classic scriptural story of doubt will offer illumination and guidance.

Thomas had mixed feelings about being a twin. The empathy he shared with his brother brought him a great sense of comfort, but at times he just needed to get away from him. Sometimes he wondered if that was the reason he left home and began following the Teacher. Still he often wished now that his brother could also experience the thrill of being close to such a holy man and know the exhilaration of being part of his noble cause. Of course, following the Master was not always easy. There was the time Lazarus died. The tearful grief of Jesus had moved Thomas deeply. Sensing the confusion of his fellow disciples and feeling great empathy for Jesus, he had blurted out spontaneously that they should accompany Jesus to Judea and be ready to die for him. When the others looked at him quizically he felt a bit embarrassed, sensing that he had overreacted.

Thomas was indeed a complex fellow, an intriguing mix of deep passion and critical intelligence. When stirred by strong emotion, he often spoke before he thought. On other occasions he maintained a cool detachment which enabled him to size up the situation and ask probing questions. Thomas had to admit that he frequently misunderstood when Jesus tried to explain that the reign of Yahweh was somehow like a mustard seed, a buried treasure and a dragnet. He always suspected that the others didn't understand everything either. But at least he was not afraid to speak up. When Jesus talked about going to prepare a place for them, suggesting that they knew the way, Thomas spoke up declaring they really did not know where he was going and therefore could not know the way. The answer of Jesus, that he himself is the way, made sense to Thomas only later after the encounter which changed everything.

The death of Jesus had completely devastated the disciples, especially the inner circle of the Twelve. They had left everything to follow Jesus and now he was gone. They had committed themselves to the cause of the kingdom and now all hope for its establishement was dashed. Paralyzed with fear, they remained in Jerusalem hiding out behind locked doors. The whole depressing atmosphere quickly got to Thomas. Despite the advice of the others he decided to go out and spend some time by himself. Furtively walking the streets of Jerusalem on a busy Sunday afternoon, he struggled to control his emotions in order to think clearly about what had happened.

After gaining some measure of the rational control which was usually part of his complex personality, he returned late in the evening to join his friends. The change in mood and atmosphere was literally unbelievable to him. His colleagues were caught up in some kind of ecstasy and kept repeating to him that they had seen the Master. Thomas was completely bewildered but maintained the cool rationality he had established throughout the day. Determined not to be hurt again, he quickly repressed a surprising glimmer of hope that his friends were indeed speaking the truth and not suffering from delusions. Although they were carried away with emotion, he would maintain his objectivity. Speaking with a firm voice, he made his position clear to all of them: "I will never believe it without probing the nailprints in his hands, without putting my fingers in the nailmarks and my hand into his side."

The next week was difficult for Thomas. He kept to himself, shielding his mind and his heart from the contagious enthusiasm and joy constantly radiated by his fellow disciples. Never had he felt so alienated, but he was determined not to be taken in by any softheaded emotionalism.

When Jesus appeared a second time to the disciples, Thomas was with them. The Master offered them all a greeting of peace and then looked directly at Thomas. Responding to the skeptical position taken by Thomas, he said, "Take your finger and examine my hands. Put your hand into my side. Do not persist in your unbelief but believe." Suddenly love broke through the barriers and faith engulfed the doubts. Without embarrassment or fear Thomas said, "My Lord and my God." The Teacher seized the moment to make a point which has echoed throughout history: "You became a believer because you saw me. Blest are those who have not seen yet have believed."

The story of the doubting twin helps us interpret all the stories of doubt which multiply in our postmodern world. It places before us the reality and the power of the resurrection in a graphic and compelling way. Because Jesus has been raised to life, our personal struggles take on a new meaning and direction. We can believe in our essential goodness and accept the ambiguities of life because the Father who raised Jesus has revealed himself as totally trustworthy. Intellectual doubts need not paralyze us because the pursuit of truth is guided by the Spirit of the risen Lord. Despite hurts and disappointments it does make sense to try to improve our personal relationships because love is ultimately stronger than selfishness.

Although the resurrection does not explain monstrous evil which haunts our world today or take away its pain, it does help us cope with it. In the midst of our sufferings we can turn to Christ with confidence because he has shared completely in the human condition. The resurrection is our guarantee that God loves us and will never abandon us. The Father who raised Jesus transforms suffering and brings us to the final fulfillment of our deepest longings. In short, the story of Thomas encourages us to believe what we desperately hope is true: despite all absurdities and contradictions, life has meaning; despite failures, our good efforts are worthwhile and have lasting validity; and despite doubts, faith eventually prevails.

17. Stories of the Spirit

We must be on alert for subtle signals of the fruits of the Spirit, mysterious manifestations of love, joy, peace, patient endurance, kindness, generosity, faith, mildness and chastity.

Today we are more aware of the power of stories and personal witness to guide our spiritual journeys. The Easter season is a good time for telling stories of the Spirit. During this important 50-day period extending from Easter to Pentecost, the liturgy provides us with an opportunity to reflect on the role of the Holy Spirit in the history of the early church. Listening to stories of the Spirit at Mass should attune us to the ways that the Spirit is at work in our own lives. Our personal stories often assume a greater depth and a new significance when we interpret them according to the biblical narratives.

A priest who suffers from the delusion that he is younger than he really is, was taking his daily half-hour aerobic walk. Shortly after the few blocks of jogging which his troublesome knees still permit, he suddenly felt a surge of gratitude which swept over him like an unanticipated wave striking a swimmer. The emotion was larger than words, but the general content was clear. He was simply grateful for being able to take a walk. It did not seem to matter that he could no longer jog very much. The ability to walk is itself a gift. Not everyone enjoys this privilege. It is an undeserved blessing to be able to walk outside on a beautiful day.

This unmistakable sense of gratitude lasted only a few minutes, but it carried a more enduring imperative. Make the most of the opportunity. Enjoy it now. Treasure the gift while it lasts.

The rush of gratitude also spawned further reflection. Gifts always entail obligations and responsibilities. If you are healthy, do not forget those who are ill. If you are emotionally stable, be strong for someone who is struggling. If you had the blessings of a good family, assist those who bear the wounds of broken homes. If you had the opportunity to study and learn, be ready to share knowledge with those who are searching. If you can walk, remember those who cannot.

These reflections included some cautions: be open to learning from those who are less fortunate, and be ready to accept help from others when your turn comes to bear the cross.

In this simple but significant experience, the priest came to know in a deeper way that the Holy Spirit is the source of all good gifts. The Father sent the Spirit to sanctify us just as He sent the Son to redeem us. The Spirit is the gift dimension of the whole of human existence. In the beginning, the Spirit hovered over the waters, bringing order out of chaos. The Spirit fills the created universe with energy and beauty and brings the process of history to its ultimate consummation. The gift of the Spirit gives life meaning, direction, and purpose. Every phase and aspect of life is a gift, including the simple act of walking. The proper response is gratitude which leads to service.

A graduate student from Burundi majoring in educational technology at the University of Toledo was crossing a busy street in late February. She saw the car coming right at her and jumped to get out of the way. The next thing she knew, she was on the sidewalk in a state of shock. She remembers that someone was quickly at her side offering assistance and comforting words. The lengthy stay in the hospital was difficult. She was separated from her family in Africa. She was in a good deal of pain as her multiple fractures healed. At times, she could not even reach over and answer the phone near her bed. And yet throughout she maintained her joyful spirit. She drew on the strength of the Catholic heritage she had received in her native country. Despite the separation from her family, she did not feel alone. She believes that her body healed faster and better because her attitude was good and her stress level was under control. Many people came to see her in the hospital, while others sent cards and flowers. Her pastor visited and asked the congregation for prayers. Many people responded generously.

Now that she is walking about again, she describes the whole experience as both bad and good. It disrupted her life and brought her physical and emotional suffering. But despite her pain and sufferings she says it has helped her "see the world with other eyes." She has developed a much greater appreciation of people and friendships. Her empathy for the handicapped has deepened. She has a strong sense of appreciation for the nurses and doctors who took such good care of her and for the friends who visited. She has been moved to examine more deeply her values and priorities.

At one point, she went to court in order to testify against the driver of the car. She was prepared to speak a comforting word, telling him not to worry about it. When their eyes met, however, she detected a heart of stone which was not open to her reconciling words. Instead, she said a prayer in her heart: "Lord, forgive him because he does not know what he is doing." Perhaps when he is older he will be wiser, she thought, and then she could say the reconciling words.

Jesus, who received the gift of the Spirit at his baptism, was so permeated by this power that he could communicate it to others. The Spirit flowed out of him, healing the sick and reconciling sinners. Through his death and resurrection, he became life-giving Spirit for all. He breathed on the apostles giving them the charge and power to forgive others. The Spirit of Jesus fired the hearts of the disciples at Pentecost and united people across national, racial and ethnic boundaries. Everyone heard the good news in their own tongue. This same reconciling, forgiving Spirit is still at work in the world today. The eyes of faith can detect it in a graduate student from Burundi. Crushed bones did not harden her heart, but surprisingly enhanced her joyful, grateful and forgiving disposition.

A retired professor who described himself as a skeptic was pondering some serious philosophical questions. For most of his life the very use of the word God had seemed ridiculous to him. Invocation of the divine name struck him as empty bombast or a platitude with no basis in reality. In the midst of his reflections, for some unknown reason, he picked up a book about Karl Rahner's theology which he had read before. This time he read it in a more reflective way. This time the impact was striking. He was transported back to the time when his first child was born. It had deepened his love for his wife and created a new sense of mutuality. When he first laid eyes on the child, the impact was explosive and "raised him to a new level of being" as he describes it. He was struck by a sentence in the theology book: "In the experience of love we feel drawn out of ourselves by a force that surprises us by its power." None of the sermons he had heard in his youth or the religious books he had read since ever really touched his heart as did that line and its subsequent explanation. Now for the first time he saw a connection between some of his deepest experiences in life and the religious language which speaks of God as the mysterious power at the very heart of things.

Jesus, in his farewell discourse in John's Gospel, tells his disciples that he must go away but that he will send the Paraclete, the Spirit of Truth, who will instruct them in all of his teachings. It is not difficult to see this promise played out when an agnostic professor takes the first steps toward finding God in his most significant experiences.

Stories of the Spirit, whether found in the Bible or rooted in the continuing human adventure, have a genuine revelatory power. They prompt further reflection on how the Holy Spirit, sent by the Father through Christ, is at work in our own lives.

It is easy to miss the presence of the Spirit in our ordinary activities, however, because divine grace always engulfs us like the air we breathe. We must be on alert for subtle signals of the fruits of the Spirit, mysterious manifestations of love, joy, peace, patient endurance, kindness, generosity, faith, mildness and chastity, as Paul suggests (Gal 5:22-23). But on other occasions we may be responsive to the Spirit without feeling any positive emotions or experiencing any consolation or seeing any clear results. A man did a favor for a friend knowing full well that she would not appreciate it and that he would feel used in the process and probably never know if his efforts did any good. Karl Rahner has suggested that experiences such as these are among the clearer signs we have that the Holy Spirit is at work. With this in mind, we may have more stories of the Spirit to tell than we usually realize.

18. The Virtue of Truthfulness

The witness of Fr. Vaclav Maly prompts reflection on our own postmodern situation. We must become more aware of the subtle distortions which affect our self-understanding and the half-truths which impede interpersonal communication.

Fr. Vaclav Maly, the Czech priest who played a significant role in the 1989 revolution overthrowing Communism, is a living example of the Gospel teaching that the truth will set us free. The life and teaching of this courageous revolutionary now serving as the pastor of St. Gabriel Parish on the outskirts of Prague constitutes a powerful reminder that Christian faith is not based on an abstract theory, but is rooted in a deep commitment to Jesus Christ who empowers his disciples to live wholeheartedly and authentically. When Fr. Maly proclaims the overriding importance of speaking the truth in all situations, he is not mouthing a pious phrase or suggesting a clever slogan. He is rather expressing a deep conviction, born in personal suffering and shaped by his courageous efforts to preach the Gospel in a totalitarian state.

My initial perceptions of Fr. Maly were formed during a long interview I had with him in his one room apartment in Prague in the spring of 1990. The significance of this man and his insights has periodically occupied my attention ever since. The encounter not only disclosed something of the man but also put a face on the amazing events which culminated in what President Vaclav Havel, a close friend of Maly, called the "Velvet Revolution."

Maly was ordained a priest in 1976. One year later, he joined about 1,000 others in signing Charter 77, which demanded that the Communist government in Prague live up to its own agreements in the area of human rights. Because Maly not only signed the statement but preached his vision of a more humane society, he was a marked man. In January of 1979, the authorities revoked his priest's license and imprisoned him for seven months. After being released he was constantly followed and harassed by the police. His apartment was bugged and a camera photographed everyone who came to visit him. He was interrogated more than 250 times and often thrown into jail for a couple of days. On one occasion he was alone and naked with brutal and vulgar guards who tortured him. He told me that at that time of terrible aloneness he learned to rely completely on God – a trust which has enabled him to avoid hating those who persecuted him. He continues to draw on this horrible but grace-filled experience in his preaching and teaching.

With his priestly license revoked, Maly worked stoking boilers. He now considers that period of his life a great learning experience because he came to a deeper understanding of people who knew nothing of Christianity and never heard of Jesus. In that setting he gradually learned how to present the Gospel message not as a series of pat answers, but as an offer to follow Christ into a fuller life.

On November 17, 1989, some students in Prague organized a legal demonstration to commemorate the 50th anniversary of the killing of a student by the Nazis. The large gathering marched to Wenceslaus Square chanting "freedom" and singing protest songs. Suddenly the police attacked, beating the demonstrators. This brutal action sparked a widespread response which in just 24 days toppled the Communist regime. Fr. Maly was deeply involved in this whole remarkable process. On November 20th he met with other Charter 77 signators and helped establish Civic Forum, the organization that guided the revolution. The next day Havel and Maly addressed a large crowd, demanding the resignation of the Communist leaders. Later in the week before a crowd of 300,000, Maly read a message from Cardinal Frantisek Tomasek which endorsed Civic Forum and declared that the Catholic Church stands with the people in the struggle. The Communist government responded with some compromise measures, but Civic Forum, represented by Maly, made a public demand, before still another huge crowd, for free elections by June 1990. On the 24th day of the revolution the government capitulated to almost all the demands of Civic Forum. The following June, right on schedule, Vaclav Havel was elected president by a popular vote. Vaclav Maly could have had an important position in the new government, but he chose to return to his vocation as a parish priest. Now as pastor of St. Gabriel's, he tries to relate the Gospel to everyday life and to form leaders who will be involved in public affairs. Large crowds, including many who are not Catholic, attend his Masses even during the week.

In my conversation with Fr. Maly, I tried to uncover the theological and cultural influences as well as the spiritual resources which have enabled him to act with such admirable courage and amazing freedom. He has read many of the important contemporary theologians, including Rahner, Congar and Schillebeeckx. From Rahner, he learned the importance of relating theology and prayer and of reflecting on the concrete situation in the light of the Gospel. Maly's response to liberation theology is revealing. He appreciates its efforts to examine the social situation but considers the use of Marxist theories to be very dangerous. His own experience with Communist repression alerts him to the insidious character of a philosophy which denies the transcendent dimension of human existence. Although Maly recognizes the existence of social sin and the alienating power of institutions, he insists that personal sin is the root of all evil in the world. The starting point for social reform is in the human heart and in the process of personal conversion. We move toward greater maturity by following the example of Jesus, the liberator, who was open, tolerant and willing to listen to others. The risen Christ continues to appeal to his disciples today to work for justice. The church cannot be an island which celebrates its own good fortune, but must be a community which forms disciples who work to transform society. Christian leaders in the world do not always have to speak about Jesus, but they should strive to practice his message and to work with others of good will in creating a more open and just society. In this regard, Maly's relationship with President Havel is instructive. They remain good friends and are in regular contact. He sees Havel as a moral man whose high values influence his political decisions. He has grown from a typical liberal agnostic to a theist who recognizes the importance and greatness of Jesus, although he is not yet ready to affirm him as Son of God. To my suggestion that Havel fits Rahner's notion of the anonymous Christian, Maly agreed and went on to emphasize the great contribution Havel was making by bringing moral values to the political task of reconstructing society. My own impression is that Maly has kept some distance between himself and the government so that he can offer constructive criticism, if that becomes necessary.

One of Maly's great strengths is his understanding of the way the Gospel must be preached in a culture severely damaged by decades of Communist totalitarianism. Although Marxism failed as a system, it affected the spirit of the people by encouraging passivity and breaking down their sense of personal responsibility. The party line that religion is a nostalgic escape from reality may have struck some responsive chords among the Czechs who tend to have a more reserved and rationalistic attitude toward religion than the Slovaks who have deeper roots in traditional Catholicism. Christian preaching today must counter the common notion that forgiveness of others is a weakness by demonstrating that it is an opportunity for growth. In order to overcome the pervasive distrust engendered by a repressive government, parishes must build up a sense of community where people can learn to trust one another. The church must emphasize the importance of the common good to people who responded to totalitarianism by concentrating on their own private space. Maly is convinced that the revival of religion and the growing respect for the church evident at the time of the revolution, especially among the young intelligentsia, was related to the spiritual vacuum created by Communism.

Maly has great respect for Pope John Paul II as one who understands the nature of Communism and who represents the unity of the whole church. The unity theme is especially important for the church in Czechoslovakia which has endured so many years of isolation. The Pope's visit to Czechoslovakia in the spring of 1990 was a great success. Maly was especially pleased that John Paul II followed his advice and spoke positively about Jan Hus (1369-1415), the church reformer who was executed as a heretic but who continues to affect the consciousness of the Czech people. It was a clear signal that the Pope took the Czech culture seriously.

When I asked Fr. Maly about his own spiritual life, he told me that he spends an hour each morning before his busy day begins praying and meditating with special concentration on listening to God. The fruit of this regimen seemed evident to me as I observed the peaceful intensity and the humble confidence of this impressive man. He is indeed passionate about seeking the truth. He has a profound distrust of generalizations, platitudes, slogans, cliches, stereotypes and ideologies. His great desire is to express the truth, to call things by their real names, to give an exact context to words. He wants to create faith communities which promote authentic communication among all the members. Believers must properly and accurately name all instances of oppression as the first step in transforming them. Social progress demands that we challenge every lie and all deceptions perpetrated by institutions. For Maly this intense and challenging struggle for truth is the basis for personal and societal freedom.

The witness of Fr. Vaclav Maly prompts reflection on our own postmodern situation. We must become more aware of the subtle distortions which affect our self-understanding and the half-truths which impede interpersonal communication. We must learn to recognize the contradictions and inequities in our own society. Our challenge is to disavow the easy accommodations which enable demonic forces to thrive. Our task is to unleash the transforming power of divine grace. Christians living in a free pluralistic democracy do not have the same specific challenges as the brave believers who remained faithful under Communist persecution. Our situation may be more complex and ambiguous, but we still are bound by the Gospel imperative to live as authentic disciples committed to truth, freedom and justice. A postmodern spirituality must continue to find guidance and encouragement in the words of Jesus: "If you live according to my teaching, you are truly my disciples; then you will know the truth and the truth will set you free" (Jn 8:31-32).

19. A Story of Conversion

We will all benefit by keeping in mind the full story of Malcolm X's conversion process, including his life of disciplined commitment and his final, more inclusive vision.

Spike Lee's important movie *Malcolm X* performed the useful service of bringing to public attention once more an important African-American leader, who made headlines in the 1960s. The movie presents a fairly faithful and rather dispassionate overview of Malcolm's life: born in Omaha, Nebraska in 1925; spent his childhood in a rural area a couple miles outside of East Lansing, Michigan; suffered through the murder of his father by white racists and the subsequent mental deterioration of his mother; attended a predominately white grade school; went to live with his half-sister, Ella, in the Roxbury section of Boston, where he started gambling and pushing drugs; moved to Harlem where he sank deeper into a life of crime; arrested for burglary, shortly before his 21st birthday, and sentenced to eight-to-ten years; converted in jail to the teaching of Elijah Muhammad, head of the Nation of Islam, often called the Black Muslims; paroled in 1952 and became an extremely successful minister for the Nation of Islam; married Betty Sanders in 1956; broke with Elijah Muhammad in 1963 for complex reasons including Elijah's sexual promiscuity and internal jealousies; made a pilgrimage to Mecca where he had a startling conversion experience; founded the Organization of Afro-American Unity; murdered on February 21, 1965 by Black Muslims as he began a speech in the Audubon Ballroom in Harlem.

The movie presents Malcolm not only as a victim of societal racism and Black Muslim perfidy, but also as a forthright spokesman for the rage simmering in the black underclass. His hatred of whites and disdain for the black leaders of the civil rights movement are portrayed vividly. Spike Lee's Malcolm is a man of action: hustling in the streets, studying in prison, preaching in the temples, traveling the world. His message to Afro-Americans is clear and pointed: overcome the self-hatred induced by a white racist society through black pride and solidarity.

The film devotes less attention to the inner journey of Malcolm X, the man. To enter this world, we must turn to the *Autobiography of Malcolm X*, written in collaboration with Alex Haley. Here we find the fascinating story of a remarkable conversion process punctuated by two major turning points and a tragic, premature ending.

The inner journey of Malcolm was set upon a fateful course when he was in the seventh grade. A white teacher, discovering that Malcolm wanted to be a lawyer, told him that he should be realistic about being a "nigger" and strive to become a carpenter instead. From that moment, it is possible to trace Malcolm's steadily increasing dislike for white people, which eventually led to his fierce opposition to integration and his condemnation of all whites as devils. The first major turning point in Malcolm's conversion process occurred in 1948 when he was in prison. His blood brothers, Philbert and Reginald, introduced him to the "natural religion for the black man" called the Nation of Islam. They explained to him that the one God, Allah, had come to America and revealed himself to a black man, Elijah Muhammad. Elijah taught that the original human beings were black and that white people were devils who enslaved and brainwashed the Africans. His brothers implored him to submit to the will of Allah and adopt the extremely strict moral code of the Nation of Islam, which prohibited smoking, alcohol, gambling, sports, eating pork, fornication and adultery. Later in his life, after much reflection, Malcolm could still not fully comprehend what happened at that point. In essence, he did surrender and everything changed. It was as though all his previous life of vice and crime was wiped away "without any remaining effect or influence." The "very enormity" of his previous guilt enabled him "to accept the truth." He read the story of Paul's conversion on the road to Damascus over and over, with the startling realization that he had experienced something similar. From that moment till the end of his life, Malcolm X remained faithful to the strict moral code enjoined by Elijah Muhammad, whom he regarded as "the Messenger of Allah." The hedonistic hustler from Harlem became an exemplary model of Islamic moral virtue. After his conversion, his previous thinking patterns slid away from him "like snow off a roof." With his new-found discipline, he threw himself into serious study. He read for as much as 16 hours a day, devouring books on history, linguistics and philosophy. As the months and years passed, he hardly realized he was in prison. Later he noted that he had never "been so truly free."

The second great turning point for Malcolm X occurred in 1963 when he made the prescribed pilgrimage to Mecca. As a result of worshiping in solidarity with millions of pilgrims from all over the world, Malcolm experienced a "radical alteration" in his whole outlook, a genuine religious conversion which complemented his moral conversion in prison. He understood in a completely new way the power of the One God to gather people of all races and colors into a unified family. His fundamental thought patterns had been rearranged once again, propelling him into a new phase in his search for truth. When he returned to the United States, he placed his usual pleas for black solidarity in the context of a Pan-African outlook. He continued to speak out forcefully against racism and the white establishment, but there was a new vision which he gradually began to articulate. He said that he would never again be guilty of sweeping indictments of all white people. He began talking more about creating "the true brotherhood" and working for justice which "benefits humanity as a whole." Some of his comments began to sound more like those of Dr. Martin Luther King. Malcolm now admitted, "Men are attracted by spirit. By power, anxieties are created." The authentic Islamic tradition had taught him that "it takes all of the religious, political, economic, psychological, and racial ingredients or characteristics to make the Human Family and the Human Society complete." His new friends included "Christians, Jews, Buddhists, Hindus, agnostics and even atheists" who, as he said, came in all colors including white. Answering a lingering question about the role of liberal whites, he said, "In our mutual sincerity, we might be able to show a road to the salvation of America's very soul." Tragically, Malcolm's own opportunities to refine, test and implement this grand design were cut short by assassins' bullets on February 21, 1965.

It is important to keep Malcolm's religious conversion in perspective. He experienced an initial breakthrough to a more universal perspective, but he did not have time to work out its full meaning or implications. His thought patterns were altered, but he continued to search for a new identity. His heart was transformed at Mecca, but he had to spend his last months on earth coping with the threats of the Black Muslims against himself and his family.

Although some of Malcolm's later rhetoric is reminiscent of the vision of Martin Luther King, the two remained sharply divided on goals and strategies. Malcolm's second conversion was from the distorted version of Islam taught by Elijah Muhammad to a more authentic form based on the

Qur'an. Faithful to his Islamic tradition, Malcolm did not share King's Christian outlook which celebrates Christ the suffering servant, believes in redemptive suffering and enjoins love of enemies. To the end of his life, Malcolm thought that nonviolence was a foolish tactic which benefited the oppressors and weakened the oppressed. It is true that after his conversion, Malcolm tried, unsuccessfully, to visit Dr. King in a Selma jail and sent a message to him through Coretta King that he wanted to make Martin's mission easier and not more difficult. Nevertheless, the two leaders remained separated by background, experience, temperament and religious vision. Martin enunciated a great dream of human unity rooted in biblical teaching and national ideals; Malcolm spoke of an American nightmare dominated by injustice and racism.

Some black commentators want to play down Malcolm's religious conversion because it might be used to emasculate an important symbol of black defiance and pride. In the movie, Spike Lee keeps a hard edge on his hero in a number of ways: by leaving out some of Malcolm's most striking conciliatory comments as well as his outreach to Dr. King, and by concluding the movie with one of Malcolm's stark inflammatory phrases, "by any means necessary." The black theologian James Cone thinks it is vital to keep alive the harsher memory of Malcolm as a corrective and complement to Martin's dream. In listening to black students discuss the movie, I heard the message, don't try to whitewash Malcolm; don't pretend he was reconciled to racist America. Let us have Malcolm as the voice of our rage and as the exemplar of black manhood.

I also heard another message in the student discussion: don't just see the movie; read the autobiography. This strikes me as wise advice for a society in which race remains such an intractable problem. Harsh rhetoric and separatist strategies may have their place, but they cannot be the final word. To his great credit, Malcolm X came to see this precise point in his Mecca experience. I believe we will all benefit by keeping in mind the full story of his conversion process, including his life of disciplined commitment and his final, more inclusive vision.

20. A Story of Abuse and Healing

Julie's experience of healing grace brings to light the God hidden in suffering who remains the source of our hope.

At the age of 29, Julie, a bright and engaging single woman, encountered a relative who tried to force her into having sex with him. She successfully fended off the attack, but the assault triggered intense feelings of anger, depression and anxiety which seemed out of proportion to the event. After wrestling unsuccessfully with these negative emotions for a couple of months, she sought help from a counselor. With guidance, she tried various therapeutic approaches: expressing her anger, dwelling on positive images, overcoming negative thoughts and getting involved in uplifting activities. Despite her persistent efforts, nothing helped. At this point, her counselor advised her to look more carefully at her childhood experiences. Soon she began to have vague recollections of being sexually abused. Through long and often painful counseling sessions stretching over a year's time, she gradually remembered in detail an incident that happened when she was five years old. She rode her bicycle over to the house of a neighbor who lured her into the garage where he began to stroke her hair and fondle her. He then took her into his bedroom, undressed her and forced her into performing oral sex on him.

After finally recalling this painful event, Julie tried to make sense out of it. It was especially difficult for her to come to terms with the mysterious mix of pain and pleasure involved in the experience. She had responded positively to the attention and the fondling, experiencing intense pleasure which she later associated with sexual arousal. At the same time, she had felt like she was going to choke to death and surely die when forced into the oral sex. As an adult remembering the event, she felt tremendous shame because she had experienced the pleasure. Her body had betrayed her at this crucial point. Now her emotions were telling her that the whole event must have been her own fault.

After abusing Julie, the attacker warned her that she must never tell anybody what happened. Upset and confused, she had an accident on her bicycle heading back home and ended up in the hospital. She had always remembered most of what happened in the accident, but now during therapy other important elements came back to her. She was in the emergency room, desperately seeking comfort from her father, but afraid to tell him about the abuse. At that point, despite her protests, he walked out of the room, leaving her alone with strange people who might hurt her. It was too much for a five-year-old to endure. She simply shut off all her emotions and stopped feeling anything. As an adult, she described it as "disassociating" herself from her body and living merely in her head.

For the next 24 years, Julie lived in this bifurcated state. Adopting an artificially optimistic view of life, she always appeared bubbly and enthusiastic. She kept very busy and spent almost no time in introspection. Out of touch with her own inner struggles, she had great difficulty appreciating the problems of other people. Her relationships lacked spontaneity and mutuality. Her sexuality both frightened and fascinated her. Most of the time, she felt totally divorced from her body. Now and then while dancing, she would feel more integrated, but this only raised perplexing questions which she was afraid to examine.

Given her history, it took tremendous courage for Julie to enter counseling. Perseverance was even more difficult because of the great pain that accompanied remembering her childhood traumas. While trying to recall the past, she would suffer from severe headaches. When she was actually able to relive the sexual abuse in great detail, she felt an immense sense of relief and a new sense of integration. It was as though she moved from living only in her head to inhabiting her body once again. Unfortunately, she was able to sustain this sense of integration for only brief periods of time. For awhile she would feel a proper sense of anger and indignation towards the man who abused her, but then her sense of shame, especially over the pleasure she had experienced, would force her back into blaming herself. As the therapy progressed, she was able to sustain her sense of integration for longer periods of time.

After making progress on the abuse problem, Julie spontaneously turned to the image of her father walking out of the emergency room in the hospital. Facing this trauma was more difficult than dealing with the abuse. It raised even deeper questions about fundamental trust and unleashed a surprising hatred for her father which frightened and confused her. Furthermore, this phase of the therapy shattered the rosy image of God which she had rigorously maintained throughout her life. All sense of the divine presence left her. Prayer became a frustrating monologue. Going to Mass was an agony. Her rage against this capricious deity periodically erupted during counseling sessions. On one occasion, feeling totally abandoned by God and completely alone in the cosmos, she experienced something like a searing fire on her back which terrified her. The counselor urged her not to resist the flames, but to let them spread and consume her. In an heroic act of courage, she did indeed stop resisting the flames. They quickly spread over her whole body, but in the process, the fire burned itself out. She experienced an intense moment of release. She felt liberated. Her body and spirit felt more united. God was present once again. A serene smile came to her face as she lingered silently over her new-found sense of peace.

For months afterwards, Julie carried in her heart an immense feeling of gratitude. She loved to go to church and thank God for blessings. She felt more integrated than at any time in her life. At times, the sense of gratitude was so overwhelming that her heart felt as though it would burst. She was convinced that her new sense of well-being, which was for her beyond imagination,was a special gift from God.

But the most trying cross of all was still to come. The demons returned to the attack. She began to have doubts again that perhaps the abusive incident was her fault. Negative feelings toward her father resurfaced. After a few months, even God disappeared once more. Having known a brief period of peace, she found it almost intolerable to feel so alone and confused again.

In the midst of this horrible reversal, Julie found an amazing strength and courage that defied rational explanation. She continued to work on her problems in a determined and systematic way. She read books on the topic of abuse and wrote incessantly in her journal. Despite the absence of any comfort or divine consolation, she continued to pray and attend Mass regularly. This perseverance has enabled Julie to make solid progress on many of her problems. Instead of blaming herself for the abuse, she has properly assigned the responsibility to her attacker, venting her anger at him in the process. Without fully understanding her bodily responses during the abuse, she now accepts the physical pleasure as something beyond her control. She has learned to accept her father's limitations, and this has freed him to respond to her in a more loving and caring way. Recalling her own struggles, Julie has become extremely empathetic toward other people. At times she can feel within her own body the pain and suffering of those around her. Her compassion for emotionally wounded children includes a realistic sense of sadness as she recognizes the challenges they face.

Julie's personal progress has enabled her to improve her relationships with men. She still regrets situations in the past when she either mistrusted men or demanded too much of them. Now she feels capable of real love and is confident that she can form mutually enriching relationships. Having achieved a greater sense of integration with her own body, she is more in touch with her emotions and more aware of her sexuality. All of this progress has prepared her to make good judgments about her relationships with men in the future.

During this recent period of growth, Julie's image of God has expanded and deepened. She has become much more aware of a female wisdom figure residing within herself. This wise woman has guided her throughout her therapy. At each crucial point, this inner feminine voice has prompted her to move in constructive directions. Julie has learned to trust this voice and associates it with the maternal God. She also has retained a more traditional image of God as a robed male authority figure. She has not yet achieved an integration of the male and female aspects of God, but she does feel a tremendous sense of gratitude to the Source of her continued growth. She knows that the Mystery has always been present throughout the horrible ordeal, empowering her to survive and to grow.

After five years of therapy, highlighted by amazing breakthroughs and hard-won progress, Julie achieved a solid basis for continued growth. When she assesses her life, she believes that it has been encompassed by the love and care of the compassionate God. She would not wish such a horrible experience on anyone else, but she feels that it has enabled her to become a more empathetic and compassionate person. She knows the tragic dimension of life, but is also aware of the power of divine grace. She is well aware of the perversities which can distort the human heart, but she also knows that there is an inner voice which leads to healing and reconciliation. Throughout her therapy, Julie found encouragement and enlightenment in reading stories of individuals who had dealt with sexual abuse. She is happy now to have her story told as a way of helping others with similar problems.

But Julie's story has even broader significance. It reminds all of us of the power of divine grace to heal our wounds. Her example of courage and perseverance can strengthen our resolve to bear our own crosses even when we feel abandoned by God. We too can learn to tap the power of the Wise Spirit in complex and confusing situations. Julie's experience of healing grace brings to light the God hidden in suffering who remains the source of our hope.

21. Sojourn in an Alien Land

Even brief excursions into an unfamiliar world can broaden horizons and deepen perceptions. My sojourn in the hospital, for example, intensified my respect and gratitude for the healers of this world.

A number of years ago I made a short sojourn in an unfamiliar world which proved to be not only disruptive but also revelatory. Pastoral duties and writing deadlines had so occupied my attention that little time and energy was left for preparing for my encounter with this alien place. This was all to the good since it prevented excessive anxiety and undo worry. Arriving early Monday morning, my first order of business was to write a check to cover some amazingly large expenses. I couldn't help but think of those who were staying longer and who had fewer resources to fall back on. With business affairs taken care of, a gentleman led me to a large room with individual cubicles. A strange dress code seemed to be rather rigorously enforced in this place. Not wishing to be out of place, I quickly donned a short gown with rather impractical ties in the back. It was now clear to me that I had entered a world where other people who knew the rules of the game were calling all the shots. Lying on a cart as instructed, I began to ponder my situation. An image from my youth emerged into my consciousness. I was standing on a diving board listening to a swimming instructor urging me to jump. Driven by peer pressure and a vague faith or hope that I would, indeed, come back to the surface after plunging to the bottom, I made the leap. This would be my strategy now – take the plunge, confident that some benign forces would buoy me up. Just then, a fellow appeared who had the task of injecting a needle into a vein in my arm. After one unsucessful try, he announced that he would not attack me again but would leave this task to a doctor. Despite this encouraging news, I began to feel faint and was preserved in consciousness only by the sage advice to lie back and relax. It was at this point that I had to admit to myself something long feared – I did not have the "right stuff" for this world. My strengths were no help; my weaknesses were magnified. My mind moved to relatives and friends who knew this hospital world all too well. While facing serious operations and long convalescence, these people had demonstrated great courage and amazing resilience. My admiration for them multiplied as I braced myself for the next onslaught of the needle. After only two tries, the doctor got the IV in place, while I rejoiced in the amazing accomplishment of retaining full consciousness throughout. This seemed to give me new confidence that I could handle this situation – a minor operation to repair a diverticulum or small pouch in my throat which had been impeding my swallowing for the last ten months.

My next memory is vague, filled in by eyewitness accounts which graphically described my wild behavior in the recovery room – one more indication of my difficulty in adjusting to this unfamiliar world. Evidently, I was convinced that the recovery room was not being run properly and that my services as a friendly consultant were needed to improve it. In addition, it was not clear to me why my wife was being kept from my side in this moment of crisis. A strong dose of demerol seemed to calm my rampaging preconscious self, while the understanding nurse who held my hand brought some measure of reassurance.

After a couple of hours in the recovery room, they wheeled me to my room where a nurse asked if I could help get myself from the cart to the bed. My initial half-joking response was "no," but then I decided that cooperation was a better approach. My new environment was largely shaped by more of those marvelous people committed to nursing the sick. They proved to be an unfailing source of hands-on help, practical advice, and positive motivation. With a great liberating compassion, they seemed to accept those of us who lacked the "right stuff" and who were struggling with our limitations in this unfamiliar world. "Wash what you can and I'll do the rest," said one especially efficient nurse. Another with a practical bent prodded me to start walking as soon as possible because this would get the bodily functions going. With a certain sternness, one suggested that it was a big mistake to refuse to take the pain medication. The comment that made the most impact on me, however, came from a philosophically-oriented nurse who declared that one should never take for granted the ability to wipe oneself after a bowel movement. This was one of the few times (a passage from a John Updike novel also comes to mind) that I have heard this particular bodily function placed in a religious-spiritual context. It seems to me that the easy familiarity of the nurses with bodily processes made the verbalization of this insight possible.

The day after the operation was the worst. All my nasal and throat passages were swollen, making breathing very difficult. My reaction was panic. The intern who visited me did not seem to understand that I was in great and imminent danger of suffocating. His logical assurances were of little help as my left brain seemed to close down. Drawing on my vast medical knowledge, I was convinced that nasal spray would help. I talked a friend into getting me some, but it did not help my breathing and the cloud engulfing me darkened. I considered praying for help, but somehow that seemed inappropriate. Prayers seemed much more appropriate for the gentleman in the bed next to mine. He had been suffering for five years and was flat on his back, waiting for some bones to knit. His upbeat, optimistic spirit both inspired and shamed me. Late in the afternoon with the help of moist oxygen, my nasal passages opened a bit and my panic subsided. I shared my relief with a nurse who had been extremely sensitive to my irrational fears. And then it was time to pray. Sentiments of gratitude merged with a dark foreboding which periodically returns. "Thank you, Lord; please be with me as courage and strength when this demon next attacks."

On the third day, the highly respected surgeon who had performed the operation appeared, surrounded by his entourage. With the self-assurance I had come to expect from this impressive and generous man, he declared that I could go home the next day, Christmas Eve, after only four days in the hospital. Suddenly the structure of this alien world was a bit clearer to me. A hierarchial system with a clear chain of command prevailed here. Some were learning from the master, while others were making sure that his directives were carried out. I had not been able to observe his skill in the operating room, but the attitude of the staff proclaimed his competency. As an outsider, I presumed that he enjoyed the respect of the whole healing team and had their full cooperation.

After the doctor left, a nurse told me that patients with such throat surgery always stayed at least seven days. Quickly reorienting herself, she allowed that I could probably manage and went on to explain in great detail how I was to feed myself through the tube in my nose. I listened carefully to everything she said, fascinated both by her teaching skills and her practical know-how.

The next day, a familiar woman appeared in my room. She claimed that she had nursed me before and could handle the task again. I decided to accept her kind offer and to continue the mode of dependency established after my surgery. As we left the hospital, she carried the box of supplies and drove the car. At her home, she prepared the couch, mastered the feeding aparatus, and administered the medication. Later, in the midst of a snowstorm, she drove me fifty miles to the hospital and back so that the doctor could remove the stitches and the feeding tube. Still her task was not yet complete. She had a week-long challenge of preparing soft foods, appealing enough to get a man in need of more nourishment and calories to eat properly. Homemade soup proved to be the matchless remedy. With the wise and respectful prudence I admire so much, my mother supported and guided my recovery. Sometimes she cautioned against overwork and too fast a pace, but at other times she suggested more exercise and greater self-reliance. Maternal love at its best not only offers support but also fosters a spirit of independence.

Even brief excursions into an unfamiliar world can broaden horizons and deepen perceptions. My sojourn in the hospital, for example, intensified my respect and gratitude for the healers of this world who bring skill and compassion to their valuable service. The experience also serves as a forceful reminder to me to respond with empathy and compassion to those who find my world of religion and church alien, bewildering and frightening. Finally, it is clear that "good health" can become as much of an idol as status, riches, power and pleasure. In a properly ordered world there is only one legitimate ultimate concern, the Gracious God who is the source of both the gift of health and the courage to deal with illness.

22. Fundamentalism: A Worldwide Movement

A broad analysis of global fundamentalism reminds us of the importance of developing constructive attitudes and strategies for dealing with the fundamentalists in our midst.

For most Americans, the term "fundamentalism," which was first coined in 1920, refers to a particularly aggressive brand of Christianity which takes the Bible literally and considers it free from all error. Many of us have been tempted to dismiss fundamentalism as a naive method of interpreting the Bible advocated by unenlightened Christians in the United States with a strong psychological need for security.

This assessment has recently been challenged by the outstanding work of the Fundamentalism Project, a scholarly undertaking supported by a $3 million grant from the American Academy of Arts & Sciences and directed by the renowned Lutheran historian Dr. Martin Marty. This project enabled over 200 scholars to study fundamentalist movements in seven major religions around the world. The study is divided into six large volumes. The first volume, entitled *Fundamentalisms Observed*, edited by Martin Marty and R. Scott Appleby (University of Chicago Press, 1991), has chapters covering a wide variety of topics, including Roman Catholic traditionalism, Protestant fundamentalism in Latin American, Jewish Zionist fundamentalism, Islamic fundamentalism in South Asia and fundamentalistic movements in Theravada Buddhism. The other volumes examine the social, economic, educational and political consequences of fundamentalism; the motivations of leaders and followers; the roles that women play; and the implications for public policy questions.

This massive study makes a compelling case that fundamentalism broadly defined is a pervasive and powerful force in our world today, which must be treated with great seriousness. Far from being confined to unenlightened Americans, fundamentalism is a major competitor in the global battle to shape the consciousness of the human family. The fundamentalist mentality exists in all religions and secular worldviews. In countries such as Iran and Sudan, Islamic fundamentalism is the dominant political power. Jewish fundamentalist groups adamantly oppose any accommodations with the Palestinians. Guatemala is moving rapidly toward becoming half fundamentalist by the turn of the century. Hindu fundamentalists want to make India into a Hindu nation. Buddhist fundamentalists in Thailand are striving to clean up the political system and to establish religious principles as the basis for the political order. In Russia, Marxist fundamentalists are trying to block the democratic reforms. The confident predictions of secular analysts that fundamentalist religions would wither under the onslaughts of the modern world have obviously proven to be totally inaccurate. With the end of the Cold War, it is becoming more evident that the growing popularity of fundamentalism cannot be ignored in the quest for world peace, national harmony and ethnic reconciliation.

Although it is difficult to come up with a concise definition of fundamentalism, it is possible, following Martin Marty, to identify certain "family resemblances" or general characteristics shared by the various fundamentalist movements around the world.

In a crucial move, Marty broadened the standard interpretation of fundamentalism, favored by James Barr and other scholars, who see it as a specifically Christian movement based on biblical inerrency. For Marty, fundamentalism is a worldwide phenomenon found in all religious traditions. The various fundamentalist movements have in common an aggressive response to the perceived threats of the modern world. In other words, fundamentalists are beleaguered persons, convinced that certain elements of modernity are threatening their personal identities and the very existence of their traditions. Their reaction is to fight back vigorously, often with great emotion and harsh methods, as happened in the Islamic revolution in Iran. Paradoxically, fundamentalists who reject modernity often use modern methods of communication as weapons in the battle. A good example is the skillful use of television by well-known preachers.

In the struggle against modernity, fundamentalists typically employ certain essential truths taken from the normative stage of their own sacred history. Although they ordinarily have roots in a conservative tradition, fundamentalists do not embrace the whole tradition as genuine conservatives do, but rather selectively retrieve the elements which serve as the best weapons for combating the threats from the modern world. These truths are used to set clear boundaries between believers like themselves and the enemies on the other side. Protestant fundamentalism, for instance, puts great stress on belief in biblical inerrancy as a way of distinguishing authentic Christians from false ones and of fighting against the relativism found in contemporary culture. Catholics can understand this strategy by reflecting on the way papal infallibility has been used as a distinguishing mark and a defense against destructive modern errors. In retrieving certain truths from their founding documents, fundamentalists deny that they are involved in a process of interpretation. They believe that the basic truths have a clear, objective meaning, which common sense can easily determine. They seldom advert to the fact that selectively retrieving certain truths is already an act of interpretation.

Persons who join fundamentalist groups are especially threatened by modern historical consciousness which, they believe, deprives people of reliable guides for thought and behavior by denying the existence of absolute truths and values. Modern pluralism is also dangerous because it undermines certitude and promotes doubt by insisting that there are various perspectives from which we can understand and interpret reality. At the beginning of this century, Christian fundamentalists adamantly opposed modern evolutionary theory and the use of historical-critical methods in analyzing the Bible because these scholarly approaches threatened their essential self-identity and their static worldview. This is why they now fight so vigorously for the right to teach creationism in the public schools. In the moral realm, fundamentalists are keenly aware of the collapse of absolute norms and values in the modern world. As an antidote, they insist on a strict moral code which promotes family values and opposes abortion, fornication, pornography, divorce, drinking, drugs, and gambling.

Persons with a fundamentalist mindset readily believe that they have a special mission in life, often as agents of God in bringing history to its predetermined end or goal. This naturally leads to an exclusive and separatist mentality. They live in the light, while others inhabit the darkness. As an elect people, they have no need for dialogue with other groups and must reject all compromises with the modern world. Their harshest judgments are often reserved for conservatives who are willing to cooperate with the enemy. The Christian fundamentalist Jerry Falwell, for example, has in the past viewed Billy Graham as a dangerous man because of his compromises with the culture.

In summary, fundamentalism is a reactive, dynamic, growing global movement composed of individuals and groups who feel threatened by modernity and are fighting back with basic truths drawn selectively from their traditions. It is important to remember, however, that fundamentalism itself is pluralistic. Biblicists like Jerry Falwell and Pentecostals like Pat Robertson refuse to be lumped together. Christian fundamentalists disavow the violent tactics used by Egyptian Muslims. Religious fundamentalists reject the atheism of Marxists. Some groups are more moderate, tolerant and open to dialogue than others.

A broad analysis of global fundamentalism reminds us of the importance of developing constructive attitudes and strategies for dealing with the fundamentalists in our midst. On the positive side, we can surely admire their personal courage and appreciate their promotion of family values. We can learn from their criticisms of modernity, their promotional techniques and their community-building skills. Since fundamentalists are one of the few groups still considered fair game for jokes and insults, it is especially important to treat them with respect and to make balanced judgments about their positions. Mainline Christians have a responsibility to hold open the door for possible dialogue and cooperation, recognizing that some groups are more receptive than others.

On the other hand, conservative and liberal Christians should unite in exposing the dangerous aspects of the funda-

mentalist mentality. Thus, we should point out the destructive consequences of religious exclusivism and denounce violence of any kind perpetrated in the name of religion. It is
also important to present an alternative understanding of
Christianity which can compete for the mind and soul of the
postmodern world. To make this vision attractive, we Christians should be involved in the political process as dialogue
partners, bringing the wisdom of our tradition to bear on
public policy issues. We must celebrate the positive achievements of modernity such as freedom, tolerance and democracy, while working with others to transform its distortions,
especially individualism, consumerism and prejudice of all
kinds. Our parishes and congregations should function as
genuine communities where individuals find support and
challenge. We ought to promote ecumenical and interfaith
dialogue and cooperation as essential factors in the quest for
world peace. Finally, we must demonstrate in word and deed
that we trust the process of life and place our ultimate security in the God who calls us to help transform the world.

23. Medjugorje and Marian Apparitions

*Keeping these theological perspectives in mind should
promote dialogue between devotees and skeptics so that
the Blessed Virgin can continue to play her traditional role
as a powerful symbol of unity and harmony.*

In 1981, six young peasants in the remote village of
Medjugorje in Bosnia began reporting visions of the Blessed
Virgin Mary. Over ten million pilgrims visited the village
during the next decade until the war made the trip too dangerous. Hundreds of cures have been claimed. Almost all the
pilgrims report that their faith has been strengthened, and
many have become more committed to the cause of peace. In
the United States alone, over 300 local groups of Medjugorje
devotees gather regularly for prayer and periodically come
together for national conferences.

Medjugorje is part of a larger Marian movement, rooted
in the famous apparitions at Lourdes in 1858 and Fatima in

1917, which has seen a dramatic increase in visionary claims during the last few decades.

Unfortunately, these Marian apparitions are at times a source of tension within the Catholic community. In Medjugorje itself, the local bishop, Pavao Zanic, has strongly questioned the authenticity of the apparitions, charging that the parish church run by the Franciscans had been turned into a tourist attraction. Such opposition fits into the pattern of other Marian apparitions. For example, Lucia, one of the visionaries at Fatima, was at first accused of lying by the local priest and by her mother, who used violence to get her to recant. In some parishes today, tensions exist between Marian devotees, who want more emphasis on Mary, and their pastoral leaders, who are committed to maintaining the Christocentric focus of Vatican II. Even families find themselves split. A husband who was inspired by his pilgrimage to Medjugorje is at odds with his Catholic wife who thinks the visions border on the superstitious. There is no doubt that the Catholic community is divided over the significance of the modern Marian apparitions. The question is whether these differences will eventually enrich the church or whether they will congeal into polarized positions which undermine its peace and harmony. Establishing a solid theological perspective for analyzing the apparitions is an important step in making these tensions more fruitful.

At the very beginning, it is important to recognize that the Marian apparitions are considered to be private and not public revelations. Already in the 18th century, Pope Benedict XIV insisted that claims of private revelations had to be investigated carefully before being given approval and that not everyone was obliged to assent to them even after approval. Out of the hundreds of apparitions claimed in the past two centuries, only seven have been approved by local bishops and gained international attention: Rue du Bac in Paris in 1830; La Salette, France, 1846; Lourdes, France, 1858; Pontmain, France 1870; Fatima, Portugal, 1917; Beauraing, Belgium, 1932; and Banneux, Belgium, 1933. Medjugorje has not been given official approval, but the Vatican has continued to investigate the claims. All Christians are obliged to assent to the fundamental truths revealed by Christ and recorded in the Scriptures. All that we need to know for salvation is contained in this public revelation. Private revelations add nothing new to the deposit of faith. They are not guaranteed by inspiration as are the Scriptures. The church's approbation means that the faithful can venerate Mary in a special way at the shrine. Private Marian devotions cannot be imposed on any church member.

For all Christian people, Jesus Christ is the one and only mediator between God and the human family. Christian piety is necessarily Christocentric. Our fundamental commitment is to Jesus Christ and his teachings. Authentic visionaries have never denied this. In fact, this is made explicit in one of the early messages from Medjugorje given on October 7, 1981: "There is only one mediator between God and man, and it is Jesus Christ." Devotions to Mary must strengthen and not weaken the unique role of Christ. Pope John Paul II, quoting the Second Vatican Council, insisted that all of the influences of the Blessed Virgin "flow forth from the superabundance of the merits of Christ, rest on his mediation, depend entirely on it and draw all their power from it. In no way do they impede the immediate union of the faithful with Christ, rather they foster this union." Individual Catholics who put so much emphasis on Mary that it undercuts the role of Christ are not only opposing the official teachings of the church, but also the fundamental insights of the Marian visionaries themselves.

Mary played an indispensable role in salvation history and is worthy of honor and respect as the mother of Jesus Christ. She is not a goddess, but she is the most influential woman in Christian history. Mary plays an especially prominent role in Luke's Gospel. Her informed and receptive response to the Angel Gabriel makes possible the Incarnation. Her Magnificat sets the tone for the whole Gospel, which celebrates God's reversal of worldly values. Like Jesus Christ, who was humble and obedient, Mary gladly accepted her role as handmaid of the Lord. Luke completes his picture of Mary in the Acts of the Apostles, portraying her as a key person in the community which gathered around Christ after his death and resurrection. In 431, the Council of Ephesus proclaimed Mary to be the *Theotokos,* the Bearer of God, or as it came to be phrased, "Mother of God." Although many Protestant thinkers have objected to placing too much emphasis on Mary, the great Calvinistic theologian Karl Barth, affirmed that Mary's title, Mother of God, is not only permissible but necessary in order to understand properly the nature of Christ. A Presbyterian theologian once said that Protestants in the past had the strange notion that they honor Christ by dishonoring his mother. Today, Catholics who have adopted a more Christocentric piety since the Second Vatican Council can enrich their faith by recalling the traditional role of Mary and recognizing the enduring power of Marian symbolism.

In all religious experiences, including authentic Marian apparitions, it is important to distinguish the original encounter with the Sacred and the distinctive cultural forms used to describe and articulate it. In this regard, modern Marian visionaries have often had a difficult time interpreting their initial experiences and have arrived at the full explanation presented to the public only after a long and complex process. For example, the young visionaries Maxamin and Melanie, who had a single experience in 1846 at La Salette, at first interpreted their vision as a woman who had been attacked by her son. It was only later at the suggestion of someone else that these two youngsters, both from troubled homes, interpreted the woman in the vision as the Blessed Virgin Mary. Bernadette, who began having her experiences February 11, 1858 at Lourdes, at first was not sure who was addressing her in the visions. It was only after numerous requests that the woman revealed herself as the Immaculate Conception, a title which Bernadette said she did not understand, even though the dogma had been proclaimed in 1854 by Pius IX. The primary visionary at Fatima, Lucia, at first had doubts herself about the authenticity of the first two appearances.

The modes of expression used by the visionaries to express their deep experiences are always historically, culturally, and personally conditioned. Furthermore, the messages are inevitably influenced by the authority figures surrounding the visionaries and by the general public which receives them. The story of the famous Fatima secrets exemplifies this point. Despite the threats of violence by local governmental officials, the three youngsters, Lucia, Francisco and Jacinta, at first refused to reveal the secrets entrusted to them by the Virgin Mary, although they did say that people would be sad if they knew them. With the early death of her two cousins, Lucia became the sole interpreter of the secrets. About a week after the sixth and final vision on October 13, 1917, Lucia was interviewed by Dr. Manuel Forimio, a seminary professor, who reported that she had trouble remembering the circumstances surrounding the experiences. Lucia composed her first written account of the apparitions almost five years after the events and it was another 19 years, in August of 1941, before she revealed the first two of the three secrets given by the Virgin. The first secret involved a terrifying vision of hell complete with fire, demons and suffering souls. The second one, originally revealed in 1917, indicated that the war was going to end, but that a worse one would break out during the pontificate of Pius XI. This secret also included the promise that if Mary's request for communions of reparation on the first Saturdays of the month were honored, Russia would be converted and there would be a period of peace in the world. Lucia refused to reveal the third secret in her memoir of 1941, but in 1944 relented and wrote it down for Bishop de Silva who sent it on to Rome in 1957. Some respected commentators believe that Pope Pius XII left the message unopened, but that subsequent Popes John XXIII, Paul VI and John Paul II did read it. None of them, including the current holy Father, chose to reveal its contents. For years, there has been great speculation about the message of the third secret. One of the more intriguing stories appeared in a German magazine in 1968, reporting that Pope Paul VI had arranged in 1963 for the secret to be read by President Kennedy and Premier Khrushchev and that this led them to the historic agreement to ban atomic experiments in the atmosphere. It is possible to believe that visionaries such as Lucia have had genuine encounters with the Holy without necessarily accepting all of the diverse articulations and speculations surrounding the experiences.

Keeping these theological perspectives in mind should promote dialogue between devotees and skeptics so that the Blessed Virgin can continue to play her traditional role as a powerful symbol of unity and harmony.

24. Learning from Confucius: Harmony through Discipline

The Confucian tradition reminds us that strict discipline and systematic effort are vital for spiritual growth.

Why should we Americans pay any attention to the Chinese religious traditions of Confucianism and Taoism? For one thing, they continue to shape the imagination of the Chinese people even after almost half a century of Communist rule. Confucius will be revered and studied in China long after Marx is totally abandoned. Our own political and economic interests demand that we know something about the fundamental attitudes of the 1.1 billion Chinese (one quarter of the world's population) who constitute a powerful nation and form the largest market in the world. Moreover, Chinese wisdom offers perspectives and insights which could help us develop a more balanced spirituality and a more harmonious society.

Learning from the wisdom of China demands that we pass over to a distinctive worldview quite different from our own. The Catholic theologian Hans Kung distinguishes "three great religious river systems" operative in the world today. One river system is composed of the three prophetic religions of Semitic origin in the Near East: Judaism shaped by Moses and the Law; Christianity centered on faith in Jesus the Christ revealed in the New Testament; and Islam guided by belief in Muhammad and the Qur'an. All three religions trace their origin to the patriarch Abraham and hold a common belief in the one God who speaks through the great prophets. A second system includes the mystical religions of Indian origin, Hinduism and Buddhism. They are characterized by the immediate experience of the undifferentiated unity of all things achieved through meditative practices. Finally, the third river system arose in China and includes the wisdom traditions linked to the sages Confucius and Lao-tzu, known as the founder of Taoism. While the prophetic religions offer salvation from sin through God's initiative, and the mystical religions promise serenity through enlightenment, Chinese wisdom holds up the prospect of human happiness through harmonious relationships.

Although this distinction between prophetic, mystical and wisdom traditions is useful, it clearly is not airtight. Within Judaism and Christianity, for instance, there is a strong wisdom tradition. Buddhist teachings and meditation practices have made a great impact on Chinese religions. A more complete treatment of the world religions would have to discuss these common elements.

The most influential of the Chinese sages is Confucius (551-479 B.C.), which is the Latin rendering of K'ung Fu-tzu or Master K'ung. He was born near modern Ch'u-fu (Shantung) and served as an ordinary public official, becoming at age 50 a commissioner in his home state. After failing to find a ruler who would implement his theories on government, he devoted himself to the arts and teaching disciples. His disciples collected his aphorisms in the *Analects*. In the past, scholars also attributed to Confucius the Five Classics: *The Book of Change, The Book of History, The Book of Poetry, The Classic of Rites* and *The Spring and Autumn Annals*. Contemporary scholarship is more aware of the historical development of these texts, although many of the core ideas may go back to Master K'ung. From the second century B.C. until the Nationalist revolution of 1911, these classic Confucian texts served as the basis for the state examinations required for all those aspiring to the life of scholarship and public service. This practice, combined with the spread of Confucian thought to other parts of Asia including Japan and Korea, made Master K'ung one of the most influential persons who ever lived.

In the *Analects*, we find a revealing self-description of Confucius: "At 15 I set my heart on learning to be a sage. At

30 I became firm. At 40 I had no more doubts. At 50 I understood Heaven's Will. At 60, my ear was attuned to this will. At 70 I could follow my heart's desire, without overstepping the line." Master K'ung devoted himself to the pursuit of wisdom and in the process developed a profound humanism and a comprehensive ethical system. At the core of his teaching is a spirituality with universal significance and enduring power.

Some contemporary scholars recognize a religious dimension in Confucian humanism. In his book *Confucius: the Secular as Sacred*, Herbert Fingeratte argues that Confucius had a profound spiritual sense of a transcendent power. He usually referred to this power as Heaven which suggests a personal God, but also called it the *Tao*, a more impersonal, ultimate principle at work in human affairs. Confucius taught his disciples to set their heart on Heaven which gives significance to life. He also said, "If you learn the *Tao* in the morning and die in the evening," your life is not wasted," but if you reach the age of 40 and have not heard the *Tao*, "there is nothing worthy of respect in you." Furthermore, by insisting on the strict observance of all the proper rituals and traditional gestures, Master K'ung established a climate in which his followers could hear the *Tao* and experience the holy in ordinary human life.

For Confucius, spiritual growth depends not only on living in harmony with the *Tao* but also on study and disciplined effort. We need a constant "cutting, filing, carving, polishing" to become fully human and to function as effective participants in society. The task is to develop virtues so that proper behavior becomes second nature. Thomas Merton identifies a "four-sided mandela" of Confucian virtues which guide all human relationships (cf. *The Way of Chuang Tzu*). The key virtue is *Jen*, a universal benevolence which inclines an individual to love others and to treat everyone as a "very important guest." *Yi* is a type of justice which moves a person to treat others fairly, not for personal gain but out of moral obligation. The third virtue, *Li*, which does not have an obvious Western counterpart, is the ability to lose oneself in the proper ritual forms and traditional conventions so that they are genuine expressions of the proper respect due to others. Finally, *Chih* or wisdom gives direction to all the other virtues by orienting individuals to "Heaven's Will" and allowing them to act spontaneously in the pursuit of good. Through arduous discipline, wise persons cultivate these virtues so that they can live in harmony with themselves, other people and with the *Tao*.

The Confucian ideal is a profound humanism which is religiously rooted, spiritually motivated and ethically oriented. It requires loyalty to one's own heart combined with respect for others. Growth as a person requires mastery of emotions and a refusal to act like a victim. In the *Analects* Master K'ung offers insightful descriptions of superior persons who live virtuously. They love their souls and not their property, are broad minded and not partisan, are at ease and not excessively worried, are always candid and not proud, seek the truth and not material comfort, blame themselves and not others, follow the path of moral rectitude and not the opinions of others, speak honestly and avoid glib talk. Confucius insisted that his followers put these ideals into practice: "Superior persons are ashamed that their words are better than their deeds."

Some neo-Confucians, such as the contemporary Japanese scholar Okada Takehiko, insist that regular meditation must be part of a comprehensive program for spiritual growth (cf. *The Confucian Way of Contemplation* by Rodney Taylor). The mystical river system of Buddhism, which flowed into China in the fourth century, brought a new interest in meditation among Confucians. But the followers of Master K'ung have always been leery of a monastic spirituality which withdraws from the real world of daily life. Therefore they developed distinctive approaches to meditation designed to promote wise living in the world. Since the 11th century some Confucians have advocated the practice of "quiet sitting." In contrast to the formal Buddhist meditation practices, neo-Confucians advocate taking time each day simply to be quiet. Do not worry about bodily posture; it can be done sitting or lying down. Do not try to force distractions away; just relax and let quietude come about naturally. Do not stiffen the mind or body; rather, gently cultivate a serene reverence for the self. Do not reflect on the method or the outcome of the meditation; just concentrate on experiencing the sights and sounds of life as they are.

The goal of this practice, ideally repeated a few times throughout the day, is "the realization of the Principle of Heaven wherever one is." This requires maintaining a sense of quietude in the midst of daily activities. Regular quiet sitting has a cumulative effect, gradually enabling a person to feel a greater sense of integration, to remain more focused and to act with greater patience.

In may ways Confucian wisdom resonates with Americans. We can appreciate its practical, down-to-earth approach to spirituality. Its emphasis on ethics rather than doctrine fits in with our pragmatic orientation. The call for full human development through enriching personal relationships sounds very familiar to us.

But the Confucian tradition also presents us with strong challenges and helpful correctives. It reminds us that strict discipline and systematic effort are vital for spiritual growth. We need to hear its call for compassion and respect in human relationships. Busy people might cope better with stress by trying some of the simple techniques of neo-Confucian meditation. Confucian humanism challenges the assumptions of our hedonistic culture. We could surely use a strong dose of Confucian civility in our political process. The great religious river system of Chinese wisdom holds the promise of hydration for our parched culture and dry spirits. Let the dialogue flourish.

25. Learning from Taoism: Harmony with Nature

The solution of Chuang-tzu is to abandon totally the competitive drive and let go completely of the need to succeed.

Our highly competitive, success-oriented culture can take its toll on our physical and spiritual health. Stress increases the risk of heart disease and other illnesses. Busyness undercuts our best intentions to maintain a balanced lifestyle. Unbridled competition fosters destructive behavior ranging from insensitivity to violence. The hunger for success makes it difficult to handle limitations, failures and intractable problems. Immersed in the whirl of everyday life, we can fail to discern these threats to our health. The great blessings of freedom and abundance can blind us to the destructive patterns in our society. It is easy to accept the distortions, contradictions and imbalances as perfectly normal. Our affluent culture tends to eclipse our need for salvation.

In this unhealthy situation, dialogue with another religious tradition can provide perspective and healing. The Chinese tradition known as Taoism (pronounced Dowism) has some distinctive teachings which could be especially therapeutic for us today. Taoism is a complex movement which includes philosophical, hygienic, mystical and religious elements. Together with Confucianism it contributes to the great tradition of Chinese wisdom which has been a major influence in Asia for centuries. In contrast to the Confucian emphasis on humanistic virtue and political organization, Taoist spirituality is concerned with personal wholeness and harmony with nature. Historically, it also has functioned as an esoteric mystery religion attractive to rebels and revolutionaries and as a popular religion of salvation appealing to the masses. Today a form of Taoism, which includes ritualistic worship of various divine beings, flourishes in Taiwan.

The Taoist spiritual tradition which is most helpful to us is rooted in the best known of the Chinese classics, the *Tao-te ching* or *Book of the Tao*, a 5,000 word collection of epigrams attributed to Lao-tzu. Not much is known of this legendary figure who is usually dated in the sixth century B.C. One legend suggests he was a royal librarian who retired and traveled to the West, leaving behind this small volume of his teachings. Whatever its precise origin, the *Tao-te ching* provides an excellent entree into the spiritual core of Chinese wisdom.

The Taoist worldview is quite different from our own. Fundamentally, it prefers complementarity over competition, harmony over tension, acceptance over success. In contrast to the tension-filled dialectical dualism of Western thought, Chinese wisdom holds a complementary dualism that sees the world as an integrated whole in which apparent opposites are ultimately harmonious. This viewpoint invites human beings to live in harmony with nature and its ultimate principle.

The *Tao-te ching* names this ultimate principle the *Tao*, and describes it as the "Origin of Heaven and Earth," the " Mother of All Things," the "Cosmic Mystery," and the "Secret of Life." It is the unchanging first principle which existed before the universe came to be. It is the Way which functions as a model for human behavior. Contemplation of the universe leads to the discovery of the *Tao*, but it remains ultimately mysterious, "fathomless like the fountainhead of all things." The sage searches for the *Tao* with eager eyes, but sees nothing, for it inhabits the realm of the imperceptible and remains nameless. This language reminds us of the Christian mystical tradition which emphasizes the ineffable character of the divine. But we cannot equate the *Tao* with the God of Moses, Jesus or Muhammad. Lao-Tzu says nothing about a personal relationship with the *Tao*, nor does he advocate worship or prayer. He does teach that human beings should live in harmony with this Cosmic Mystery and that this is the only way to happiness. Happiness cannot be achieved through success or progress or accumulating possessions. It comes only as a gift or as a byproduct of a proper relationship with the Secret of Life.

The harmonious life results from following the laws of nature and staying in touch with the rhythms of the natural world. For Taoists the harmony of the whole universe results from the interplay of the primal powers *yin* and *yang*, traditionally represented by the familiar circular symbol, divided equally into black and white segments, each containing an opposite color dot. *Yang* is the source of the hot, active, masculine, light and dry elements of the world; while *yin* grounds what is cold, passive, feminine, dark and moist. The interplay between *yin* and *yang* brings the whole universe into existence and maintains it in a harmonious flow. This explains the alternations between warm and cold, summer and winter, day and night. Human beings flourish when they live in harmony with these alternating rhythms of the natural world. Chinese landscape painting represents this outlook by depicting serene natural settings which gently envelop small human figures. This Taoist perspective offers the basis for an eco-spirituality which calls human beings to live in harmony with nature and not to dominate or destroy it.

The Taoist *yin-yang* theory also forms the basis for holistic Chinese medicine which has lately gained greater respect in the Western world. Chinese doctors see illness not as the result of a particular diseased organ, but as the consequence of disharmony and imbalance within the total human organism. They do not try to cure a particular disease, but rather treat the whole person, who is always embedded in a network of relationships with others and with the environment. Their goal is to facilitate a more harmonious flow of vital energy currents among various organs. Over the centuries, Chinese medicine has developed a whole series of therapeutic strategies to achieve greater balance, including diet, acupuncture, breathing techniques, exercise programs and massage.

The holistic approach fostered by Taoism reminds us that personal health requires a balanced life. As embodied spirits, our physical health is essentially rooted in our spiritual and psychic well-being. We find more strength and energy by respecting our bodily rhythms and by living in harmony with the laws of nature and the Cosmic Mystery. The Taoist teaching on proper balance, harmony and rhythm provides helpful insights for those of us who live busy lives filled with stressful challenges.

Taoism also offers a counterpoint to the Western success ethic in its teachings on *wu-wei*, which literally means nonaction. This notion is developed in helpful ways by the Taoist sage Chuang-tzu, who lived around the fourth or third century B.C. Not much is known of his personal life, but a popular legend claims he turned down a very lucrative offer to become the minister to a king because he wanted to avoid the restrictions of a high position and maintain his freedom. His classic work, known simply as *The Chuang-tzu,* contains philosophical reflections and humorous anecdotes which develop the thought of Lao-tzu and criticize the formalism often associated with Confucian rituals and politics. The Trappist monk Thomas Merton has popularized the thought of Master Chuang through a very free translation or interpretation of some of his best anecdotes (cf. *The Way of Chuang-tzu*).

For Chuang-tzu, and the whole Taoist tradition, the path to happiness is not through achieving success or wealth or even virtue, but through *wu-wei*, or nonaction, which avoids conscious striving for results. Conscious efforts to achieve self-fulfillment are destructive because they promote egocentric selfishness and distort the harmonious relationship with the *Tao*. Master Chuang makes the point in personal terms: "My greatest happiness consists precisely in doing nothing whatever that is calculated to obtain happiness." More positively, *wu-wei* suggests perfect action which is effortless and spontaneous because it is in harmony with the Cosmic Mystery. It is action which is genuine and without artifice. Wise persons who live out the principle of nonaction do not overreact or intervene needlessly in human affairs. They live simply, but with great vitality and deep joy. Because they are immersed in reality and not their own ego, they instinctively discern the proper course of action in various circumstances. Artists manifest the power of nonaction when they move beyond rules and calculations and simply allow their creative intuitions to take over. So do superior athletes who at times get into a zone where they perform flawlessly with no thought and little strain.

Chuang-tzu insisted that the need to win diminishes a person's ability to act spontaneously and effectively. My adaptation of one of Merton's renditions of Chuang-tzu conveys this insight. When a golfer who has not learned the wisdom of nonaction plays for nothing, he has all his skill. If he plays for a dollar, he is already nervous. If he is playing in a tournament, he loses focus and his swing betrays him. His skill has not changed, but the prize has destroyed his concentration and the need to win has eroded his skills.

The point is applicable to life as a whole. The competitive drive for success, so prevalent in our culture, can diminish our ability to function as balanced and effective human beings. The solution of Chuang-tzu is to abandon totally the competitive drive and let go completely of the need to succeed. If this seems impossibly radical, then we could at least listen to the correctives suggested by the Taoist tradition: slow down and stay in touch with the rhythms of nature; care for the body through proper diet, exercise and meditation; concentrate more on making a good effort and less on achieving results; strive for a better balance between work and leisure; put more emphasis on fulfilling our own potential and less on surpassing others; and most of all, live in harmony with the Cosmic Mystery.

Chapter 3

Love of Neighbor: Deepening Personal Relationships

1. Moral Relativism

In Veritatis Splendor, *Pope John Paul II wants to restore the organic character of personal and societal existence by promoting the Christian understanding of freedom and responsibility.*

Pope John Paul II's encyclical *Veritatis Splendor* (*The Splendor of Truth*) generated a good deal of discussion when it first appeared in 1993. Initial reactions focused on the controversial aspects of the lengthy encyclical, especially the Pope's rejection of the moral theory known as proportionalism. Important Catholic moral theologians who espouse proportionalism responded by insisting that they do not hold the views that the Pope condemns. Some were upset that the encyclical lumped them together with secular authors who embrace moral relativism. Cardinal Ratzinger, who heads the Vatican congregation charged with maintaining doctrinal orthodoxy, said that the encyclical, more moderate than many expected, was not intended to close off debate. Indeed, leading moral theologians have continued to discuss the proper methods of moral decision-making.

But there is another way of reading *Veritatis Splendor* which is less polemical and has more relevance for most people today. The encyclical gathers together important elements of traditional Christian wisdom and makes them available for reflecting on the serious societal problems that we all face. The Pope has presented the example and teaching of Jesus Christ as an antidote to the moral relativism which threatens our postmodern culture. The encyclical highlights perspectives and principles from Catholic moral theology which could help in combating the permissive individualism and the social injustices which spawn family violence, street crime, drug abuse, economic greed and political corruption. Throughout the document we find inspiring reflections on the story of the rich young man who asks Jesus about eternal life and receives an invitation to give up all his possessions for the kingdom.

The Pope offers a sustained and insightful analysis of human freedom as a foundation for his moral prescriptions. Following the lead of Vatican II, he recognizes that freedom is a crucial concern today for people around the globe. With growing insistence, persons demand the right to make their own decisions without external pressure or coercion, even in the sphere of religion. After noting the positive achievements of modern culture in expanding the scope of freedom, the Pope warns that "certain currents of modern thought have gone so far as to exalt freedom to such an extent that it becomes an absolute, which would then be the source of values" (Number 32 in the text). In this view, the individual conscience becomes the "supreme tribunal of moral judgment" which independently determines what is good and evil. This individualistic ethic ends up denying that there are any moral norms which have a universal binding character. The Pope is convinced that these misunderstandings of freedom contradict the true dignity of human beings and lead to the ills which plague our society.

For John Paul II, freedom is not a matter of license to do whatever one feels like doing. Nor is it simply the power to choose among various alternatives. Reflecting the deeper analysis found in his doctoral work on modern phenomenology, later published as *The Acting Person,* the Pope insists that freedom is the root capacity to create ourselves and to decide definitively about ourselves as a whole. In establishing this position, which accords with the thought of contemporary theologians such as Karl Rahner, the Pope quotes St. Gregory of Nyssa: "Thus we are in a certain way our own parents, creating ourselves as we will, by our decisions" (71). We are acting persons who shape our personalities and determine our fundamental characteristics through our free decisions. Our freedom involves a self-transcendent quest for a final fulfillment which will satisfy the deepest longings of our hearts. This philosophical analysis constitutes a radical response to those who understand freedom as license to pursue pleasure or expediency. It also challenges the position of behaviorists such as B.F. Skinner who claims that human behavior is totally determined and that freedom is an illusion. Neither license nor determinism can bring genuine fulfillment because they do not accord with the true nature of human freedom.

From a theological perspective, John Paul II insists that freedom is a gift from God, "one to be received like a seed and to be cultivated responsibly" (86). Recalling the words of Paul to the Galatians, "You were called to freedom" (5:13), Christians today can understand their freedom as a vocation, a divine summons to achieve fulfillment by serving others. Prompted by the Spirit within, disciples of Jesus are called to live the Gospel wholeheartedly so as "to possess the full freedom of the children of God" (Rom. 8:21). Becoming free is a process which demands continuing conversion. We move only gradually toward greater maturity which involves a responsible use of freedom. "For freedom Christ has set us free; stand fast therefore, and do not submit again to a yoke of slavery" (Gal 5:1). Thus Paul reminds us that our freedom is hard won and continuously threatened by sin. Our fundamental option for God, which is always exercised through conscious, free decisions, can be revoked by choosing selfishness over love and the slavery of vice over personal freedom. Genuine freedom is motivated by love, seeks communion with others and serves the common good. This Christian understanding of freedom as a generous response to the call of God challenges the modern assumption that human liberty is primarily a matter of the individual's right to be free from constraints.

The cultivation of freedom is essentially connected to the pursuit of truth. The Pope insists that many of the destructive tendencies which threaten the moral order of society, including subjectivism and individualism, are rooted in "lessening or even denying the dependence of freedom on truth" (34). When freedom is divorced from truth, individuals tend to assume that they can independently determine what is good and evil. Instead of being guided by traditional wisdom or moral principles, many people today make their moral judgments solely on the basis of being sincere, acting authentically and feeling at peace with themselves. In this approach, conscience is too subjective and morality loses its objective character. Such an individualistic ethic taken to extremes denies the very idea of a common humanity and destroys the moral foundation of society.

In responding to the moral crisis of our time, the Pope directs our attention to Jesus Christ who is himself the "splendor of truth." In Jesus, we see the flowering of genuine freedom. His closeness to the Father freed him to serve the cause of the human family. The beatitudes which he proclaimed invite us to growth in freedom, and provide us with an inspiring "self-portrait" of the Lord. Jesus lived what he taught. He is "the true and final answer to the problem of morality" (85). The Pope finds special significance in the passion and death of Jesus: "The Crucified Christ reveals the authentic meaning of freedom; he lives it fully in the total gift of himself and calls his disciples to share in his freedom" (85). The personal example of Jesus gives special power to his claim: "If you make my word your home you will indeed be my disciples; you will come to know the truth, and the truth will set you free" (Jn 8:31-32).

The relationship between truth and freedom proclaimed by Jesus comes to focus for us in the call of conscience. The Pope understands conscience as "the sacred place" where God speaks to us. This inner dialogue with God leads to a practical judgment which makes known what we must do or not do in specific circumstances. But conscience is not "an independent and exclusive capacity to decide what is good and what is evil" (60). On the contrary, the judgment of conscience must be formed by the pursuit of truth and by a process of continuous conversion to what is good. It must take into account the call of God, the example of Jesus and the promptings of the Spirit. An informed conscience which remains "the proximate norm of personal morality"(60) puts us in accord with the eternal law of God written in our hearts. Through the practice of virtue we can develop a "connaturality" or harmonious conformity between our consciences and the true good. The person who has put on the mind of Christ is well prepared to cooperate in building a morally sound society.

For the Christian conscience, the law of God is not a burden, but an expression of divine wisdom which enables us to live in accord with our own nature as creatures oriented to the Creator. Conscience is not totally autonomous, but must respond to the natural law which, according to a long tradition, is the eternal law of God implanted in our hearts and known by reason. Biblical revelation and a living faith enable us to understand the law of God with greater facility and to make it the "interior law" of our own hearts. The Pope repeatedly insists that law and freedom are not in opposition; on the contrary, acceptance of God's law is the only way to achieve genuine freedom.

The secularism rampant in our culture is destructive because it denies the deepest truths of human existence. In promoting the autonomy of personal conscience, secularism effectively denies the essential connections between faith and reason, freedom and truth, conscience and law. Understanding the depth of the problem, Pope John Paul II wants to restore the organic character of personal and societal existence by promoting the Christian understanding of freedom and responsibility. His positive message deserves a hearing as we search for ways to maintain and strengthen the moral foundations of society.

2. Healthy Relationships

Christians are called to cooperate with the omnipotent Lord by using our God-given power to nourish others and to create healthy communities.

The question of power is crucial to our personal and societal existence, as ordinary conversation suggests. "He is too powerful for me and I feel intimidated when talking to him." "I want to find out where the real power in this organization is so I can get some things accomplished." "Politicians certainly exemplify the principle that power corrupts." "The powerless must be empowered so they can take charge of their lives." "I feel safer since there is only one superpower left in the world." "When I get into a power position then I will be able to do more good." "Power is frightening; I am afraid I will misuse it." "I love power. It makes me feel secure." "Powerful nations have a responsibility to help weaker countries." "Black power is the answer to our racial problems." "Our police need more fire power to control our streets." "After my power walk, I am going to put on my power suit and go to a power lunch." Our personal and cultural preoccupation with power invites further analysis.

There is a dark side which sometimes appears in the actual exercise of power. Compulsive individuals grab at power in order to ward off insecurity and anxiety. Criminals use force to attain their ends. Spouses engage in a power struggle which wounds their children. Politicians misuse their power for personal gain. Ordained clergy lord it over the laity in violation of Gospel mandates. Terrorist groups use violence to subvert the established order. Nations get involved in the arms race which takes food out of the mouths of the poor. Some individuals ruthlessly seek power for its own sake. Others callously struggle to maintain power as a means of control and domination. Persons tinged with sado-masochistic tendencies link power with sexual activity and fantasy. Intelligent individuals use their verbal skills and word power to intimidate the less articulate. Most of us are appalled by the gross misuse of power by others. But we also know the temptation to misuse power ourselves.

One reaction to the power struggles of life is to retreat into utopian idealism which disavows all power relationships. Persons who adopt this standpoint believe power is evil and force is never justified. They try to avoid all types of ranking and strive for strict equality. For them competition is harmful because it produces winners and losers. Confrontation should be avoided at all costs. It is unseemly to seek directly a position of power or authority. They believe that politics with its built-in power struggles is less than honorable. In their ideal world, human beings would relate on the basis of charity and society would function harmoniously. The young Karl Marx envisioned just such a harmonious world in which the classless society would replace the power relationships of the capitalistic system. Even with all the failures of Marxist experiments, some people of good will still think we can move toward such a utopia by renouncing all competitive relationships.

The problem with utopian idealism is that it is not rooted in a solid understanding of human existence. In reality, we are social creatures living in mutual interdependence. We have the root power to assert ourselves, to act freely, to shape the environment and to change situations. Often this necessary and healthy self-expression affects others prior to their own consent. By their attitudes and decisions, parents influence the psyches of their children; important authors supply guidelines and categories for thinking; politicians set the framework for public debate; natural leaders create the tone for small groups; insightful and articulate individuals provide direction for ordinary conversation. In all these cases, persons inevitably exercise power by influencing, moving, and shaping others, apart from their own volition. Power, understood as influencing other people before their free consent, is an unavoidable aspect of human interaction.

In analyzing power it is important to consider the Christian doctrine of original sin. We live in a flawed world shaped by personal sin and institutional injustice. The temptation to misuse power is universal and permanent. No structural change or conversion process will ever eliminate power relationships or totally preserve us from the misuse of power.

The utopians who want a noncompetitive society have forgotten the impact of original sin on human affairs.

It is more realistic and productive to begin by admitting that power always plays a role in human relationships. Our task then is to learn to use power in more constructive and humane ways, while overcoming the temptation to exploit and control others. In his book *Power and Innocence,* psychologist Rollo May offers helpful guidance on this task by distinguishing five forms in which power is exercised.

1. Exploitative power or coercion involves the use of physical force. Most would admit that such an exercise of power over others is necessary in some cases; for example, to keep little children from running into a busy street or to prevent a psychopathic killer from murdering innocent people. The real danger, however, is that we develop a coercive mentality which presumes that force is a legitimate element in all human relationships. The increasing violence in our society gives graphic and frightening witness to the destructive power of the coercive mentality. We all need to examine how we are influenced by the television culture which constantly portrays violence as the way to solve disputes. It is crucial that our society find ways to reduce violent crimes such as child abuse, spouse battering, and gang shootings, but it is also important to uncover and transform the coercive tendencies in our own hearts.

2. Manipulative power uses psychological means to attain power over other persons. Individuals can be on either side of this problem. Some are tempted to control and dominate; others are prone to being manipulated. Those tempted to domination can easily use strengths to control other persons. Consider how wit, intelligence, money, status, beauty and sex can be used to gain power over others. The temptations to use manipulative power are often very subtle. It would be helpful in this regard to train a critical eye on the mass media and the world of advertising to see how they influence our attitudes and behavior.

3. Competitive power involves the confrontation of one power with another of near equal strength. Such power is exercised, for instance, when leaders vie with one another to get a community to adopt their plan of action by employing various strategies such as forming coalitions or arguing against alternative views. This type of process, which may lead to winners and losers, is inherently healthy and helps to produce better results. Consensus is not always possible. Sometimes the use of cognitive power is the best way to separate shoddy arguments and inferior proposals from those which are more solid and adequate. This analysis can be translated to other areas of life. The competition between political parties can lead to better public policies. Athletic competition can bring out the best efforts and finest skills of the opponents.

On the other hand competitive power can easily be misused. Parents can be in a destructive contest for the affection of their children. Co-workers can harm themselves and the company by fighting too aggressively for higher positions. Major college sports can get out of control, and individual competitors can be obsessed with winning. This analysis of competitive power suggests the need for self examination. Some may find that they are too fearful of playing and losing, too timid about taking risks, too afraid to assert themselves. Others may discover the need to win is too great and that they have extended the competitive mode to all their relationships.

4. Nutrient power is exercised for the benefit of others. It involves setting up situations, devising plans, organizing activities and structuring relationships so that other persons are empowered to grow and develop. For example, teachers control the learning process by setting goals and determining the methodology so that their students can become self-motivated learners. Those exercising nutrient power must make sure they are really enabling others to move toward greater personal responsibility and not directly or indirectly fostering a sense of dependency.

5. Finally, Rollo May identifies integrative power which strives to engage the freedom of the other person in a mutual cooperative effort. This creates a situation in which two individuals are working in partnership to accomplish some good. A parent exercises integrative power by gaining the support of the other spouse in responding to a problem presented by their children. Effective leaders use this type of power to gain consensus and to mobilize a common effort. Our society needs to overcome the isolation of special interest groups and to find more cooperative modes of working for the common good. Personally, we need to multiply the situations in which we use power in this healthy life-giving way.

In the Christian tradition, we speak about our God as all-powerful and we read in our Scriptures that Jesus exercised power in healing and casting out the demons. Christians, therefore, cannot consider power as simply negative. On the contrary, we are called to cooperate with the omnipotent Lord by using our God-given power to nourish others and to create healthy communities.

3. Sexual Morality

The Spirit of love prompts sexual expression which is socially responsible, life-serving and joyous.

We human beings face the continuing challenge of achieving a healthy sexual integration so we can relate to others in a constructive and a life-giving way. We are called to live out this moral demand in an age of transition which has questioned many traditional sexual prohibitions. Fundamental societal changes have established a new context for sexual morality. For example, the modern population explosion and the development of effective contraceptive techniques have prompted Christian moralists to rethink the relationship between the personal aspects of sexuality and its function of procreating children. Today young people face more difficult problems than previous generations in dealing with premarital sex because they reach puberty sooner and delay marriage longer. Thus for about a decade they are expected to abstain from sexual intercourse while receiving a great deal of sexual stimuli from the culture as well as confusing signals about the importance of sexual freedom and fulfillment. The societal changes also affect married life. In 1860, married couples who did not get divorced spent an average of 12 years together, most of them in the company of their children. Over a century later similar couples spend 42 years together, about half of that time after their children have left home. This new situation obviously puts different kinds of strains on the marital relationship and highlights the need to cultivate the interpersonal aspect of marriage.

In our age of transition, the mere repetition of moral absolutes from the past does not prove to be very helpful. Many good people struggling to live responsibly in our changing world are looking for wisdom and guidance that goes beyond a summary of moral prohibitions. It is not good enough simply to repeat that all artificial birth control is wrong, that divorce can never be tolerated, and that premarital sex is always a mortal sin. Merely proclaiming absolute moral prohibitions often leads to a clever search for exceptions rather than a genuine engagement with the intent of the moral teaching.

Rejecting legalism does not have to lead to total relativism. The Judeo-Christian tradition has developed a fund of wisdom on sexual morality which can be expressed in terms of values and ideals rather than absolute laws. Back in 1977, Father Anthony Kosnik and other members of the Catholic Theological Society adopted this approach by suggesting that morally good sexual acts should embody seven values conducive to personal growth and healthy relationships (cf. *Human Sexuality*, Paulist Press).

First, sexual activity should be self-liberating which means that it helps individuals achieve personal development and avoid enslaving behavior patterns. This value recognizes a legitimate self-interest in sexual involvement. To think of sex in totally altruistic terms is unrealistic and sets the stage for distorted attitudes and destructive behavior.

Thus, it is personally unhealthy for a woman to submit to the sexual advances of her boyfriend simply because she does not want him to be frustrated.

Second, healthy sexual involvement is other-enriching. It helps the partner to develop greater freedom, maturity and integration. It encourages other persons to grow in self-confidence and self-esteem. Expressed negatively, sex should not be used to control or manipulate the other person. Violence and abuse of all types are obviously ruled out, as are sexual conquests. More subtly, it is wrong to gain sexual favors by exploiting the other person's weaknesses or shadow side, for instance, poor self-esteem or masochistic tendencies. Sex should not enhance passive-dependent tendencies nor intensify feelings of superiority.

Third, sexual activity should be honest, expressing openly and truthfully the depth and commitment of the relationship. Sex is a language, a mode of bodily expression which should communicate as accurately as possible the genuine love shared by a couple. This value suggests that casual sex is wrong because the act of intercourse in itself speaks of total giving and complete commitment. Honesty guides a couple to engage in gradually greater physical expression as their love for one another grows. The Christian tradition teaches that intercourse makes sense only after a couple has achieved the kind of total commitment associated with marriage. This value reminds us of the symbolic character of sex and prompts serious questioning about the deeper meaning of all sexual activity.

Fourth, sexual involvement should be faithful, demonstrating a consistent pattern of interest and concern for the other person. This value obviously excludes adultery and promiscuity in both heterosexual and homosexual relationships. It underscores the folly of one-night stands which leave a person waiting for a follow-up phone call which never comes. The value of faithfulness also reminds married couples of the importance of surrounding sexual activity with a consistent pattern of mutual care and expressions of endearment. The proper language of sexual love is fidelity forever.

Fifth, sex must be socially responsible. Couples are not isolated entities but are unavoidably situated in larger communities. They relate to families of origin, parishes, neighborhoods, nations and finally the whole human family. It is socially irresponsible for couples to bring children into the world that they cannot properly raise. As the AIDS epidemic has painfully taught us, irresponsible sexual behavior is not a purely personal affair, but has grave social consequences. From the Christian perspective, the proper response is not simply safe sex based on preventive techniques, but responsible sex rooted in virtue. This value also broadens the thinking of unmarried couples making decisions about sexual involvement. They should not, for instance, simply ignore the wishes and advice of their parents in deciding about living together before marriage.

Sixth, sex should be life-serving. For married couples this may mean responsibly bringing children into the world and nurturing them with genuine love. The challenge for single persons is to channel their root capacity for love and their desire for intimacy into healthy relationships and constructive service to the community. This value excludes sexual activities which are deadening and isolating. Persons dealing with a habit of masturbation should examine whether it is symptomatic of self-preoccupation or is inhibiting their ability to relate to others.

Finally, sexual activity should be joyous. Sex is a gift from God and thus possesses an essential goodness. According to biblical anthropology, we are not an accidental combination of body and soul but inspirited bodies or enfleshed spirits. As integral persons, healthy sexual activity should involve the whole person, bringing spiritual and bodily delight. Guilt gets in the way of joyous sex and it is important to distinguish appropriate from neurotic guilt. Our culture celebrates sexual performance, symbolized by the quest for simultaneous orgasm. The joy of sex emanates not from performance but from an honest and loving abandonment to union with the partner. Joy is a byproduct of a committed, faithful relationship which allows intimacy to flow spontaneously and naturally.

These seven values provide a useful framework for evaluating the morality of sexual behavior. They have application to married and unmarried individuals as well as heterosexual and homosexual persons. Sexual conduct which is self-destructive, manipulative, dishonest, inconsistent, promiscuous, irresponsible or repugnant creates serious obstacles to achieving the moral ideal of personal growth and loving union. We all have a serious obligation to avoid these destructive actions.

Drawing on recent studies in moral theology, I find it helpful to place this discussion of values in the larger context of the virtues which shape our life story. Virtues give us the assured capacity to draw on practical wisdom and to engage in responsible behavior in various circumstances. They are crucial to dealing with the mysterious strength of the sexual drive as well as the rapidly shifting cultural scene. Virtues acquired over a long period of time create a second nature which enables us to trust our intuitions and to act with pleasure and ease. A virtue-centered approach to sexuality reminds us of the importance of a solid formation in ethical habits through participation in the life and vision of a moral community. Persons who cultivate Christian virtues prepare themselves to act in accord with traditional values even when strongly tempted to violate their sexual ideals.

We can explore the efficacy of this approach by applying the traditional cardinal virtues of fortitude, temperance, justice and prudence to contemporary sexual concerns. We need to learn fortitude from an early age as a bulwark against anti-Gospel values in the culture. This kind of courage enables persons to resist the playboy philosophy which reduces sexuality to pleasure seeking and claims that the only moral norm is mutual consent by adults. Fortitude strengthens persons who do not really want to be sexually active to say no when facing great pressures to violate their ideals. It encourages us to fight against destructive cultural tendencies such as sexism, homophobia, and sexual stereotyping.

The virtue of temperance enables individuals to enjoy sexual pleasure in a free and spontaneous manner without worrying about performance. Temperance teaches us that immersion in the moment and genuine concern for others is what makes joyful pleasures possible. Acquiring this virtue prompts a variety of positive behaviors. Married couples talk freely about what brings them pleasure in their lovemaking. Persons learn to place their sexual drive in the larger context of being able to enjoy a great variety of bodily pleasures. A married man with sadistic tendencies overcomes them by treating his wife with respect and pleasing her in many ways.

The virtue of justice is rooted in the conviction that we are all equal subjects before God and participants in the common journey of life. This suggests that we have responsibility to care for one another and to work for the common good. If we acquire the general habit of respecting persons as individuals, it is less likely that we will exploit them as sexual objects. A sense of justice attunes us to the destructive consequences of sexual activity which is dominating, manipulative, and abusive, as well as the potential harm flowing from promiscuous or casual sex. Persons who have developed the virtue of justice have added motivation to avoid the spread of sexually transmitted diseases. They are also more inclined to speak out against the evils resulting from sexism and homophobia.

Prudence is the regulator and guide for all the other virtues. It provides practical wisdom to guide us in relating to ourselves and others. This habit, acquired gradually through experience, encourages persons to gain a deeper understanding of their own sexual drive and how to channel it constructively. Prudent persons are aware of new sexual attractions and any dangers they entail. They are self-critical and able to see through the rationalizations which can so easily distort sexual attitudes and activities. Prudence prompts a variety of constructive behaviors. An engaged couple talk regularly about how they are going to maintain their ideal of saving intercourse for marriage. A married woman monitors her sexual fantasies to reach a better understanding of her needs, desires and attractions. A married man, aware of his growing sexual interest, decides to treat an attractive female co-worker with extra restraint.

The moral virtues are held together by charity which combines love of God, self and neighbor. Charity gives a distinctively Christian slant to the whole discussion of sexuality. It directs us to the life and teachings of Jesus Christ for guidance. Charity prompts generous self-giving, proper care for self and openness to the gift of the Spirit. Sex achieves its full meaning and purpose only in a context of love. Physical expressions should match the degree of loving commitment which has been achieved. Intercourse is a symbol of a faithful, committed love which is struggling for authentic communication in a variety of ways. The virtue of charity gives deeper meaning to all the values and virtues which guide sexual conduct. Jesus Christ exemplifies for us the kind of love which cares for the well-being of the beloved and finds personal enrichment in the process. The great God calls us to be honest and faithful lovers. The Spirit of love prompts sexual expression which is socially responsible, life-serving and joyous. By cultivating the virtues of fortitude, temperance, justice and prudence, we prepare ourselves to become better lovers. These virtues help clear away obstacles so that we can enter into truly loving relationships. Sexuality rooted in Christian love can achieve its goal of personal growth through intimate union. In this process we come to know the love of God revealed in Jesus Christ.

4. Advice to an Engaged Couple

I pray that the dreams and ideals you feel so deeply now will continue to guide and motivate you both throughout your married life.

Dear Mary,

I want to thank you and Scott for the invitation to your wedding, but, as you surmised, I will not be able to get away and join you that day. Since presence is not simply a function of physical proximity, I will be with you in prayer and spirit as you joyfully celebrate your love for one another and take the awesome step of publicly pledging lifelong fidelity.

Your invitation to offer some advice for enriching your marriage is most welcome and provides an opportunity to reflect on what I have learned about that topic over many years of talking to couples before marriage and helping them handle their problems afterwards. Since I have never been married, my insights lack the experiential basis of one who knows the struggle to make a marriage work from the inside; on the other hand, many hours spent counseling troubled couples gives me a perspective which you may find valuable.

One of the most striking facts to me is the great contrast between the optimistic idealism which couples bring to marriage and the tempered realism that sets in so quickly. A familiar scene comes to mind. A young couple comes to my office announcing they want to get married. They sit there holding hands, obviously enjoying each other's presence. When I interrupt their reverie with a question about what they think the biggest problem in their marriage will be, they are hard pressed to give an answer and speak instead about how they seldom fight and how well they communicate. If I detect a potential problem and bring it to their attention, they are extremely reluctant to consider the matter. If I suggest that they might want to give the relationship a longer time to prove itself before getting married, they tell me of their great desire to be together and that waiting would just be too painful.

Now, I picture this same couple a few years later. Their marriage is in trouble and they are back in my office seeking advice. They do not hold hands and seem uncomfortable in each other's presence. They tend to address their remarks to me instead of their partner. It is a struggle for them to maintain a civil tone with one another. They speak of numerous unresolved conflicts. She says she is tired of giving more than she receives. He has been deeply hurt and strikes back with harsh words. They are in my office because they cannot even talk about some of their problems. Without help their next step will be the divorce court.

When I ask about what went wrong, they both agree that marriage magnified their problems. He says he saw those distressing faults in her before, but thought she would change after marriage. She says she sort of knew about his abrasive personality traits, but chose to ignore them during the engagement period.

Mary, it is this composite scene which prompts my advice to you and Scott. It pleases me and bodes well for your marriage that you are seeking guidance. This suggests to me that you have seen through the cultural myth that marriages are made in heaven, that they work automatically as long as you are in love, and that they provide an assured path to security and happiness. The reality is that happy marriages are difficult to achieve and require systematic and intelligent effort. The very intimacy of marriage creates the problem: closeness involves abrasiveness, openness reveals weaknesses, receptivity creates vulnerability, and expectations bring disappointments. The truth is that marriage is among the harder human relationships to make work, as the divorce statistics clearly indicate. Simply realizing this fact is a healthy starting point and something you have going for you.

Mary, I really do not want to dampen your idealism. To me, the dreams you have for a happy marriage are both beautiful and revealing. Your love allows you to see goodness in Scott that others may miss. The romantic sentiments you share give spice to life and allow your spirits to soar. They help you to perceive something of the way that the gracious Mystery cares for all of us. Your admirable idealism reveals the marvelous possibilities of human existence: the satisfaction inherent in generous giving, the growth made possible by wholehearted commitment, the fulfillment found in sharing love, the joy that comes from being in tune with the God who is the source of all love. In other words, because you are in love you have gained insight into important secrets of human life. You know firsthand that we are not imprisoned in our selfishness. Love has taught you that persons are essentially mysterious and worthy of respect. Together you are discerning that the human adventure with all of its risks is filled with opportunity.

My intent, as you can see, is not to puncture your romantic dreams, but to put them at the service of a successful marriage. The real task is to keep your idealism alive so that it influences your daily life together. You want your high expectations to keep you from settling for mediocrity. Your intense romantic feelings should light up the inevitable routine and ordinariness that will pervade your life together. Put in another way, your romantic love must grow into a mature love that overcomes the disappointments that marriage unavoidably brings, and remains generous even when not fully reciprocated. Such love prompts forgiveness in the face of real hurts, and sustains the effort over a lifetime together.

Mary, I can hear you saying, "Yes, but how are we going to do this? How do we connect our dreams with daily life? How do we avoid getting in a rut or getting overwhelmed by our problems?" I have, of course, no simple answers to these crucial questions. It is clear, however, that good communication is one of the keys to making a happy marriage. Dialogue is your great tool for managing the inevitable disagreements, confusions and hurts. You need to share your deepest joys, small victories and positive feelings for one another. It is not possible to predict all the problems that might develop in your marriage. But whatever the precise shape of your challenges, there is no substitute for honest conversation in which you search for a deeper understanding than either of you can achieve alone.

In trying to improve your communication skills, I suggest you concentrate on understanding rather than winning an argument or achieving absolute certitude about a particular matter. It is important to strive for empathy, to hear behind the words, to catch the tone of voice, to be aware of presuppositions and to recognize the other's dominant worldview. In other words, you want to crawl behind Scott's eyes in order to see the matter from his point of view. In turn you can encourage him to pass over to your viewpoint so he can sense something of what you feel and think about the topic under discussion. This is, of course, difficult to do, especially if you are feeling threatened or defensive and thus tempted either to withdraw or strike out. The secret seems to be to get your own needs under enough control so that they do not prevent you from entering into reasonable dialogue. This may mean postponing your conversation till a time when you are both receptive and have had time to deal with your initial anger or hurt. I can imagine, for example, a situation in which you are stewing about a problem all day long and want to discuss it as soon as Scott gets home from work. But realizing he is often tense when he first gets home, you wait until after dinner to bring it up when he is more relaxed and receptive.

Effective dialogue demands that you are in touch with your own emotions, to have some sense of their appropriateness, and are able to express these feelings to each other. I suspect Scott is going to have more trouble doing this in an open and honest way, but you both have to work at it. Problems occur when assumptions are unclarified and when needs are unexpressed. It is difficult to respond appropriately when you are only guessing as to why your partner is in a bad mood. Suppressing or hiding negative emotions often backfires. Likewise, it is not healthy to pretend you feel something you don't. Sometimes it helps to have agreed upon signals alerting the other that some deeper feelings are difficult to communicate. You might, for instance, use a set phrase such as "I am really nervous about bringing this up" or "I am in a rotten mood so bear with me."

You both must remember that your communication will never be perfect and you are not marrying the perfect respondent. By combining high idealism with realistic expectations, you will find the wisdom and strength to work at your marriage without getting overly disappointed at the failures. I know that you two pray together regularly, and I encourage you to keep up that practice. It is an effective way to deepen your relationship and to recognize your total dependence on the Mystery that sustains the love you share.

Mary, there are so many other things I would like to say and this bit of advice seems paltry compared to the awesome character of the vows you are going to make. My prayer is that the dreams and ideals you feel so deeply now will continue to guide and motivate you and Scott throughout your married life.

5. Weddings: Celebrating Dreams

"If you have hope, this will make you cheerful" validates the dream of lovers that a life of mutual commitment and firm trust in God will bring a deep and abiding sense of joy and satisfaction.

Everything about the ceremony contributed to the dreamlike character of the event – the colorful stained glass window depicting the Assumption of Mary, the attractive royal blue dresses of the attendants, the familiar wedding songs and hymns. The bride and groom, well-disposed after a year of careful planning, brought an especially lofty idealism to the occasion as well as optimistic hopes for a happy married life together. My familiar role as celebrant of the wedding Mass took on added significance since the groom was my oldest nephew. On this occasion I felt especially proud of David, a good and sensitive young man, who has always evoked a special fondness in my heart. Hours of conversation with him and his devoted fiancee, Michele, gave me a good sense of the dream they shared. They seemed to appreciate the awesome character of making vows of lifelong fidelity before God and of placing their happiness in the hands of another human being.

David and Michele carefully chose the Scripture readings for the wedding Mass and, at my request, wrote insightful comments on the significance these texts had for them. In my homily, I used this material to articulate their distinctive vision of married life, confident that it would have a more universal message for those attending the wedding. I began by recalling occasions when my nephew and his two younger brothers visited me for a couple of days. At those times we had only two rules: they could do whatever they wanted, and they could not tell their mother. Presumably this quasi rite of passage did not do irreparable harm to his character.

My comments on the second reading, Romans 12:1-18, related Paul's powerful statements on the ideals of the Christian life to the dreams of the bride and groom. "Do not let your love be a pretense" suggests a vision of married life based on genuine caring. "Do not model yourselves on the behavior of the world" indicates that the real pattern for Christian marriage is not found in the individualism and consumerism fostered by our culture, but in the generous sacrifical love exemplified by Jesus Christ. "Have a profound respect for each other" forms the basis for a true partnership in which both spouses overcome their desires to control or to produce a clone and concentrate instead on encouraging the beloved to develop as a unique individual. "Treat everyone with equal kindness" and "live at peace with everyone" encourages married couples to allow the love they share to flow over into service to the world and care for the less fortunate. "If you have hope, this will make you cheerful" validates the dream of lovers that a life of mutual commitment and firm trust in God will bring a deep and abiding sense of joy and satisfaction. The couple told me they wanted to place this passage from Romans on the wall of their apartment. I hoped they would write it upon their hearts as well, since it contains not only high ideals, but also practical wisdom for married life.

At weddings I often have the urge to call on married couples in the congregation to stand up and give honest expression to the trials, crosses, difficulties, temptations and failures they have experienced in their lives together. Resisting this urge, I tried to summarize some of the common problems I have heard expressed over many years of marriage counselling. He won't share his feelings with me. She does not respect me or the work that I do. My spouse is always around and I have no space for myself. We fight over how to spend the money. We seem to have fallen out of love. It is hard to keep showing the little signs of endearment which used to flow so easily. The infidelities and lies have destroyed my trust. I get tired of dealing with my partner's main faults. We are so busy we don't have time for one another. Our sex life moves between routine and nonexistent. We have trouble meshing two careers. Our disagreements on how to raise children are a continuing source of tension.

These familiar comments remind us that marriage is an extremely difficult relationship to make work. Furthermore, the problems built into the marital relationship are intensified by trends in contemporary culture such as frequent divorce, dual careers, busy lifefstyles, stressful jobs, unreal expectations and the prevalence of drugs. The beautiful dream shared by David and Michele will inevitably encounter the harsh realities of life. Their idealism will be assailed by the same kind of dark forces which attack all modern marriages. The marriage vows demand a resolute effort to avoid cynicism and indifference. The challenge is to face the problems and to mobilize love and intelligence in search of workable solutions. The eyes of faith discern hidden resources in this struggle. In John's Gospel (15:12-16) Jesus says he calls us not servants but friends because he has revealed to us the wisdom learned from the Father. He has given us the command to love one another as he has loved us. He has commissioned us to go forth and to produce fruits which have an enduring significance. Christ walks the path with married couples, sustaining and enriching their love. It is the power of his Spirit which provides daily energy and surprising resources for avoiding cynicism and keeping the marital dream alive. I expressed the hope that my nephew and his bride would use the inevitable clash between their ideals and reality as a means of deepening their love.

Over the years I have learned to appreciate the remarkable power of weddings to evoke memories from the past and to stimulate the imaginative process. Based on this insight, I invited the married couples present to activate their imaginations by remembering their own wedding day and recalling the visions, hopes and ideals which brightened that moment. I suggested that today's beautiful wedding could be a catalyst for reactivating their own dream and for making a new effort to embody it in their daily lives. No matter what their age or how long they have been married, couples could use the occasion to renew their commitments to live in mutual and lasting fidelity. Guided by their original vision, they could work together to improve their communication and to heal the wounds inflicted on each other. Recalling their better encounters, they could search together for ways to bring back some of the zest and chemistry to the relationship. Spouses could try again to get rid of a fault or vice which hurts their partner. They could initiate dialogue on some of the continuing areas of disagreement and conflict. Couples could resolve that they will not settle for mediocrity in their marriage. Remembering the religious character of their wedding, they could make a more vigorous effort to grow together spiritually and to make Christ a more intimate part of common journey. Stirred once again by their wedding dreams, every couple present could find ways to enrich their relationship and deepen their love.

Experience tells me that many married couples do think seriously at weddings and some do seize the moment by following up with constructive actions. Comments after my nephew's wedding solidified this conviction: "My wife poked me in the ribs when you talked about recapturing the chemistry." "The whole ceremony provoked some genuine soul-searching on my part." "You got us thinking." "I got teary and then realized I was reliving my own wedding." "You get so busy that you forget about the dreams you had in those first years." "We talked after the ceremony and decided to work on improving our communication." "Thanks for speaking to us as well as to the bride and groom." "I am glad you brought in the realism – it has been a struggle for us." "My husband said he feels like renewing our vows." "We never have prayed together much; maybe we should do more of that; it might help."

I concluded my homily by thanking my nephew and his bride for arranging such a beautiful and meaningful ceremony that challenged all of us to reflect more deeply on our own relationships. In turn, I asked the congregation to pray that the Lord will grant David and Michele the wisdom and courage to maintain their idealism and to live out their dream.

6. Becoming Better Lovers: Advice from Scott Peck

Love is rooted in self-discipline and demands constant effort and prudent risk-taking in order to achieve mutual growth.

I remember when I first encountered Bob and Terry. They wanted me to officiate at their wedding and so we began a serious conversation about the strengths and weaknesses of their relationship. They spoke easily and intensely about the positive aspects. They could talk about anything; it was exciting to explore each other's thoughts and feelings. Being together and sharing activities were a lot of fun. During those times they felt so close and yet so free it was hard to describe. Each one found a great deal of satisfaction in doing tiny favors for the other. Bob, for instance, felt great when he took her to a new restaurant and could tell by her face that she really liked it. It was very easy for Terry to pay him honest compliments and she did so frequently. Yes, they were sexually involved, but it felt so right for them. Intercourse expressed the deepest feelings they had for one another and brought them closer together.

They were less articulate about weaknesses and potential problems in their relationship. They almost never argued, and when they did the joy of making up overshadowed the painful side of the quarrel. No, they didn't talk very much about religion, nor did they pray together. And religion wouldn't be a problem because, after all, they were both Catholics. There wasn't anything particular about their prospective spouse which irritated them and if there were any minor difficulties they could be straightened out as they went along. Fidelity would not be a problem; she was not even interested in dating anyone else and he seldom noticed other women any more. They concluded by assuring me that they were in love and could handle any potential difficulties.

I responded by offering my usual reminder of how hard it is to make marriages work and by spelling out for them my own perceptions of what usually goes wrong. They went on to complete the marriage preparation course and we celebrated a beautiful and inspiring wedding ceremony.

Three years later they were back in my office. It was all so strikingly different. They did not hold hands as they had before. Their language was hardly civil, let alone endearing. Honest communication about their problems had come to a halt. Bob was tired of doing all those nice things for her; she never appreciated them anyway. Terry did not feel like complimenting him anymore; he thought he was so self-sufficient and didn't need anyone. It had been months since they had intercourse. He usually was not interested and she hated it because it seemed so mechanical. He said he was not interested in anyone else, while she admitted that there was a guy she liked to talk to because he at least listened to her. After going downhill for almost a year they were not sure they even loved one another anymore and were thinking seriously about divorce.

This distressing story, which the couple is willing to share for the benefit of others, is repeated in varying forms all too frequently in our postmodern world. In trying to understand this common phenomenon, I find enlightenment in the immensly popular book by M. Scott Peck, *The Road Less Travelled* (Simon and Schuster 1978). Drawing on his experience as a practicing psychiatrist, Peck makes a sharp distinction between falling in love and genuine human love which he defines as "the will to extend one's self for the purpose of nurturing one's own or another's spiritual growth." Falling in love, in contrast to true love, is not an act of will nor a deliberate choice, but rather a spontaneous response to another person who is perceived as sexually desirable. This romantic response is effortless and produces a sense that one has finally discovered the key to happiness. The heart soars and the world looks brighter because one has found that special person who will satisfy all desires and needs. This experience, however, does not guarantee the kind of fruits which accompany genuine love, such as the expansion of personal horizons, reduced selfishness, and mutual growth. On the contrary, romantic lovers sometimes feel that they have reached the peak of personal fulfillment and have no need to pursue the path of spiritual growth. Their relationship may become dependent and closed, thus effectively precluding the opportunities for personal development provided by other persons and situations. Falling in love can also retard mutual growth by creating the illusion of permanency. The couple in love simply assumes that the positive feelings of attraction and liberation which are so intense now will automatically continue. Our culture fosters this illusion through popular stories of lovers who marry and live happily ever after. This assumption prevents people from preparing for the time when their romantic feelings fade. Unprepared for this terrible disappointment, couples like Bob and Terry often drift toward divorce without ever appreciating the positive potential for growth which accompanies the changing character of their relationship.

As a psychiatrist, Peck offers a psychological explanation of these changes. When individuals fall in love, their ego boundaries or perceptions of psychological limits collapse as they merge their identities. By pouring themselves into one another, they overcome loneliness and experience an ecstatic sense of unity. Reality, however, soon attacks these illusions of total unity. Daily experience reveals that one's partner still possesses a unique personality with distinct desires, interests, thoughts, feelings and goals. Spouses have their own concerns which absorb their attention and prevent them from being totally present to one another. When couples recognize the inevitable limitations of their relationship, they reconstruct their ego boundaries and accept again the need for psychological constraint. In other words, they fall out of love in a process which is both natural and predictable.

The death of this kind of romantic love is not only a tremendous disappointment, but also a marvelous opportunity to grow in genuine love. To appreciate this point, it is helpful to analyze the nature of love in the context of Christian faith. While Peck defines love in terms of will and decision, it seems better to me to describe it as a total-person response which has emotional and intellectual dimensions as well as the admittedly important volitional ones. Ideally, love prompts an individual who has achieved a sufficient degree of self-possession to reach out freely to another person. In this way, we are able to establish mutually enriching relationships which enable us to do good for the other and, at the same time, actualize our potential by breaking the bonds of selfishness. Our intelligence should guide this free decision to risk our autonomy for the other and we should be receptive to the new knowledge which only love can bring. Our desires and hopes initiate and sustain the loving relationships which bring us joy and a sense of liberation. Genuine love does not rule out romantic feelings, but places them in a larger context of mutual care. The delights of love as well as its disappointments throw us back on the gracious Mystery which sustains and allures us. Because God has first loved us, we can take the risk to love others and make the effort to become better lovers. Belief in a God of love gives us confidence that our love is always worthwhile and ultimately full of meaning. For Christians, this belief becomes concrete in the life of Jesus of Nazareth, whose unsurpassed love of God and human beings brought him to his obedient death and victorious resurrection. Jesus Christ remains our model of love generously given and fully rewarded.

With this theological framework in mind, we can return again to the psychological insights of Scott Peck. For him, true love involves work and demands constant effort to overcome our inherent laziness. Mature lovers freely decide to overcome both inertia and the natural tendency to take the easy way out by generously extending themselves for the purpose of spiritual growth. They modify their own needs so that they can attend to the needs of others. Since exercising such attention is so difficult, it requires a conscious decision, constantly renewed, to move beyond laziness and selfishness. Being a good listener is the most common way of attending to others and Peck offers helpful advice on developing this important skill. We should, for example, learn the "discipline of bracketing," which means temporarily setting aside our own views, assumptions and categories in order to enter as fully as possible into the world of our dialogue partner. If we act in this loving way, we not only help to liberate others but experience an expansion of our own horizons.

Love which is fully human requires courage as well as work. In genuine acts of love, we bravely extend ourselves for mutual growth despite the normal fears which such risks generate. True self-love prompts us to choose the path of personal growth despite the frightening possibility of having to make substantial changes in our behavior. Marital love demands a lifelong commitment, despite the fear of losing autonomy and being submerged by the other. Authentic love moves us to risk painful confrontations with friends and family members when it seems wise or necessary to offer advice or make suggestions for their spiritual welfare. Successful confrontations require humility which recognizes our own limitations and prudence which discerns the best method of truly helping the other person.

For Scott Peck, love is rooted in self-discipline and demands constant effort and prudent risk-taking in order to achieve mutual growth. Drawing on his experience as a therapist, he has articulated traditional religious notions of love in new and attractive psychological categories. His realistic portrayal of love is a much needed corrective to the romantic and sentimental notions which prevail in our culture. When placed in a comprehensive theological framework, his insights provide the kind of solid advice which couples like Bob and Terry need in order to understand their problems and move to a more mature stage of love.

7. Healing Broken Hearts

My prayer is that in the midst of your disappointments and frustrations, you will find comfort and guidance from your faith in God who will never abandon us.

Dear Theresa,

I have just read your letter describing your breakup with Larry. It touched me deeply. I know from your previous letters how much in love you were and how you had committed yourself completely to him. I still recall your comment that being with him gave you "a high and an exhilaration beyond words." At the time it seemed to me that a wedding was coming up soon. And now this crushing news. I noted the finality in your comments about the breakup and I agree that any talk of patching it up is really out of place. On the other hand, your description of your psychological state does call for comment. The resentment toward Larry is surely understandable and I'm glad you expressed it in such strong and graphic terms. I think that time and perspective are going to be important healing factors in this area. The anger you feel toward yourself, however, has to be examined more closely. Your statement that you "felt like a fool because you gave your love to someone who really didn't treasure it" is typical of what so many rejected lovers have felt. I know you feel it intensely and it is indeed a very understandable response. Nevertheless, I believe that you must eventually rethink your emotional reaction because it seems to me that it is finally inappropriate. First of all, to say Larry simply toyed with your feelings misses part of the reality. My sense is that he had some genuine care for you which helped trigger your positive response, but he did not attain the depth of commitment or intensity of love which you did. Surely it is painful enough to be more committed and more in love than your partner. My guess is that he also found this disparity troubling and uncomfortable. But I think it is both wrong and harmful to see him as a manipulator who had no feelings for you.

The second and more important point is that loving another person deeply is a good and beautiful achievement which is valuable in itself. You have great potential as a lover and that lies close to the center of what makes us human. Sometimes our love is not reciprocated, but that does not necessarily make it foolish. Great saints have described God as almost foolish in His love for us as He constantly pursues us despite our sinful refusal to love in return. Like the best of mothers, God embraces us with tender care which strikes us as mad and improbable in its generosity. Perhaps you could allow your own sense of foolishness to be embraced and healed by the compassionate God. This faith perspective could help you transform the self-hatred and loathing you feel into more positive feelings about yourself and your great power to love another person. It is indeed better to reach out to another in love, risky though it is, than to remain locked up in oneself, shielded from the hurt of possible rejection. To me, your love seems beautiful and noble, not foolish.

You have asked me to help you to get perspective on this whole experience. I do not believe your statement that you know nothing about love and relationships is really true, but I know it all seems very confusing in the midst of your pain. Let us start with your question about why people fall in love when it can lead to such frustration. This question takes us to the core of human existence. On such profound matters there are no simple answers, but wrestling a bit with the question may be helpful. Even though we humans are "the question for whom there is no answer" as Karl Rahner often insisted, we are not absolved from the task of making sense out of our experiences, even the very painful ones.

You have often heard me talk about our search for the perfect lover. We do indeed passionately long for a respondent who will know our heart, resonate with our moods, support us in the difficult times and rejoice with us in the good moments. Our hearts cry out for a companion who will help us achieve both intimacy and success. And when an individual encounters a potential partner who begins to satisfy some of these deepest needs, the stage is set for falling in love. This experience of interpersonal union seems so unique that the lover may imagine no one else has ever experienced such a marvelous transformation. Persons preparing for marriage who believe they have found the perfect lover weave a great web of expectations out of the finest aspirations of the human heart.

The deep sadness of the human adventure is that such lofty dreams always remain unfulfilled. Even the ideal lover eventually disappoints, often in minor ways, but sometimes with shattering force, as in your case. The degree differs, but the web of romantic expectations is always sundered by the reality of personal limitations and daily demands. The whole story includes both liberation and restriction, exhilaration and routine, high expectations and frustrated dreams. The drive for the perfect lover propels us out of ourselves and provides us with some of our most significant experiences, but it also can bring the deepest frustrations and disappointments. Theresa, learning to manage this inevitable tension is clearly one of the great tasks of life, and that burden rests heavily on your shoulders now.

I found some other ideas on your question in an insightful and poetic theological book by Sebastian Moore entitled *The Fire and the Rose Are One.* Moore develops the thesis that the central human need is "to be myself for another." He argues that our great desire is to have self-worth, to feel significant, to be someone, and that guilt, or the deep sense of isolation and unworthiness which results from failing other persons, is the great barrier to achieving this sense of personal value. Only a positive relationship with another human being can break us out of this guilt-ridden frustration. In other words, we need other persons to accept our love, to reciprocate our feelings for them, to desire us as we desire them. We know we are significant because a friend or a lover values us. Falling in love means that barriers come down, that the blockage to receptivity is reduced, that the reluctance to give melts away as the heart softens. The exhilarating sense of liberation comes when the spirit is released from the bondage of self-centeredness in a genuine act of love which affirms the essential worth of the beloved. When this kind of love is reciprocated, lovers find their self-doubts transformed into a more confident love of self. We know we are valuable persons when we are able to give and receive love. Of course, these treasured peak experiences also set up the possibility of desolate pit experiences. We seldom feel so insignificant as when our friendship is rejected, so alone as when our love is spurned, and so worthless as when we are treated like non-persons.

Theresa, this whole analysis of the relation between love and our sense of self-worth seems to speak to your situation. You have known the heights that come from genuinely giving yourself to Larry; it is very understandable that you feel so confused and unsure of yourself now that you are struggling to climb out of the dark pit. I know that it is from such darkness that your heart cries out, "Why fall in love when it brings such frustration?" You realize, of course, that simple and compelling answers escape us here. We can say that it is

built into the human predicament. The combination of infinite longings and finite capabilities which constitute our very
being inevitably brings frustration. Experience suggests that
managing hurts and suffering can build a stronger character
and more flexible personality. Christianity teaches us that carrying the cross of disappointment is to walk in the footsteps
of the Master who gives us a more abundant life. When you
push the question further, however, it recedes into the inexhaustible mystery of the divine-human relationship. We are
thrown back on the faith conviction that the process of life
can be trusted and our restless and disappointed hearts will
one day find ultimate satisfaction in union with the gracious
God. Our model is Christ who knew the desolation of love
betrayed, and yet found the emptiness ultimately filled by
one whom he trusted and called Abba.

Once we accept the mystery surrounding the question of
why, we are in a position to deal with the question of how:
how to cope, how to pick up the pieces, how to restore a
sense of self-confidence, how to cooperate with a God who
calls us to be better lovers. Theresa, I want to be present to
you as your healing process continues. I am hoping you find
ways to transform your pain and anguish into more positive
feelings about yourself and your capacity to love. My prayer
is that in the midst of your disappointments and frustrations,
you will find comfort and guidance from your faith in God
who will never abandon us.

8. Improving Family Life

*Our common task is to embody our optimistic dreams in
the realities of everyday family life.*

It is a sad tale. Emily, a popular collegian, hates to go
home during the school breaks. Most of her problems stem
from the depressing relationship she has with her father. She
longs to hear an encouraging or complimentary word from
him, but all he ever does is yell: "I pay good money to send
you to college and all you do is goof off. Why can't you get
As like your brother did?" The harsh comment is especially

cutting because the young woman is a hard working student who happens to have only moderate academic talent. In her whole life her father has never praised her. Sometimes he just completely ignores her, and then she has the horrible feeling that she is of no account, not real, unworthy of love. In an odd way she prefers the yelling to being treated as a non-entity. It is unbearably distressing to be a non-person in her own family setting.

We all can empathize with the pain of this young woman. Our own experience suggests that profound frustrations and deep wounds can result from failed family relationships. All the books and articles about dysfunctional families have expanded our awareness of the depth and extent of the problems created by destructive dynamics within the family setting. The postmodern world has been hard on family life. Those of us who spend a good deal of time listening to people's problems know how often they are rooted in unhealthy familial relationships. But we all know the disappointments of family life from the inside. Marital relationships are seldom as easy or satisfying as couples anticipate on their wedding days. Many children do not attain the kind of success envisioned for them by parents. Offspring have to deal with the inadequacies and limitations of their parents. Sibling rivalries can be ugly and destructive. Communication within families often gets distorted; misunderstandings cannot be totally avoided.

Our pain and distress over failed or disappointing family relationships is sharpened by our intense longing for a happy family life. We seem to have a desperate need for the warmth and comfort associated with a peaceful home life. Our collective dreams and fantasies include hopeful images of family activities: stimulating conversations around the dinner table, peaceful holidays at home, enjoyable picnics at a park, and harmonious liturgies at church. These images represent our desire for a setting where we can be ourselves, find acceptance, experience love and know intimacy. It is interesting to note the great emotion that home Masses often evoke. Perhaps on these occasions people sense a partial fulfillment of these deep longings for an open, comforting, supportive family life. Even people who say they no longer care about failed family relationships often maintain a powerful, if masked, desire for a successful reconciliation with alienated relatives. The drive for a nourishing and peaceful family community continues to be operative, even in the midst of failure.

Given the great gap between ideals and reality in family living, we might anticipate a certain cynicism about the whole project. Contemplating all the tarnished dreams, broken relationships, resentful children and wounded individuals could easily lead to despair over the possibilities of a happy family life and to a search for alternative communities. There are young people who vow they will never marry because their home life was so miserable. Some divorced people say "never again." Some married couples decide the task of raising children is too daunting. A few radicals claim the family is an essentially enslaving institution and must be abolished. Popular articles tell us things are getting worse and that we can expect the demise of the family.

The more remarkable phenomenon, however, is the prevailing optimism about family life, even in the midst of so much pessimism about other societal institutions. Almost all the young couples that I help prepare for marriage are convinced they can make a success of it. This is true even of those with unhappy experiences growing up. The percentage of divorced people who get remarried is higher than that of eligible singles in the same age bracket. Despite the talk of alternate approaches to child rearing, 98% of all children in the United States are raised in a family setting. Many people report that their most satisfying experiences are with their families. When tragedy strikes, members of the family often huddle together, expecting comfort and support from one another. In short, the dream of a fulfilling family life seems to be more powerful than all the reality of failure.

Our common task is to embody this optimistic dream in the realities of everyday family life. Such an effort will include proper preparation for marriage, adequate marriage counseling, and available support systems for troubled families. It is important to integrate religion into family life and to educate children for responsibility and freedom. The church has a crucial role to play in sustaining and enhancing family life. In their 1993 pastoral message *Follow the Way of Love*, the American bishops encourage families to reflect on what kind of support they need from the church and how they are cooperating with God's grace to make family life work. As the bishops' document suggests, we need a balanced vision of both the possibilities and the limitations of family life. We must celebrate the deep joys of loving family relationships and the genuine satisfactions in meeting family responsibilities. Those of us who have received the free gift of a loving and nourishing family life can perform a great service by sharing the fruits of this experience with others.

But given the utopian dreams surrounding family life, it is important to emphasize the limitations and challenges encountered by contemporary families. First of all, on a societal level, it is unrealistic to expect a massive return to the traditional family life of the past in which the father works, the mother cares for the home, and children are raised in a stable atmosphere. Today more than 54% of married women with school age children work outside the home, compared with 26% in 1948. The rate of divorce is up 700% since the turn of the century, and today four out of every ten children spend part of their childhood in a one-parent family. Around one million mothers each year begin to raise their firstborn children by themselves. Scholarly books have appeared in the 1990s which emphasize the staying power of the American family and suggest that the changes we are experiencing are not all that bad. Other scholars insist that the American family is getting weaker, primarily because of the breakup of the two-parent home. From a Christian perspective, we must certainly deplore the breakup of families and must work to create more stable marriages. On the other hand, charity and realism dictate that we respond to the new situation in which nontraditional families do exist in great numbers. They need guidance and support to function as effectively as possible.

Secondly, the family cannot satisfy all of the members' needs, and it is destructive to expect this. No spouse is the perfect lover, and superwomen are as rare as supermen. Each partner will have needs and interests which the other cannot satisfy. Children profit from having adults other than their parents as models of human behavior. A family turned in on itself will soon be involved in a stultifying group narcissism. The love shared in a family should become fruitful by spilling over to other people and groups. Families can profit by being an active part of larger communities such as the neighborhood or church. Individual members of the family need healthy relationships outside the family circle. Children obviously need good friendships as a part of the maturation process. Spouses also need friends of both the same and opposite sex to meet their own needs and to call forth their gifts of care and love. The dangers inherent in opposite sex relationships are real, but ruling them out is unrealistic and potentially fustrating. Good outside relationships can be a source of enrichment for the whole family.

Thirdly, it is impossible to avoid strife in family relationships, and it is healthy to begin with this premise. There is an abrasiveness built into day-to-day contact among people who have faults and rough edges. It is often harder to be nice to people with whom we are intimate. We learn the foibles and weak points of the other family members and know how to wound them. Since children do not choose their family of origin, they often run into conflicts as they develop their unique personalities.

Given these factors, it is important to anticipate conflicts and to develop methods to deal with them. Family members need strategies and skills for resolving daily disagreements. It is vital to maintain civility during arguments. Working on better communication during the happy times is good preparation for dealing with more stressful situations. When anger flares, it is crucial to avoid personal attacks and language which wounds the other. Genuine efforts to overcome personal faults are especially valuable because they signal to the rest of the family a willingness to change and a desire for more harmonious relations.

Finally, family life will never be as simple or easy as young lovers imagine. Recent research confirms that clinging to excessive and unrealistic expectations of married life is a major factor in the breakup of marriages. The romantic bias which dominates our culture must be countered by strong doses of realism. Parents can help by talking openly and realistically about some of their own problems and how they try to solve them. We can use more realistic homilies at Mass about family life. Marriage preparation classes taught by couples who honestly present the challenges as well as the joys of married life provide an excellent stimulus for engaged couples to examine realistically their own relationships.

Accepting these and other limitations is not an invitation to passivity. It does make us more reliant on the gracious Mystery which inspires the great dream of a happy family life and energizes us to make it real.

9. Differences Between Men and Women

Men and women can relate on the basis of mutual understanding because they both know the struggle to balance the various tensions built into human existence.

A few years ago, scientists at the Yale Center for Learning and Attention discovered that women use both sides of their brain when doing simple verbal tasks, while men use only the left side. Reports of this and other scientific studies have sparked a renewed debate on male-female differences. At least four different approaches or models are evident in this ongoing discussion.

Some traditionalists continue to defend a patriarchal system based on gender differences. According to this outlook, men are more aggressive, independent, dominant, active, competitive, logical, worldly, adventurous and direct. They are non-emotional, skilled in business and proficient in math and science. These characteristics make men more competent for managing the affairs of the world. On the other hand, women are more affectionate, cheerful, compassionate, gentle, loyal, sympathetic, tender, understanding, warm and yielding. They are eager to sooth hurt feelings, loving toward children and sensitive to the needs of others. In short, women possess traits well designed for the nurturing tasks in the home. Contemporary proponents of this patriarchal model generally insist that men and women are equal but different. The differences dictate, however, that men function as leaders in society and women concentrate on raising children. Nature has decreed that men be defined by their careers and women by motherhood.

The patriarchal model encompasses diverse proponents. Pope John Paul believes it is important to protect women from the distortions of modern culture by celebrating their distinctive nurturing skills and enhancing their roles in the home. Many evangelical Christians support a patriarchal system on the basis of certain biblical texts, such as Ephesians 5 which admonishes wives to be subject to their husbands. Some men insist on traditional gender differences in order to maintain their privileged position in our society. Finally, those who defend family values often insist on the traditional roles of men in the workplace and women in the home.

Many of the criticisms of this patriarchal approach center on the harm done by gender stereotypes which keep men from developing their nurturing capacities and deprive women of leadership roles in society.

A second approach to gender questions, developed in reaction to the perceived abuses of patriarchy, denies the existence of any significant differences between men and women. Proponents of this unisex model are convinced that continued attention to specific male or female traits will perpetuate sexism. They insist that apparent differences are culturally conditioned and can be eradicated by even-handed child rearing methods. Their initial reaction to recent scientific studies on gender differences has been to deny the significance of the research and to insist on justice for women in all aspects of contemporary life. If they had their way, funding for research on biologically based differences would be diverted to understanding and overcoming sexist attitudes and patriachal practices.

Gloria Steinem is representative of the feminists who vociferously reject all talk of gender differences as detrimental to the cause of women. She even rejects the significance of physical strength in doing certain jobs, such as firefighting. Her solution is to change the way these jobs are done, so upper body strength is not a consideration. Some Christian feminists argue that gender dualism is the real original sin, the root cause of much societal evil and personal suffering. But Christ has healed this destructive division so that in him there is neither male nor female. The unisex model also includes some men who reject the privileges of a patriarchal system as well as those fighting for male custody rights on the grounds that men can nurture children just as well as women.

This approach has certainly raised consciousness on the evils of sexism, but its unisex solution flies in the face of common sense and the mounting scientific evidence of gender differences. In the long run the battle against patriarchy cannot be won with a questionable unisex anthropology.

Avoiding the extremes of the patriachal and unisex models, many authors have proposed a complementarity approach to gender questions, which involves two critical assumptions about human existence. One assumption, drawn from the psychological theory of Carl Jung, is that men and women each possess latent opposite sex characteristics which must be developed for full human functioning. In order to achieve full individuation, men must develop their *anima* or feminine pole which includes the ability to nurture and achieve intimacy. Women are called to develop their *animus* or masculine side of their personality which is more aggressive and independent. The other assumption is that men and women are incomplete and come to their fulfillment only through intimate relationships with persons of the opposite sex. The two sexes are different, but complementary. They need each other in order to be complete and to find fulfillment. The great Protestant theologian Karl Barth espoused this position based on the second creation account in Genesis which emphasizes that Adam felt alone and found fulfillment only with the creation of Eve. Elements of this approach often appear today in popular spiritual writing. For instance, men will find liberation by learning from women to face and express their emotions. Women can move toward greater maturity by asserting themselves as men do. Christian marriage offers a secure setting which enables wounded and incomplete spouses to find healing and fulfillment.

The complementarity model has indeed provided helpful guidance and inspiration for many men and women serious about spiritual development. But it has also contributed to gender stereotyping by naming some human traits masculine and some feminine. Furthermore, the model suggests that gays, lesbians and single people are doomed to an incomplete existence because they do not experience the fulfillment of heterosexual marriage.

Finally, the current discussion includes a more integrated approach to gender questions found in various authors, including the Protestant theologian James B. Nelson who makes helpful suggestions in his book *The Intimate Connection* (Westminster 1988). The holistic model assumes that both men and women have the root capacity to achieve personal integration and to relate to one another on the basis of mutual maturity. It begins with the presupposition that every person is a complex mixture of dialectically related energies, for example, a need for intimacy and independence, a drive to succeed and nurture, a capacity to think and feel. The task for each person is to find a fruitful synthesis of these apparently opposed tendencies. For men, the goal is not to get in touch with their feminine side, but to appreciate and enhance their own distinctive ways of feeling, relating and nurturing. Women are not called to manifest masculine traits, but to develop their own distinctive way of thinking, striving and achieving. According to the holistic model, human relationships work best when men and women come to them as whole persons ready to capitalize on their strengths. Marriage is not primarily a remedy for incompleteness or therapy for woundedness; it is a partnership which thrives on the personal maturity and integration of each spouse. Healthy relationships are based not on dominance and submission, but rather on sharing generative power which leads to greater interdependence and personal growth. Men and women can relate on the basis of mutual understanding because they both know the struggle to balance the various tensions built into human existence, such as the drive for independence and for intimacy.

The holistic model does recognize statistical differences between men and women in our culture, for example, that women generally put more emphasis on intimacy and men on independence. But it does not force individual men and women to conform to these statistical norms, nor does it promote gender stereotypes by naming some human traits masculine and others feminine. On the contrary, it celebrates the unique character of each individual's struggle to achieve personal integration. This approach deserves greater attention in the continuing discussion of gender differences.

10. Abortion and Christian Compassion

Christians must insist on the good news that God accepts us as we are.

A young woman is in my office obviously nervous and distressed. Haltingly, the story comes out. She met this guy, thought she loved him, got involved sexually and found herself pregnant. When she told him, he seemed cold and distant and said he would pay for an abortion. She was a Catholic and had often spoken against abortion in discussions with her girlfriends. But after the conversation with her boyfriend, she felt panicky and unsure of herself. Some of the details of what happened next are now blurred in her memory, but she knows she did not seek any advice from parents, counselors, or priests. She was too frightened and embarrassed. Disappointed and angry with her boyfriend, she decided to go ahead on her own and get the abortion. She called an abortion clinic advertized in the campus newspaper and made an appointment. Afraid to go alone, she got her roommate to go with her. Her friend suggested she talk to a priest or someone, but she declined because she just wanted this horrible nightmare to end right away. At the clinic everything seemed so businesslike and routine. The other girls were so young.

Then the deed was done and she was back at school. She seemed to put the whole thing out of her mind. Her girlfriend didn't talk about it and her former boyfriend was nowhere to be seen. Life returned to normal though she was, at times, slightly depressed.

Recently she met a really great guy. It appeared that the relationship might have a future and she was feeling very good about it. Then suddenly, after more than a year, the events surrounding the abortion came flooding back into her consciousness. Thoughts of her brief pregnancy dominated her waking hours while images of the abortion clinic appeared in her dreams. She alternated between feeling horribly guilty and imagining that it was really someone else who went through the whole experience. It was these intense and volatile emotions, so threatening to her current relationship, which brought her to my office.

My encounters with individual women whose stories filter into this composite picture prompt these reflections on proper Christian responses to women who have had an abortion. With an estimated 1.5 million abortions each year in our country, more and more people find themselves interacting with family members, friends, and clients who have had an abortion and feel the need to talk about it.

We need to begin with a sense of compassion which reflects our perception of both the love of a merciful God and the weakness of human nature shared by all. From this perspective, judgmental attitudes and self-righteous indignation are obviously out of the question. We need to respond to these women by listening well, empathizing with their intense emotions, and expressing genuine care. Our responses should reflect the Gospel mandate to be compassionate as our Heavenly Father is compassionate (Luke 6:36). We live in a society which not only permits abortions, but fosters a "do your own thing" morality. The pressures in such a society to escape the responsibility of a pregnancy are obviously intense, but are known in their full power only to women in this situation. By recalling our own weaknesses and listening with empathy, we can strengthen the natural compassion we sometimes feel for those tested in difficult circumstances. A compassionate response helps to create a climate of mutual trust which allows women who have had an abortion to speak more openly about their feelings.

Christianity also insists that we must accept responsibility for our free and blameworthy actions. Repressing genuine guilt feelings often leads to vague anxiety and even to an unconsciously motivated self-loathing. Healing cannot occur when sinful behavior is blocked out of consciousness. Women who have had an abortion must face the reality and admit their proper responsibility. Common experience contradicts the "enlightened" assumption that abortion is a simple procedure with no lingering consequences. Although there are debates among therapists about the extent and nature of the "post-abortion syndrome," there definitely are women who experience delayed fears and depressions after an abortion.

Friends and counselors provide a valuable service for these women by allowing them to tell their story in detail with honesty and emotional intensity. They may need to vent their pent-up anger directed at themselves, at those who failed to support or warn them, or even at God, who put them in this predicament. Opportunities may arise to help them distinguish a healthy sense of responsibility from possible neurotic guilt feelings. In moral matters, outsiders can never make judgments about sinfulness. Even from within our own experience we often find it difficult to discern our culpability. When doubts about responsibility persist, it seems helpful to place the whole matter before the merciful God who knows the secrets of the human heart.

Our Christian faith is good news because it insists that forgiveness is always available no matter what we have done. Thus, acceptance of responsibility should lead to acceptance of forgiveness. At times, however, women anguished over an abortion find it hard to accept God's forgiveness and even more difficult to forgive themselves. They need repeated reminders that God's love is both unconditional and unlimited. Regular meditation on Scripture passages portraying divine mercy can make this message more available and concrete. I recall a woman who was experiencing debilitating guilt feelings long after an abortion. After meditating every day for several months on the Prodigal Son parable in the 15th chapter of Luke's Gospel, she came to see herself as the prodigal daughter, embraced by the loving arms of her Heavenly Father. Her guilt feelings lifted and she returned with renewed energy to her ordinary activities. Regular imaginative recall of experiences of human love, such as a striking instance of acceptance by a friend or loved one, can help construct an emotional base for accepting the divine love always mirrored in human love. Some women have found that going through a systematic grieving process for their lost child prepared their heart for accepting forgiveness. It is helpful to recall the destructive character of continued self-loathing as well as the importance of accepting forgiveness in order to prepare for the new challenges of life. Participating wholeheartedly in a supportive community is a good way of increasing self-acceptance. The Sacrament of Reconciliation is our official way of symbolizing not only our desire for forgiveness, but also our faith in the power and scope of divine mercy. Celebrated at the proper stage in the process of acceptance, the sacrament is a powerful vehicle of grace and a striking reminder that the merciful God is always ready to forgive and to offer a fresh start.

An abortion cannot be forgotten: remorse and sorrow often remain, and the process of healing may take surprising turns. Christians, however, must insist on the good news that God accepts us as we are. Divine acceptance implies forgiveness and invites a more faithful response to the Gospel message.

11. Sexual Harassment and the Clarence Thomas Hearings

The New Testament provides helpful perspectives and powerful motives for avoiding all forms of harassment and establishing healthy relationships between men and women.

Despite its great emphasis on human rights, modernity made only limited progress in overcoming the evils of patriarchy. An effective postmodern spirituality must uncover the root causes of sexist attitudes and promote greater equality and mutuality in relationships between men and women.

The Senate Judiciary Committee hearings on the nomination of Judge Clarence Thomas to be an associate justice of the Supreme Court initiated a new phase in this continuing effort. For 30 hours on the weekend of October 11 through 13, 1992, television provided a mirror for examining our national psyche. Although some were repelled by what they saw and tuned out, many others were absorbed in the intense drama which had such important sexual and racial overtones. In fact, the hearings captured the national attention as no other event since the Watergate affair. Although the proceedings sometimes had the character of a bizarre soap opera, the whole event has prompted some serious reflection on various forms of sexism in our culture. We have been able to face in a more sustained fashion the shadow side of our national psyche. During the hearings, our traditional Puritan preoccupation with sin and guilt played a prominent role. We seemed to need public confession in order to exorcise the demons that inhabit our collective soul. Since then we have had the opportunity to reflect in greater depth on the meaning of the hearings, especially the issue of power.

In our enlightened culture we still have a great deal of difficulty establishing and maintaining healthy relationships between men and women. Traditionally, male-female relationships were tightly regulated by custom and societal constraint. During the relatively brief period of greater freedom, we have not yet developed a common wisdom to guide us. Many of us would readily admit that we do not understand gender differences in much depth. The early feminist strategy to avoid all talk of male-female differences may have had understandable and even laudable goals, but it actually retarded the process of understanding one another. In order to get along better, we need to understand the different ways that men and women function imaginatively, emotionally, intellectually, morally and religiously. We need open dialogue which enables us to discuss gender-based differences in attitudes, perspectives and approaches. In this process, it is crucial to recognize the inequities that currently exist between men and women. We cannot ignore the fact that men in our society are generally more secure economically, better positioned socially and better represented politically.

It is within this patriarchal world that contemporary forms of sexual harassment occur. Unequal power relationships create an environment in which women often experience unwelcome and persistent sexual advances. Some acts of sexual harassment are clearly and blatantly offensive, such as demanding sex as a condition for employment. In other cases, the harassment can be much more subtle. Sometimes men compliment women on their appearance in order to coerce them into conforming to arbitrary standards of beauty or to demean their intelligence. In order to develop a balanced perspective on this issue, we should carefully distinguish harassment from innocent flirting and banter which is mutually acceptable.

The televised hearings offered a rare opportunity to hear the distinctive perspective of women on this question of sexual harassment. Intelligent and articulate women described the shame and self-doubt they experienced after being abused. They explained how fear made them reluctant to report unwelcomed advances. Many of them linked harassment to a power struggle in which men with greater authority and strength tried to dominate and control them. The women generally expressed frustration because men so often ignore or misunderstand the problem. The often repeated phrase "you just don't get it" summarized much of their frustration and anger.

Men responded to the hearings in diverse ways. Some dismissed or played down the claim of widespread sexual harassment. They think women are overreacting to normal interactions and innocent flirting. They find it hard to believe that women feel powerless or are afraid to report serious cases of abuse. Their feeling is that women should not take offense if nothing harmful was intended. Other men responded more constructively. They appreciated learning about women's fears of abuse and the way they often feel powerless when men are in control. They can now see that a casually flirtatious comment can strike women as insensitive, demeaning and coercive. Their good intention is to be more sensitive in their dealings with women. They also are more aware that an unscrupulous woman acting out of spite or frustration could easily ruin their reputation by bringing false charges of harassment.

After the hearings, many people expressed the hope that the testimony of Anita Hill and those who supported her would raise public awareness of the problem of sexual harassment and move us to constructive action. When the full Senate approved the nomination of Judge Thomas, Professor Hill said that the whole unpleasant experience was definitely worthwhile because of its long-range constructive consequences. There is no doubt that in the short run the hearings produced a great deal of conversation on the topic. More women shared their stories of sexual abuse. Some men became more sensitive to the feelings of women. A good number of businesses and agencies established more protective policies.

But it remains to be seen whether we can continue to make progress. Some claim that the harsh treatment of Anita Hill has made women more reluctant to initiate harassment charges against men. Perhaps a few deviant men have become more aggressive, convinced that they can get away with abusive behavior because their victims will not be able to prove it. Despite all the testimony given at the Judiciary Committee hearings, only three Senators changed their previous positions on whether Judge Thomas should be approved for the Supreme Court. Individuals on each side found a plausible explanation in the diametrically opposed testimonies to justify their previous positions. Supporters of Judge Thomas focused on the supposed holes and inconsistencies in the story of Professor Hill and judged him to be more truthful. Those who originally opposed Judge Thomas believed Professor Hill because they could find little or no motivation for her coming forward with totally false accusations. As new books and articles appear analyzing the debate, public opinion continues to be as polarized as before. This is a striking reminder of how much we are all influenced by our assumptions and previous convictions in searching for the truth. Long term progress on the sensitive issue of sexual harassment will not come easily. Nevertheless, the hearings did raise consciousness and open up new possibilities. Success will require a disciplined and sustained effort. We need constructive discussions of gender differences and practical guidance on how men and women can form relationships on the basis of mutuality rather than power. We must overcome the social and economic inequities that foster sexual harassment. Women need to gain greater power and status in all our major institutions including the government, the corporate world and the church.

As Christians we look to the Scriptures for guidance on this difficult question. The Gospels portray Jesus rising above the patriarchal patterns of his own day by interacting with women in public and including them in religious discussions. He treated women with respect and benefited from their loving service, suggesting a healthy pattern of mutuality. Jesus taught us to love others as we love ourselves and to have special care for the powerless. He identified himself with those who suffer and insisted that our salvation depends on how we treat those in need. According to Mark's Gospel, the risen Christ first appeared to Mary Magdalene and the other women, sending them forth to spread the good news to the other disciples. Paul taught that in Christ there is neither male nor female. In the church, we are still in the process of understanding the implications of this provocative statement which suggests a fundamental equality between the sexes. Paul also taught that we are all members of one body and must have respect for the distinctive contributions of others.

Despite being written in a patriarchal culture, the New Testament provides helpful perspectives and powerful motives for avoiding all forms of harassment and establishing healthy relationships between men and women.

12. Magic Johnson and AIDS

Through his dramatic public disclosure in 1991, Magic Johnson opened up a new phase in the battle against the virus which breaks down the immune system and leads inexorably to AIDS.

When Magic Johnson made his announcement in 1991 that he had been infected with the virus that leads to AIDS, it functioned like a much needed dose of reality therapy for important segments of our population. It can happen to anyone. Even the rich and famous are not immune, and neither are the strong and agile. Homosexuals and drug users are not the only ones at risk. A new awareness struck the land. AIDS hotlines were deluged with calls from heterosexuals. Young people, who normally feel invulnerable, were forced to face the threat posed by HIV infections. It was as though Magic had spoken directly to those who thought they were safe. His message: wake up – don't gamble with your future. One young man spoke for many when he said, "If this can happen to Magic, then I'd better quit fooling around."

Although some were leery of making the real life person, Earvin Johnson, with all his failings, into a hero or role model, the Magic Man of legendary court deeds did provide us with an unexpected and unparalleled opportunity to deal constructively with the HIV epidemic. In characteristic fashion, Magic had suddenly dominated the scene, opened up the action and made possible a new team effort in the life and death struggle against an uncontrolled and volatile foe.

Grim statistics had long been available: worldwide as many as 10 million infected and in the United States alone more dying in one year than in the whole Vietnam War. But it seems that AIDS has to have a face before it hits home: a loved one, a family member, or a friend. I know that my own sense of the disease is shaped largely by ministering to particular infected individuals who have fought valiantly, suffered greatly and with the help of family and friends died peacefully. When Magic, with his engaging smile and upbeat public persona still intact, came forward to tell his story, the demographics suddenly changed. Now we all knew someone who had tested positive for HIV and his continuing struggle with the disease would become part of our common story. The nation as a whole had a new opportunity to face this dreaded epidemic and to plan constructive action. Young people had a reason to examine their understandable, but potentially harmful, sense of invulnerability. Magic invited everyone to face the essential precariousness of life.

But our national memory is short. The dramatic announcement of Magic Johnson has faded from consciousness, and we need to remind ourselves again of the lessons his illness teaches. The heterosexual population is not immune to the HIV virus. The World Health Organization has reported that three-fourths of those carrying the virus throughout the world are infected by heterosexual contact. In the United States, there was a twelvefold increase in the disease among heterosexual persons in less than a decade. The prevailing popular opinion that AIDS is almost entirely a homosexual disease enabled many heterosexual persons to dismiss the threat and to continue promiscuous and casual sexual activity. It also made it more difficult to mobilize the public support needed for adequate prevention and care programs. Furthermore, some homophobic individuals have used the high incidence of HIV infection among members of the gay community to stigmatize all homosexual persons and to suggest that the disease is a divine punishment for their deviant sexual orientation.

The sad case of Magic Johnson undercuts the premise behind these dangerous stereotypical assumptions. No one, not even rich and famous heterosexual persons, can presume to be free from the threat of AIDS. Sexual promiscuity is dangerous, whether among heterosexual or homosexual persons. From the viewpoint of HIV transmission, to have sexual relations with a particular person is to have sex with all of that person's other partners. As the incidence of HIV infection rises in the heterosexual community, the dangers of casual and irresponsible sex multiply dramatically.

The answer to the AIDS epidemic is not to discriminate against gay persons or to force mandatory testing on them. A proper response is to recognize the disease as a common problem which requires responsible preventive action and compassionate care for all victims. We need a massive national effort to find a cure and to discover ways to prolong and enhance the quality of life for those already infected. People like Magic Johnson get the best treatment and care that money and status bring. But what about others? The severity and extent of the epidemic demands that we mobilize the talent and financial resources necessary to offer proper care for victims and to help prevent the spread of the disease.

Christians bring a faith perspective to this effort. A campaign against AIDS which insists that it is not a moral problem and which relies solely on the use of condoms is doomed to failure. It is true that we do not need moralizing or harsh statements about divine retribution directed against victims. A successful campaign, however, requires a theological dimension and sound moral principles.

Since specific actions flow from our being and character, we must work to achieve healthy attitudes and to cultivate virtues. In simple terms, people can be instructed in the use of condoms, but they are less likely to use them if they are generally irresponsible and lack respect for other people. Young persons who have cultivated the virtue of temperance and fortitude are more likely to resist peer pressure to engage in casual sex. Individuals who are inherently compassionate are more likely to treat AIDS victims with genuine care. Persons with an abiding confidence in their own sexual identity are less likely to practice discrimination against homosexuals who have the virus. A successful approach requires a strong educational and formative effort to inculcate healthy attitudes and solid virtues.

From the viewpoint of Christian morality, it is better to speak of responsible sexual behavior than to propose safe sex as the only solution. Abstinence is the best method of all. About half the young women in the United States are still virgins by the time they are 18. Most collegians reject promiscuity and maintain high ideals of fidelity in their relationships. They need encouragement to continue to act responsibly. Moreover, many young persons are in the process of deciding about the extent of their sexual involvement.

A message which concentrates solely on safe sex is harmful in the long run because it insinuates that everyone is sexually active. Responsible sex is a broader term which encompasses a variety of desirable behaviors. It insists that promiscuity violates the ideal of fidelity and commitment, and that the discipline involved in abstinence can be personally enriching and beneficial for relationships. Furthermore, it suggests that those in our society who do not accept these ideals must still act responsibly by taking proper precautions so as not to harm themselves or their partners in their sexual activity. Safe sex as an ideal is too narrow and too selfish.

Those who uphold abstinence as the best solution do not have to oppose education about the value of condoms in preventing the spread of the disease. In a pluralistic society, the moral standards of one group cannot be imposed on others. If people are going to engage in promiscuous or casual sex, then it is better that they use condoms and help prevent the spread of HIV infections. The crucial point is to place the information about condoms in the larger framework provided by the ideal of responsible sex, which includes abstinence as the best option.

Theologically, we should avoid talking of AIDS as a divine punishment inflicted on disordered and sinful individuals. The God of the New Testament is ultimately compassionate, always working for the good of the diverse human beings who crown the creative process. At the same time, the evolving created world demonstrates certain inherent and consistent laws or patterns, which are violated at human peril. Thus, a case can be made that human beings were made for faithful committed sexual relationships, and that violations of this pattern produce destructive consequences among which we now include HIV infections. When dealing with those suffering with AIDS, it is important to act compassionately and to avoid all judgments about the possible sinfulness of the behavior which transmitted the virus. Judgment belongs to the merciful Lord, who alone knows the human heart.

Through his dramatic public disclosure in 1991, Magic Johnson opened up a new phase in the battle against the virus which breaks down the immune system and leads inexorably to AIDS. With many indications that our national commitment to fight this epidemic is waning, we must try to recapture the momentum. Christians can make an important contribution by maintaining the ideal of responsible sex and by extending compassionate care to the victims of this disease.

13. Sexuality: A Christian Perspective

Our long and rich Christian tradition contains wise teachings on sexuality which our troubled culture needs to hear.

In our culture there is an ongoing conversation on the topic of sex. It takes place in various settings, ranging from the street to the classroom. Everyone has something to contribute to the discussion, including men and women, homosexuals and heterosexuals, married and single people and even celibate priests. Although the topic of sex evokes endless discussion, the conversation is often crude and uninformed. Much of it lacks depth and perspective. Many participants in the dialogue are constrained by stereotypical thinking and distorted attitudes.

The Christian tradition contains a wisdom that can enrich and deepen this conversation. Not everyone agrees with this statement. One professor who teaches a course on sexuality said she could sum up the Christian contribution in just a few words: "No, no and no." She speaks for many who claim that their Christian training left them with unhealthy attitudes toward sex. In order to counter this position we need to search the tradition more carefully for perspectives and insights which will provide positive guidance on sexual questions.

In our society, television and other mass media bombard us with the idea that sex is good and sexual liberation is important. Influential shapers of popular culture make this general message more specific. Since sex is part of being human, it is normal and natural to indulge this biological urge. Sexual pleasure is good and individuals should pursue it with zest. People who are with it have a lot of sexual experience. Abstinence from sex is unrealistic and also odd. A person who feels guilty for sexual transgressions probably needs therapy.

Christianity offers a deeper and more nuanced outlook. Influenced by modern developments, the church today also proclaims the fundamental goodness of human sexuality. But Christians add the crucial reminder that sex is not an autonomous possession which can be used as one wishes. It is a gift from God which we should treasure and use responsibly. Sexuality stamps our whole being and adds zest to life. It helps us overcome selfishness by directing our attention to another person. The sexual drive is an essential part of the divine plan for achieving human intimacy and propagating the human race. For Christians, healthy and responsible sexual activity has a sacramental character. It speaks of love, fidelity and commitment. It has a mysterious power to reveal the God who loves us with a passion beyond imagining. It reminds us that Christ has healed and transformed every aspect of human existence. We should be grateful for the good gift of sex which calls us from aloneness to communion and from selfishness to commitment.

Christianity not only rejoices in the God-given goodness of human sexuality, but it also calls us to face its dark side. Sex can be used to dominate and control others. The drive for sexual pleasure can be compulsive. Sexual liberation can become license to do whatever feels good, even if it hurts others. It is difficult to achieve sexual integration, and dysfunctions are common. The very power of the sex drive can lead to poor decisions and destructive behavior. Our culture provides strong temptations to misuse the gift of sex. Christianity insists that it is sinful to engage in sexual behavior which is culpably irresponsible and seriously harmful to others.

The popular secular account of human sexuality as a personal possession well designed for fun and pleasure fails to prepare individuals for dealing with the fundamental ambivalence of this passionate drive. Christianity, on the other hand, portrays sex as we actually experience it, with all its wondrous joys and all its dark power. With gratitude for the healing power of grace, Christians can affirm the essential goodness of sexuality without denying the realistic threat of sin.

With this general assessment in mind, we can examine what the Christian tradition has to say on more specific questions of gender, interpersonal relationships and genital sexuality.

The contemporary discussion of gender sexuality has moved between two extreme positions. At one extreme are those who defend the stereotypical images of men and women propagated by our patriarchal society. At the other are the radical feminists who react against sexist generalizations by denying the existence of any emotional or psychological differences based on gender.

The Christian tradition contains resources which challenge both positions. The Bible teaches that God has created us as unique individuals and calls each one of us by name. We are free individuals and not robots acting out a gender role. We are responsible persons impelled by the Spirit to develop our distinctive gifts and talents. If we try to force ourselves or others into predetermined gender roles or behaviors, we stifle the work of the Spirit. Stereotyping betrays the uniqueness of the divine call. Christians live under a moral imperative to fight against patriarchal attitudes and sexist practices in society and the church. Although Christianity has been used to defend patriarchy, the real thrust of the teaching of Jesus, as reflected in the best of the tradition, is for men and women to relate as equal partners on the basis of mutual love and respect.

The Christian tradition also challenges those who want to suppress all discussions of sexual differences. According to the holistic anthropology found in the Bible, human beings are inspirited bodies or enfleshed spirits. Through our sexually differentiated bodies, we live in the world and relate to one another as males or females. Sexuality permeates and affects all aspects of our lives. We can debate to what degree sexual differences are innate or nurtured, but as Christians shaped by biblical teaching we cannot simply deny all emotional and psychological differences. Our incarnational anthropology, with its fundamental appreciation of the body, necessarily assumes that there are essential gender differences which affect all dimensions of the personality. As our brief analysis suggests, Christianity sets a useful framework for a more specific discussion of sexual differences without falling into sexual stereotypes.

Our society tends to obscure the importance of interpersonal or affective sexuality by concentrating so heavily on genital sex. Much of the ongoing conversation about sex centers on performing well in bed and achieving orgasm. Persons consumed with the search for genital satisfaction find it hard to achieve genuine intimacy. As one author noted, our culture tends to place the fig leaf on the face rather than the genitals. This approach to sex which neglects interpersonal communication tends to trivialize human encounters and to diminish genuine erotic passion.

Christianity insists that God designed sexuality to lift us out of an egocentric preoccupation with self by propelling us toward intimate communion with other persons. This Christian insight puts great emphasis on developing a healthy affective sexuality which first seeks union and intimacy rather than orgasm. Achieving intimacy is an exciting and challenging task. Intimacy demands open communication and respect for the other person. Too much intimacy too soon often proves harmful. Relationships work best when persons reveal themselves gradually over a period of time. Prudent individuals disclose their deeper thoughts and feelings only if their partners prove trustworthy and are willing to reveal themselves. Since close relationships involve risk and make the partners vulnerable, genuine intimacy requires large doses of compassion, tenderness and forgiveness. By insisting that sexuality has an affective dimension, contemporary Christian teaching encourages us in the crucial task of developing healthy interpersonal relationships.

Our secular culture puts great emphasis on genital sexuality, but offers little moral guidance. It sees sex as a recreational activity in which anything goes as long as it is done by consenting adults. It encourages sexual experience and makes light of sexual restraint. One result appears to be more sex and less enjoyment. More importantly, this permissive attitude also contributes to many of our social ills: widespread promiscuity, marital infidelity, family breakdowns, the spread of sexually transmitted diseases, unwanted pregnancies, children having children, and an abortion rate totally unacceptable to many citizens.

Christianity has fundamental moral teachings on sex that our wounded society desperately needs to hear. The Christian tradition insists that genital sex is a gift from God which must be used responsibly in accord with the divine plan. Genital sexuality is true to its nature when it is rooted in healthy interpersonal relationships. Intercourse is authentic only in the context of the kind of love and fidelity associated with marriage. A good marriage offers the stability necessary for a couple to develop a satisfying sex life.

Sex is a type of language, a mode of communicating which should speak truthfully and represent accurately the depth of the relationship. Sexual activity should be honest, faithful and joyous. It should not promote selfishness, hurt other persons or do damage to society. Christianity has traditionally understood that controlling the volatile sex drive demands the cultivation of virtues or habitual ways of acting. A young woman, for example, who has developed the virtue of fortitude is prepared to say a courageous no to her boyfriend who is pressing her to have intercourse before she is ready.

The long and rich Christian tradition does indeed contain wise teachings on sexuality which our troubled culture needs to hear. Our challenge as Christians is to retrieve these insights and to demonstrate their relevance for personal development and societal reform.

14. Mary: The Great Symbol of the Feminine

The current interest in Mary provides us with a new opportunity to tap the humanizing energy of this most powerful of feminine symbols.

The Blessed Virgin Mary continues to function as a remarkably influential religious symbol in our postmodern world. The famous shrines of Lourdes in France and Fatima in Portugal together attract 10 million pilgrims a year, including a good number of young people. Pope John Paul II, who has visited Marian shrines all over the world, wrote his sixth encyclical in 1987 entitled *The Mother of the Redeemer*, which presents Mary as Mother of the Church and model of faith. The American bishops frequently invoke the example and the intercession of Mary in their pastoral letters. For example, the pastoral on the economy, *Economic Justice for All*, cites Mary's great canticle, *The Magnificat*, as an example of God's special care for the poor and the lowly. The great Catholic theologians of our time have also written about Mary. Karl Rahner explored the contemporary significance of the Blessed Virgin in his book *Mary the Mother of the Lord*. Edward Schillebeeckx discussed the modern Marian apparitions in *Mary Mother of the Redeemer*. Hans Urs von Balthasar wrote extensively on Mary as the primary example of receptive openness for the entire church. Important feminist authors, such as Rosemary Ruether (cf. *Mary: the Feminine Face of the Church*), are exploring new images of Mary for the contemporary world. Nor is the interest in Mary confined to Catholic scholars. In 1990, the Anglican theologian John Macquarrie, published a book entitled *Mary for all Christians*, which examines the topic in a broad ecumenical context.

At the popular level, many older, conservative Catholics have maintained their private Marian devotions throughout the post-conciliar period. More remarkable are the scattered, but increasingly frequent, reports of younger and more liberal Catholics shaped by the teaching of Vatican II who are rediscovering Mary. For example, a sister involved in social justice causes finds herself spontaneously meditating on Mary's *Magnificat*; a progressive married couple has recently

begun saying the rosary together; a bright collegian is fascinated by Marian devotions.

All of this interest within the church has gained the attention of the secular world. Late in 1991, *Time* magazine ran
a cover story on Mary entitled "Handmaid or Feminist?,"
which dealt with the modern apparitions of Mary as well as
her contemporary relevance. *The New York Times Book Review*
of August 11, 1991 featured a favorable, front page review of
a book by Sandra L. Zimdars-Swartz entitled *Encountering
Mary: From La Salette to Medjugorje.*

In assessing the significance of the Marian renewal, it is
important to keep the numbers in perspective. Many Christians, especially those rooted in the Protestant Reformation,
have little or no interest in Mary. Some evangelicals still feel
the need to warn against putting too much emphasis on the
Virgin. Large numbers of Catholics have abandoned Marian
devotions and are now quite content with their Christocentric
piety. Most Catholics who have grown up since the Council
have little explicit knowledge of Mary and do not participate
in Marian devotions. Nevertheless, the Blessed Virgin Mary
has maintained a remarkable hold on the religious imagination of church leaders, important scholars and millions of
devotees. What accounts for this abiding influence?

The answer is complex, because the motivations are diverse and often subtle. In times of great international crises,
some believers find themselves attracted to the Mother of
Peace. Individuals suffering from personal insecurities and
doubts may find comfort in Mary, the Mother of Sorrows.
Some are seeking to rekindle their spiritual lives by returning
to traditional images of the Blessed Virgin which touched
their hearts in the past. For others, Mary of Nazareth represents the highest ideals of spiritual development and is therefore a person worth emulating.

But there is another reason for the enduring popularity
of Mary which bears further exploration. The Blessed Virgin
symbolizes the feminine dimension of religion which has
been lost or distorted in the modern world. The Enlightenment ideal of progress through reason and science has celebrated the masculine virtues of efficiency and productivity,

while confining feminine energy to the private world of home and heart. Modernity assumed that men would concentrate on the public tasks of creating a viable political economy, while women would attend to the private function of religious formation. This societal arrangement corresponded to the patriarchal structure of the church with an all-male official leadership whose public liturgy addressed the Father through the Son. Thus in the public realm of both church and society, masculine symbols predominated. Such a one-dimensional world intensified the need to celebrate the feminine in the private realm.

Historically, Mary has been the most influential representative of such feminine imagery and energy. The Gospels, which offer very little historical information about Mary, do provide us with striking images: the awesome encounter with the Angel Gabriel in the Annunciation; the compassionate visit to Elizabeth; the tender story surrounding the birth of Jesus; the frightening flight to Egypt; the puzzling discovery of Jesus in the Temple; the commanding role at the wedding feast at Cana; and the sorrowful vigil at the foot of the cross.

The Gospel picture of Mary as Mother of Jesus has shaped the Christian imagination throughout history. In 431, the council of Ephesus affirmed Mary as *Theotokos*, the bringer-forth of God. The Fathers of the Church spoke of Mary as the new Eve, whose faith and obedience brings renewed life. In the Middle Ages, St. Bernard of Clairvaux gave emotional expression to his great admiration of the Virgin Mother. At the height of the Renaissance, Michelangelo captured something of the sword-piercing agony of the sorrowful mother in his sculpture the *Pieta*. Modern poets have continued the great hymn to Mary, ranging from our "tainted nature's solitary boast" of William Wordsworth to the "Mayhope of darkened ways" of Gerard Manley Hopkins. The official proclamation of the great Marian doctrines, the Immaculate Conception in 1854 and the Assumption in 1950, enhanced the role of Mary within the Catholic community.

Despite the great power of this traditional Marian symbolism, the modern world was very effective in confining it to the private world of religious emotion. Both men and women in the Catholic church often invested their more tender religious sentiments in private Marian devotions. Detached from a larger political and economic context, the Mary of popular devotions often appeared as a weak, submissive character with little substance.

The question today is whether the powerful symbol of the Blessed Virgin Mary can be freed from these modern constraints and can play a positive role in the construction of the postmodern world. After the proclamation of the Doctrine of the Assumption, the psychotherapist Carl Jung called it the most important religious statement since the Reformation. He was impressed with the notion that Mary, representing Sophia or Wisdom, was now united with the Godhead, introducing a feminine principle into the Deity. Although Jung's theology is questionable, his fundamental insight into the role of the feminine is worth pursuing. Mary is a human being, one of us and not a goddess. Her Assumption does not transform the Trinity into a "Quaternity." But Mary does represent the feminine dimension of human consciousness and of our religious imagination. The historical Mary of Nazareth was an active participant in the drama of salvation. Her receptive obedience enabled her to act decisively. She overcame her misgivings about the mission of her son Jesus and became a committed disciple. She grieved deeply over his sufferings and death but maintained a sense of hope. The great religious symbol of the Virgin Mary can be appropriated in many ways, but it must remain faithful to its historical roots. It should not be co-opted to justify passive-dependent attitudes or patriarchal structures. The Marian symbol does remind us that the great God transcends our distinctions between male and female and that the divine Spirit dwells in the hearts of both men and women. The one God is a source of both masculine and feminine energy. The experiences of both men and women are potentially revelatory. Our God is a Father who exercises maternal care, a Judge who has compassion, a King who serves.

Mary can speak to the postmodern world because she not only challenges the assumptions of patriarchy but also represents an integrated and attractive image of a fully functioning human being. Men and women can learn from her example. She reminds those who are overly aggressive and impatient to be more attentive to the life-giving spirit within. She prompts the timid and the fearful to act with resolute courage. As the bishops at the second Vatican Council taught, Mary is one of us – a model of faith, the prototype of the whole church. She inspires the Christian community to take an active role in spreading the kingdom in the world. Her great *Magnificat* reminds us to take seriously the work of peace and justice.

Throughout history, the symbol of the Blessed Virgin has played an ambivalent role, on one hand inspiring individuals to strive for sanctity and on the other justifying the distortions found in patriarchal systems. The current interest in Mary provides us with a new opportunity to tap the humanizing energy of this most powerful of feminine symbols.

15. Developing Interfaith Dialogue

For many Christians, members of other traditions have been transformed from enemies, heathens and betrayers to dialogue partners.

Momentous changes in our world during the last century have stimulated greater interfaith dialogue and cooperation. With the end of the colonial period, Western Christians are in a position to develop a global spirituality which draws on the wisdom found in the great literate religious traditions, including Hinduism, Judaism, Buddhism and Islam as well as the native religions, such as those practiced by Native Americans, which have no written scriptures. The possibility and success of interfaith dialogue depends on the fundamental attitudes that individuals bring to encounters with those who practice a different religion. Using broad generalizations, we can say that Western Christians have tended to categorize adherents of other religions as either enemies, heathens, betrayers or dialogue partners.

The "enemy model" has been far too prominent in all interfaith encounters, but has been especially prevalent in the relationship between Christians and Muslims. In less than a century after the death of Mohammed in 632, Muslim forces reached the Iberian peninsula in the West and the banks of the Indus River in the East. Despite setbacks, Islam remained powerful and achieved a great strategic and psychological advantage when the Ottoman Turks captured Constantinople in 1453. Christians in Europe felt threatened militarily and hemmed in economically. They had almost no accurate information about Islam as a religion, and the distorted views which were prevalent simply intensified their animosity toward Muslims. Even after Islamic power waned and better information about Mohammed and the Qur'an was available in the West, deep antipathies remained in the Christian consciousness. In our own time, the spread of Islamic fundamentalism has rekindled the ancient antagonisms. Muslims in the United States complain that the media presents a distorted image of Islam, often indicting the whole Muslim community because of a small group of terrorists. Given the current climate, it is difficult for many Christians to overcome their prejudices and to enter into genuine dialogue with Muslims.

The possibility of new conflicts between the Christian West and the Muslim East make it even more imperative that we learn to treat one another with mutual respect. Vatican II helps us in this task by reminding us that Muslims "adore one God" and "submit wholeheartedly even to His inscrutable decrees." They revere Jesus as a prophet and honor Mary his virgin mother. They prize the moral life and give worship to God especially through prayer, almsgiving and fasting. The Council insists that Christians and Muslims "forget the past" and "strive sincerely for mutual understanding" (*Nostra Aetate N 3*).

The new global spirituality must face and transform all hostile attitudes toward any other religious group. All religious traditions, including Christianity, are a mixture of grace and sin. No group escapes blame for the religious strife of the past. We must allow those previously conceived as adversaries to start over with us and to become friends. Christians can find motivation and guidance in this difficult task by recalling the challenge of Jesus to love even our enemies.

In the past, Christians generally considered Hindus and Buddhists, as well as members of native oral religions, more as heathens or pagans than as enemies. Early European colonizers, for example, tended to characterize Native Americans as noble savages or childish innocents or devil worshipers. Dialogue with such creatures was unthinkable. They adopted instead the barbaric strategies of forced conversion, enslavement or extermination. Ever since the initial contacts between Christians and Hindus in the second century, Christians have tended to see Eastern religions as exotic and mysterious on the one hand and idolatrous and inferior on the other. In the 19th century, the German philosopher Hegel claimed that the superstitious religions of India caused the physical and spiritual degeneration of the people, leading them to seek happiness through opium, an addictive drug. In our own time, Catholics were urged to contribute money to ransom "pagan babies," a quaint phrase which suggests a distorted attitude toward the religions of foreign lands. More recent developments have called these perceptions into question. The Second Vatican Council spoke generally of the "profound religious sense" instilled by these religions. More specifically the Council praised Hinduism for providing a "trusting flight to God" and Buddhism for offering a path to "supreme enlightenment." In the United States some Christians have gained a deeper appreciation of nature and the importance of caring for the earth from Native Americans.

The new global spirituality will have to build on these advances. We now know too much about these religious traditions to call their adherents heathens or pagans. These religions contain valuable insights which can help Christians in the struggle against typically Western temptations such as individualism and consumerism.

Jews have always occupied a unique position in the Christian consciousness. Unfortunately, the positive connections have often been blurred by the belief that the Jewish people are betrayers of the Lord. Influenced by the anti-Jewish bias in the Gospels, some Christians have regarded all Jews as guilty of deicide (murdering God), and therefore deserving of punishment. They believe that because Judaism failed to recognize the Messiah, it no longer has a right to exist. This attitude, which ignores important teachings of Paul on the enduring significance of the Jews, has contributed to monstrous, unimaginable crimes. Vatican II repudiated the deicide charge, insisting that blame for the death of Jesus could not be placed on all Jews living then nor on the Jews of today. The Council also called for mutual respect and understanding between Christians and Jews based on a common "spiritual patrimony."

The new global spirituality flourishes when the "other," whether perceived as enemy or heathen or betrayer, becomes a dialogue partner. Dialogue is based on mutual respect and the conviction that conversation can produce new understandings and deeper commitments. Since the 1960's interfaith dialogue has been increasing throughout the world. This development has forced Christians to rethink many theological issues, including questions about the extent and dynamics of salvation. Most Catholic participants in the dialogue reject the older exclusive outlook which claims that salvation is only open to those who explicitly accept the lordship of Jesus. Among those taking a more open approach, some hold that the world religions offer saving truth and grace to their adherents, but that this grace ultimately comes from Christ whether the recipients recognize the source or not. This is generally the position of Karl Rahner and his followers who discern an anonymous Christian grace at work in all people of good will. Other scholars (for example, Paul Knitter, the author of *No Other Name? A Critical Survey of Christian Attitudes Toward the World Religions*) have rejected Rahner's inclusive theology in favor of a pluralist approach which finds saving grace active among the followers of other religions apart from even the implicit mediatorship of Christ. Important theologians, including Hans Kung, contend that Rahner's anonymous Christian theory is offensive and an obstacle to dialogue. Knitter has gone beyond most of Rahner's critics by proposing a global theological framework calculated to promote interfaith dialogue. The key to his thought lies in his reinterpretation of the uniqueness of Jesus as the savior. Knitter challenges the Rahnerian claim that Jesus is the absolute Savior and the definitive and unsurpassable revelation of God. He proposes instead that we see Jesus as a universal, decisive and indispensable savior. "Universal" means that we Christian experience Christ as having meaning for all people. "Decisive" suggests that God could say more than was revealed in Jesus but could never contradict his message. "Indispensable" indicates that Jesus is so significant that any humans who do not know about him are in important ways unfulfilled or unenlightened. For Knitter this analysis suggests that other prophets could also have a saving significance which is universal, decisive and indispensable in the same way as Jesus. This effectively denies the contention of most Christian theologians, including Rahner and Kung, that the revelation in Christ is normative for all persons and provides a basis for judging the truth claims of other religions.

Leading theologians will continue to debate these crucial questions on the fundamental relationship between Christianity and the world religions. But great advances available to all of us have already been made. For many Christians, members of other traditions have been transformed from enemies, heathens and betrayers to dialogue partners. We can read their scriptures, admire their prophets, attend their services, learn from their good example and gain insights from their traditions. For example, Jews remind us to find God in concrete daily life; Hindus teach us about meditation; Buddhists show us the power of compassion; Muslims challenge us to surrender wholeheartedly to God; Native Americans instruct us in care for the earth. And we have so much more to learn from our dialogue partners. In a changing, shrinking, post-colonial world, we need a global spirituality which roots us more deeply in our own religion so that we can remain open to the meanings, values and practices of other traditions.

16. Interfaith Dialogue: Toward a Global Ethic

The world religions possess spiritual resources which are absolutely crucial to solving our global problems.

One of the most significant events in the history of interfaith dialogue occurred in Chicago in 1993. From August 28th to September 5th, some 6,000 religious leaders and faithful from around the world, representing 125 faiths, participated in the Parliament of the World's Religions. During the eight-day event, participants discussed their common religious convictions as well as their differences. They prayed together and listened to talks by important religious leaders, including Cardinal Joseph Bernardin of Chicago and the Dalai Lama, the exiled spiritual and temporal leader of Tibet. Near the end of the conference, about 250 religious leaders signed *The Declaration of a Global Ethic,* which proposes general moral principles shared by the world's great religions as a framework for dealing with the serious social, economic, political and environmental problems affecting the human family.

This historic conference, which commemorated and developed the groundbreaking achievements of the 1893 World's Parliament of Religion also held in Chicago, has signaled a new stage in interfaith relationships. Building on the progress in mutual trust and understanding achieved during the past century, the Parliament turned its attention outward to the collaborative task of helping to create a more just and peaceful world.

To draft a consensus statement on ethics as the basis for peacemaking, the Parliament turned to Fr. Hans Kung, the well-known Swiss Catholic theologian. After spending the early part of his theological career dealing with internal church matters, Kung has become a recognized leader in the field of interfaith dialogue. In 1986, he published *Christianity and the World Religions* (Doubleday), which focuses on his dialogues with scholars representing Islam, Hinduism and Buddhism. In this rich and provocative volume, he spelled out his now famous principle, "No world peace without religious peace." For him, dialogue among the world religions can no longer be seen as an interesting theological exercise confined to specialists. On the contrary, our troubled world demands that all believers engage in dialogue and collaborative efforts on behalf of peace and justice. Subsequently, Kung published *Global Responsibility: In Search of a New World Ethic* (Crossroad 1991), in which he culled from the world's great religious traditions some common norms, values, ideals and goals, useful for healing our wounded world. He summed up his convictions in this way: "No human life together without a world ethic for the nations; no peace among the nations without peace among the religions; no peace among the religions without dialogue among the religions."

Kung drew on his continuing scholarly studies of the world religions in drafting *The Declaration of a Global Ethic,* which was eventually adopted by the Parliament. The joint statement weaves back and forth between broad descriptions of a world in agony and summary statements of what religions can do to relieve this suffering. The agony of the world is evident to all with compassionate eyes. Millions of people "suffer from unemployment, poverty, hunger and the destruction of their families." Throughout the world, there are destructive forms of patriarchy which lead to sexual domination, exploitation of women, sexual misuse of children, and prostitution, often used as a means of economic survival. All over the world, we find hatred, envy, jealousy and violence between individuals, groups, races, nations, and even religions. Unjust institutions and systems cause unemployment, poor wages, a growing gap between poor and rich, bureaucratic corruption and theft for the sake of survival. Around our globe human beings are hurt by "endless lies and deceit, swindling and hypocrisy, ideology and demagoguery." In addition, the human family has ruthlessly plundered our planet so that we are now threatened by the collapse of our ecosystem.

Adopting the self-critical attitude that Kung insists is absolutely crucial to successful interfaith collaboration, the document explicitly recognizes ways in which religions have contributed to the global problems. Members and even leaders of religions have been known to "incite aggression, fanaticism, hate and xenophobia." Religion has been misused to the point of promoting violence and wars for purely political goals. At times, representatives of religions have preached intolerance, which leads to a lack of respect for other religious traditions.

While honestly admitting these destructive practices, the declaration insists with even greater intensity that the world religions possess spiritual resources which are absolutely crucial to solving our global problems. Rather than emphasizing the well-known differences among religions, the document enunciates a common global ethic – "a minimal fundamental consensus concerning binding values, irrevocable standards and fundamental moral attitudes." Without claiming total answers to the world's problems, the great spiritual traditions do offer "a fundamental sense of trust, a ground of meaning, ultimate standards and a spiritual home." To become credible witnesses to these truths, religions themselves must overcome their mistrust of one another and begin to demonstrate a greater respect for the "traditions, holy places, feasts and rituals" of people who follow a different spiritual path.

A solid and constructive global ethic can be founded on the crucial and indispensable principle held by all of the world's religions: "every human being must be treated humanely." This means that every person without exception possesses "an inalienable and untouchable dignity" which must be honored by every individual and all states and governments. This fundamental principle can be stated in terms of the golden rule, "What you do not wish done to yourself, do not do to others," or put in more positive terms, "What you wish done to yourself, do to others." From this great traditional principle, Kung derives four guidelines or directives for human behavior that are found in most of the religions of the world.

The first and most fundamental guideline is "You shall not kill," or more positively, "Have respect for life." This means that all people have a right to life and the opportunity to develop themselves personally. It obviously excludes "ethnic cleansing" and liquidating minority groups. It further suggests that the inevitable conflicts of life should be solved nonviolently within a framework of justice. We must try to create a "culture of nonviolence" so that young people will learn that there are other ways of settling disputes. The principle extends to care for the environment. "Limitless exploitation of the natural foundations of life, ruthless destruction of the biosphere and militarization of the cosmos are all outrages." Human beings must learn to live in harmony with nature without dominating it.

The second common principle is "You shall not steal," or more positively, "Deal honestly and fairly." This suggests that no one has the right to use personal possessions without concern for the needs of others and the well-being of the earth. We must promote global justice if we are to have global peace. Young persons must learn that having personal property carries with it the obligation to contribute to the common good. All states must work together to structure a more just world economy so that "the poorest billions of humans" can achieve a better standard of living. The spiritual traditions encourage us to have compassion for those who suffer and to work for economic and political justice for all. Religions teach their adherents to have a sense of moderation so that they will not lose their souls, their freedom and their inner peace in an "unquenchable greed for money, prestige and consumption."

The great religious traditions hold a third guideline in common, "You shall not lie," or more positively, "Speak and act truthfully." This directive applies to all, but has special significance for persons of influence. The mass media, for example, have an obligation to respect human rights and to report the truth with objectivity and fairness; artists, writers and scientists are called to pursue and express the truth; political leaders must avoid the temptation to manipulate the truth; and representatives of religions should engage in honest dialogue which seeks a truth greater than any community now enjoys.

The fourth and final directive is "You shall not commit sexual immorality," or more positively, "Respect and love one another." This teaching condemns sexual exploitation and the domination of one sex by the other. We must teach our young people that sexuality is "a life-affirming shaper of community" which "should express and reinforce a loving relationship lived by equal partners." The mutual concern and love experienced in personal and familial relationships is absolutely crucial since it helps us understand how nations and religions should interact.

After discussing the ramifications of these four ethical directives, the document insists that we cannot improve our world unless we experience a transformation in individual and collective consciousness. We need to awaken our spiritual powers through "reflection, meditation, prayer or positive thinking." To respond to the agony of the world we need a conversion of heart and collaborative action. "Together we can move mountains."

The declaration closes by inviting all men and women, whether religious or not, to commit themselves to "a common global ethic, to better mutual understanding, as well as to socially beneficial, peace-fostering and Earth-friendly ways of life."